WINDOWS™ 3.1
by PICTORIAL

PicTorial Series

Dennis P. Curtin, Series Editor

Windows™ 3.1 by PicTorial

Dennis P. Curtin

Prentice Hall Career & Technology
Englewood Cliffs, New Jersey 07632

Library of Congess Cataloging-in-Publication Data

Curtin, Dennis P.
    Windows 3.1 by PicTorial / Dennis P. Curtin.
        p.   cm.—(PicTorial series)
    Includes index.
    ISBN 0-13-026551-9 (pbk)
        1. Windows (Computer programs)   2. Microsoft Windows (Computer file)
I. Title.
II. Series: PicTorial series (Englewood Cliffs, N.J.)
QA76.76.W56C87   1994
005.4'3—dc20   93-23110
                                                        CIP

Windows is a trademark of Microsoft Corporation.

Acquisitions editor: Liz Kendall
Production editor: Cecil Yarbrough
Creative director: Paula Maylahn
Electronic production and design: Function Thru Form, Inc.
Project manager at Function Thru Form: Gwen Waldron
Art director and interior designer: Robin D'Amato
Icon design: Clea Chmela
Illustrations: Freddy Flake
Zoom art: Rita Myers
Cover design: Marianne Frasco
Cover art: © David Bishop/Phototake NYC
Manufacturing buyer: Ed O'Dougherty
Supplements editor: Cindy Harford
Editorial assistant: Jane Avery

 © 1994 by Prentice Hall Career & Technology
Prentice-Hall, Inc.
A Paramount Communications Company
Englewood Cliffs, NJ 07632

Printed in the United States of America
10 9 8 7 6 5 4 3 2

ISBN 0-13-026551-9

Prentice-Hall International (UK) Limited, *London*
Prentice-Hall of Australia Pty, Limited, *Sydney*
Prentice-Hall of Canada Inc., *Toronto*
Prentice-Hall Hispanoamericana, S.A., *Mexico*
Prentice-Hall of India Private Limited, *New Delhi*
Prentice-Hall of Japan, Inc., *Tokyo*
Simon & Schuster Asia Ptd. Ltd., *Singapore*
Editora Prentice-Hall do Brasil, Ltda., *Rio de Janeiro*

CONTENTS

PREFACE

When IBM PCs were first introduced in the early 80s, they used an operating system called DOS (which stands for "Disk Operating System"). Most IBM PCs and the millions of similar computers that have been sold continue to use this operating system. When using DOS, you enter a command by typing it in. DOS has hundreds of commands, and it can be a fairly demanding task to remember the ones you need. As computers have become faster and more powerful, it has become possible to take a lot of the difficulty out of computing by designing interfaces, or screen displays, that are not only attractive but also easy to use. These new interfaces, which make extensive use of icons (little graphical pictures) and menus (lists of commands), are called graphical user interfaces (GUI—pronounced "goo-ey"—for short). There are a number of graphical user interfaces in use today, and Windows is by far the most popular.

Windows has three immediately noticeable features. First, its graphic screen contains many icons that you can click to operate programs and execute commands. Second, it displays commands on menus so you can choose the one you want without having to remember how to type it in. Finally, it can run more than one program at a time. This is very useful, especially when you want to transfer data from one program to another. Windows also has one feature that isn't so obvious. It still uses the DOS operating system but hides it unless you want to find it.

This text introduces you to Windows without assuming that you have prior computing experience. Everything you need to know to become a proficient Windows user is presented here. You needn't bring anything to your learning experience except a willingness to explore a new and exciting way to compute.

■ CONTENTS AND APPROACH

One of the main functions of Windows is to make it easy to start and use application programs. These are the programs you use to perform work on the computer. Typical application programs are those that you use for word processing, spreadsheet analysis, graphics preparation, and database management. Windows has a number of built-in application programs. File Manager helps you manage your files; Write allows you to create, edit, and format documents; and Paintbrush allows you to create and edit graphics that you can print or include in your other documents as illustrations.

This text introduces Windows through these, and other, built-in applications. For example, file and disk management is introduced through File Manager; opening and printing files is introduced using Notepad; and copying, moving, linking, and embedding data between applications is introduced using Paintbrush and Write.

Because the built-in Windows applications introduced in this text work much like the more powerful Windows application programs such as Word, WordPerfect, Excel, Quattro Pro, 1-2-3, Access, and Paradox, the principles and procedures that you learn in this text will carry over to those programs. Learning the other programs will be easier because you will already know many of their basic operations, such as how to load them, execute commands, save files, and make printouts.

■ ORGANIZATION

This text is organized into chapters, which in turn are organized into pictorial tutorials called PicTorials. Each PicTorial begins with objectives and then proceeds step by step through a series of related procedures. The concept behind each procedure is first discussed, and then a *tutorial* guides you in exploring the concept on the computer. At the end of each PicTorial are a number of *skill-build-*

ing exercises that you use to practice the procedures that you have learned at the computer. Following the exercises is a *visual quiz* that tests your understanding of the elements you have explored in the PicTorial.

Chapter 1 covers Program Manager—how you use it to open, close, size, and drag windows and execute commands.

Chapter 2 introduces File Manager and shows you how to use it to manage disks, files, and directories.

Chapter 3 covers many of Windows' built-in application programs. Notepad is introduced first, to teach you basic procedures such as opening and saving files, printing files, and cutting and pasting. Notepad is so easy to use that it doesn't get in the way of your learning. Write is introduced in the next PicTorial, and covered in detail, because it is such a useful program for school and personal work. Finally Paintbrush is introduced, and you use paintings created with it to explore the important concepts of copying, linking, and embedding data between application programs.

Chapter 4 introduces techniques you can use to control your Windows environment and DOS applications.

■ COMPUTER ACTIVITIES

Many textbooks use a projects approach, having you work on a limited set of documents as you progress through the text. The problem with this approach is its limitation. How many procedures are required for even a complex document, and how many times need they be repeated? Without practicing procedures, and doing so repeatedly, you will not master them. This text uses a more structured approach that incorporates three classes of documents.

▶ *Tutorial documents*, used in the tutorials in the text, have been designed to teach a single procedure. They are the most effective learning tools for introducing a procedure. For example, a single document can allow you to explore all of the choices on the Character menu of Write. You can use Arial, Courier New, and Times New Roman fonts; sizes from 4 to 127 points; and bold, italic, and underlining as well as superscripts and subscripts. No project-type document would allow you to explore all of these choices that are available in a single dialog box.

▶ *Exercise documents* at the end of each PicTorial use the build-as-you-go approach. These documents are threaded through the text from the beginning to the end. As you master new procedures, you use them to revise and refine these documents.

▶ *Project documents* at the end of each chapter are like exercise documents but require an understanding of all of the procedures covered in the chapter.

■ KEY FEATURES

Windows is a visually oriented program, so this text uses a visual approach. It features two unique elements, PicTorials and VISual Quizzes, in addition to a number of other features designed to make it a better learning tool.

PICTORIAL FEATURES

▶ *PicTorials* are heavily illustrated tutorials. The visuals serve two purposes. First, they help explain concepts. Second, they tell you when you are on course as you follow the steps in the tutorials.

▶ *VISual Quizzes* at the end of each PicTorial test your understanding of the Windows environment. Unlike standard questions presented in just words, these questions are illustrated.

▶ Five different kinds of *boxes* help make the book easy to use.

Common Wrong Turns boxes alert you to where many people make mistakes and show you how to avoid them.

Tips boxes point out shortcuts and other interesting features about many procedures.

Looking Back boxes are used whenever a procedure that has been discussed earlier is essential to completing a new task. These summaries are intended to remind you how to perform a task without your having to refer back in the text.

Looking Ahead boxes are used whenever a procedure is unavoidably referred to before it has been discussed in detail. These boxes help you avoid confusion by providing a brief description and an assurance that a more detailed discussion will follow.

Pausing for Practice boxes appear periodically in tutorials when essential procedures have been introduced. They encourage you to stop at key points and practice these procedures until they become second nature.

CHAPTER FEATURES

▶ At the end of each chapter you will find a wide variety of true-false, multiple choice, and fill-in-the-blank questions to test how well you have understood the material.

▶ *Projects* at the end of every chapter give you the opportunity to practice the procedures you have learned in that chapter and demonstrate that you have mastered them.

END OF TEXT FEATURES

▶ A *quick reference section* at the end of the text summarizes the most important Windows procedures discussed in the text and some additional options. When working on your own, you can find the information you need in this section without having to dig it out of the PicTorials in the text.

▶ A *glossary* at the end of the text defines key terms. Terms appearing in this glossary are italicized in the text the first time they are used.

CONTENT FEATURES

▶ The documents used for lab activities are real-world applications. For example, in the Write PicTorial you work with the EDUCOM statement "Using Software: A Guide to the Ethical and Legal Use of Software for Members of the Academic Community."

▶ Object linking and embedding are two of the most important features of the Windows environment. Both are covered in some detail using Paintbrush and Write as the source (server) and destination (client) applications.

▶ This text covers non-Windows applications. It discusses adding DOS programs to Windows groups, opening DOS applications, PIF files, and accessing the DOS command prompt.

THE PAINT SHOP PRO APPLICATION

When developing this text, we knew we had to include a useful Windows application so you could have the experience of installing it just as you will install any new Windows applications you encounter later. After a long search, we were fortunate to have Suzanne Dougherty, a leading California computer animator, tip us off to an application called Paint Shop Pro. Designed to manipulate bitmapped images and digitized photographs, the program was much like the widely used but expensive Photoshop and PhotoStyler programs. We got a copy of the application and explored it and were amazed to find such power and ease of use in such an inexpensive program. The publishers of this program have been kind enough to grant you the right to use this program in your first introduction to Windows, and a copy is included in the *psp* directory on the *Windows Student Resource Disk*. However, this shareware program is expensive to develop and maintain. The fact that it is on the *Windows Student Resource Disk* does not imply that the publisher's charge for this text is payment for the program. Continued use beyond the duration of the course requires purchasing the licensed version of Paint Shop Pro. Your instructor should explain the concept of shareware to you, and stress how it provides one of the few remaining areas for innovation now that the software market is dominated by a few giant firms. It is important that you understand that shareware is like going to the movies and paying only if you like the film. It's a great concept, but it only works if people support the developers. Paying the low price for continued use doesn't only make you feel better; it also gets you a printed manual and notice of improved versions as they become available. An order form is contained in the file *vendor.doc* in the *psp* directory of the *Windows Student Resource Disk*.

■ SUPPLEMENTS

The following supplements to this text have been made available by the publisher:

▶ The *Windows Student Resource Disk*. This disk contains all of the files needed to complete the computer activities in this text. In addition, it contains a copy of the shareware program Paint Shop Pro that is used to demonstrate how to install Windows applications.

▶ An *Instructor's Manual with Tests,* prepared by Donna Matherly of Tallahassee Community College. The manual contains suggested course outlines for a variety of course lengths and formats, teaching tips and a list of competencies to be attained for each PicTorial, solutions and answers to VISual Quizzes and all computer activities, and a complete test bank of over 200 questions.

▶ *A Windows Instructor's Resource Disk.* This disk features two important files, created by Gray Patton of Forsyth Technical Community College, designed to be installed on your systems and help you and your students get more enjoyment from the course.

    ▶ First, an on-line help file with a built-in glossary operates just like Windows' on-line help. However, unlike Windows', this system is designed to guide students through the procedures and activities covered in this book.

    ▶ Second, a batch file restores Windows to the way it was when it was first installed. Any settings changed by students and any icons or groups that have been deleted are restored. Automatically restoring all settings should prove to be a great timesaver for the lab manager. And much instructor time should be saved because many unnecessary questions caused by system changes left over from previous users will be eliminated.

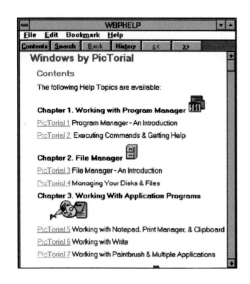

■ NOTE TO THE INSTRUCTOR

▶ When working with Windows, you can execute most commands by just pointing and clicking with the mouse. In most cases there are also alternate keyboard commands that you can use. Except where the alternate keyboard commands are obviously superior, this text discusses only the mouse commands, and the computer activities assume that computers are equipped with a mouse.

▶ The PicTorials in this text are based on the default Windows screen display that appears when you first install the program. They assume that the StartUp and Applications group windows may vary but otherwise that your systems will be set up so they look like the illustration in PicTorial 1's section "Exploring the Windows Screen."

▶ When students work with Windows, they can make changes in it that affect the next user. If these changes remain in effect, some of the hands-on activities in this text will not work as described. To overcome this problem, the *Windows Instructor's Resource Disk* contains a batch file that copies all of the important Windows files (*.ini* and *.grp*) to a hidden directory on drive C. Then each time Windows is loaded, these files are automatically copied to the Windows directory, where they ensure that the program runs as originally installed. If you make any changes to Windows that you want to preserve, you can run the *install* portion of this batch file system, and it copies the changed files to the hidden directory so they are preserved.

ACKNOWLEDGMENTS

Working on this text has been an unusually enjoyable experience. No book is ever the work of a single individual, so teams of people assemble to get the job done and then disperse to other jobs when they have finished. The development of this text has drawn together the most talented and committed group of people that I have ever had the experience of working with. Here they are, in the order in which they became involved in the project.

To begin, David Ford worked with the author during the development of the text's concept. The book's heavily visual approach required the insights of a designer such as David who could work with the author on how best to integrate text and graphics to the extent done here. At the publisher's end have been Liz Kendall and Cecil Yarbrough, both of whom have made major contributions to the text from beginning to end. On the academic end have been the reviewers and contributors who have tried to make this the best possible text. They include the following:

Cheryl L. Dukarich, Pima Community College
Sandra S. Hagman, Forsyth Technical Community College
Norman P. Hahn, Thomas Nelson Community College
Sue Higgins, Community College or Rhode Island
Sally L. Kurz, Coastline Community College
Amelia J. Maretka, Wharton County Junior College
Gray Patton, Forsyth Technical Community College
Philip J. Sciame, Dominican College
Betsy Walsh, Laney College

Finally, at the production end, thanks go to all of the people at Function Thru Form, who used the latest digital tools to take the book from raw manuscript to final published form as easily as it could be done (which is not the same as saying it was easy!). The people at Function Thru Form who contributed to the text include Clea Chmela, Robin D'Amato, Anne DeMarinis, Nelson Gomez, Keith James, Rita Myers, Lise Prown, and Gwen Waldron. Supporting the production of the text were Freddy Flake, who prepared the dozens of line drawings, and Cathy Morin, who prepared over 700 images of the screen; Jane Avery, who coordinated reviewing; and Karen Moreau, the Prentice-Hall representative in northern Florida who had some valuable suggestions for the author (as usual) which appear in this text as Common Wrong Turns boxes.

All of these people, each and every one, took a personal interest in this text; and that interest shows in the work you are now holding. Any shortcomings are of course the responsibility of the author (me) and in no way reflect on the professionalism and talent of this fine group.

DEDICATION

This text is dedicated to Paul and Dorothy Curtin, without whom none of this would have been possible (including any errors that you might find).

About the Author

Dennis Curtin's 25-plus years' business experience in educational publishing provide a rich and unique perspective for his computer applications texts. He has served in executive positions at several companies, including Prentice Hall, where he has been a textbook sales representative, an acquisitions editor, editorial director of the engineering, vocational, and technical division, and editor in chief of the international division. For the past 9 years, he has been primarily a writer of college textbooks on end user computer applications.

Dennis has been involved with microcomputers since the introduction of the original Apple II. He was a beta tester for the first version of Lotus 1-2-3 when Lotus Corporation had only 9 employees squeezed into a small Kendall Square office. In the years since, he has taught in adult education and corporate training programs, but he readily acknowledges that he has learned most of what he knows about textbooks by working with thousands of instructors during the writing, reviewing, and revising of his own books.

The primary author and series editor of the COMPASS Series and author of several popular microcomputer concepts texts, he is now spearheading and developing an exciting new series of highly visual Windows applications texts called the PicTorial Series. This title is the first book in the PicTorial Series.

Dennis welcomes feedback and suggestions from students and instructors using his books. You can write to him at the following address:

Dennis Curtin
c/o Software Skills Editor
Prentice Hall College Division
113 Sylvan Ave, Rt. 9W
Englewood Cliffs, NJ 07632

Chapter 1
WORKING WITH PROGRAM MANAGER

PicTorial 1

PROGRAM MANAGER – AN INTRODUCTION

After completing this PicTorial, you will be able to:

▶ Start your computer system and load Windows

▶ Name and describe the parts of a window

▶ Point with the mouse

▶ Click and double-click the mouse

▶ Minimize, maximize, and restore windows

▶ Change the active window

▶ Drag windows and change their size

▶ Exit Windows and turn off your equipment

The microcomputer is a versatile machine. With it you can calculate a budget for this year's college expenses, plot a graph of the results, and, finding that you won't have enough money, write a letter to your boss asking for a raise. Each of these tasks is an *application*. To perform it, you load an *application program* specific to the task. For example, WordPerfect® and Microsoft® Word are word processing application programs used to enter, edit, and format memos, letters, reports, and other documents. Excel and 1-2-3® are spreadsheet application programs used to work with numbers and make calculations.

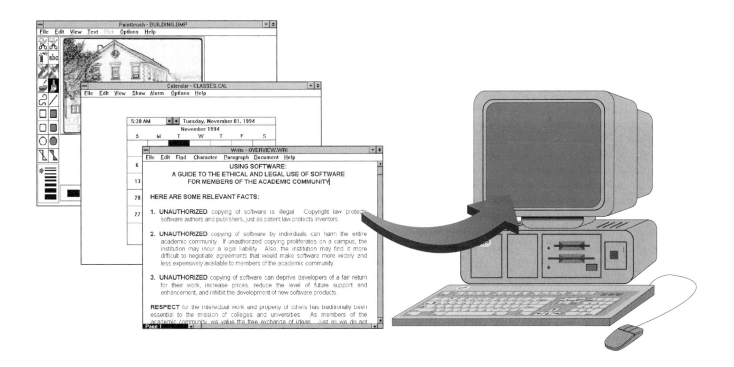

To change from one application to another you switch from one application program to another. In this sense, the computer is like an actor, and the application programs are like scripts. When the actor changes scripts, he or she can perform a different role. By changing application programs, you can make your computer perform different applications. Being *computer literate* means that you understand how to use application programs to perform useful work.

Windows is designed to make it easy to work with application programs. Unlike earlier systems where the screen just displayed a prompt such as C:\>, and you had to type commands, Windows' *Graphical User Interface* (also called a GUI—pronounced "goo-ee") allows you to choose commands from pull-down menus and run more than one application program at a time, each in its own window. Using Windows you can run a spreadsheet in one window and a word processor in another. Windows also gives a common look to most programs that are developed to take advantage of its features. Standard commands load programs; call up help; save, retrieve, and print files; enter and edit data; and quit applications. This makes it easier to learn new programs because many of your existing skills are transferable.

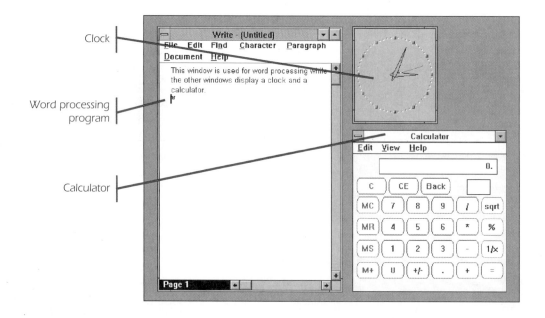

The most important Windows application program is *Program Manager*. Program Manager is important because, unlike most other applications, it remains in the computer's memory from the time you load Windows until you quit. Program Manager's sole task is to start or *launch* all other Windows application programs such as word processors, spreadsheets, and database managers. When you exit an application that you launched from Program Manager, you always return to Program Manager.

This PicTorial introduces you to Program Manager step by step. All of the procedures you learn here will also apply to other Windows applications. They are fundamental to operating Windows, so take your time. The concepts and procedures that are introduced later will be much easier if you have mastered the procedures presented here.

LOADING WINDOWS

To use Windows, you begin by loading the computer's operating system, usually DOS. This is called *booting the system*. The term *booting* comes from the expression "pulling yourself up by your bootstraps."

COMMON WRONG TURNS: ANXIETY

If you have never before worked with a computer, now's the time to *relax*. New computer users often have anxieties about things that might go wrong. These fears, all of which are unjustified, include the fear they will somehow cause damage to the computer. There is nothing you can do to blow up the computer or otherwise hurt the system, so there is no reason to be anxious. Also, don't be intimidated by others who seem to grasp the procedures more quickly. They may have had previous experience with computers or just have a knack at these things. These differences among users tend to level out after a few weeks when everyone feels comfortable.

▶▶ TUTORIAL

1. Open the door to floppy drive A or eject any disk from that drive. When you turn on a computer, it looks to the *startup drive* for the operating system files that it needs to start up. On a hard disk system like the one you are using, the startup drive is the hard drive C, but the computer still looks to the floppy drive A first. If there is a disk in that drive when you turn on the computer, you could have a problem loading Windows.

2. To boot most systems, you just turn on the computer and the display monitor. If you can't find the on/off switches, ask someone where they are.

When you turn on the computer, it may seem to be inactive for a few moments. In fact, it is running a diagnostic program to be sure the system is operating correctly. What then happens and what you do next depends on how your system is set up. Windows may be loaded automatically or one of the other possible outcomes illustrated in the box "Things That Can Happen When You Boot a System" may occur.

The Windows screen display may appear when you boot your system.

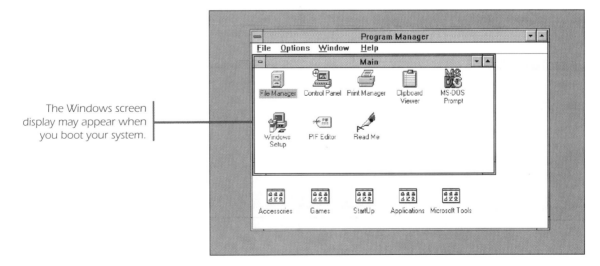

A menu designed specifically for your computer lab may appear. If it does you can usually type a number and press Enter↵ to load Windows.

The screen may be blank. If it is, turn on the display monitor or adjust its brightness and contrast.

The DOS command prompt may appear. If this happens, type WIN and press Enter↵.

An error message may read "Non-System disk or disk error." Remove the disk in drive A and follow the instructions on the screen.

COMMON WRONG TURNS: NON-SYSTEM DISK IN DRIVE A

When you boot a system, you may see the error message *Non-System disk or disk error* or a similar message. This appears when you turn on the computer with a disk in drive A that does not contain the operating system files that the computer needs. If you get this message on your system, open the drive door and press any key to continue.

TIP: ARE WE TIMING EGGS HERE, OR WHAT?

When you first load Windows, and at other times when you are using it, you will see an hourglass appear on the screen. This is Windows' way of telling you it's busy and that you should wait before expecting it to do anything else.

TIP: REBOOTING YOUR SYSTEM

Turning a computer on to boot it is called a *cold boot*. Rebooting a computer when it is already on is called a *warm boot*. To warm-boot the system when Windows isn't loaded, you hold down Ctrl and Alt while you press Del. (This command is usually written out as Ctrl+Alt+Del.) Warm booting clears all data from the computer's memory and has almost the same effect as turning the computer off and then back on again. If Windows is loaded, pressing Ctrl+Alt+Del terminates an application program, but you remain in Windows. This is called a *local reboot*. To warm-boot the system, you press Ctrl+Alt+Del again. You normally use this procedure only when you encounter a problem with your system. For example, there are times when Windows "freezes up." You may be able to move the mouse pointer, but you can't execute commands. Whenever possible, you should exit Windows before warm booting your system; otherwise you may lose data.

EXPLORING THE WINDOWS SCREEN

When you load Windows, your screen may look like the illustration shown here. Because Windows can be customized, your screen may look different, but you should still be able to find the elements we are about to discuss.

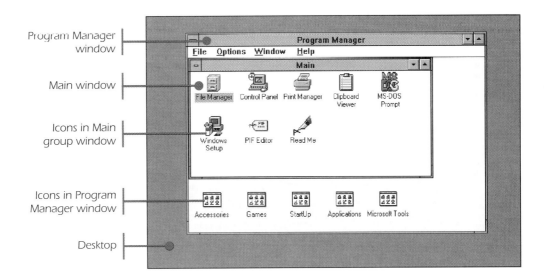

First, notice the boxlike area with a title bar at its top labeled *Program Manager*. This is a *window* about which you'll learn a lot more later. Inside this first window is another window with a title bar labeled *Main*. When working with Windows, it's common to see one window inside another like this.

Inside the Main window are graphical symbols called *icons*. Each icon has a descriptive label, and its design also gives you a visual clue to what it does. In fact, the term *icon* means "a picture, image, or other representation." Well-designed icons accurately represent their assigned function and are easy to remember. For example, the File Manager icon looks like a file cabinet because you use this application to manage the files on your disks.

Below the Main window are a series of small labeled boxes, also called icons. Your screen may display icons in this area that are labeled *Accessories*, *Games*, *StartUp*, and *Applications* and perhaps *Microsoft Tools*.

Notice that the windows and icons are occupying only part of the screen. Around them (and beneath them) is an area called the *desktop*. This desktop is simply the space on the screen available for the display of Windows' various elements. As you'll see, you can add items to this electronic desktop, move items about on it, or take them away from it just as you can on the top of a real desk. In fact, some systems may display one or more icons on the desktop (and not in other windows) when you start Windows. For example, you may see an icon labeled *Vsafe Manager*. This application continually scans the system for signs of viruses that may damage data. If your desktop displays icons, you might ask what they are for.

EXPLORING PROGRAM MANAGER

Windows gets its name because it displays application programs and documents in boxes called windows. All of these windows have many of the same features.

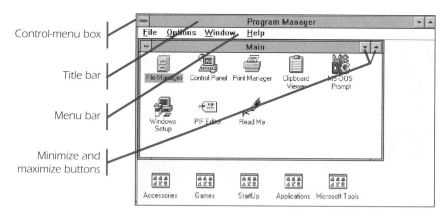

Control-menu box

Title bar

Menu bar

Minimize and maximize buttons

At the top of each window is a *title bar* that lists the name of the application program running in the window or otherwise describes the window's contents.

Every window displays up- and down-pointing arrowheads to the right of the title bar. These are called the *Minimize* (▼) and *Maximize* (▲) *buttons*. As you'll soon see, they are used to change the size of the window.

The upper-left corner of every window displays a *Control-menu box* that displays a Control menu when you click it with the mouse. This Control menu is discussed in the next PicTorial.

A *menu bar* immediately below the title bar displays the names of menus. These menus list commands that you execute to operate your program. Menus will be discussed in detail in the next PicTorial.

EXPLORING YOUR MOUSE

Although Windows can be operated from the keyboard, it is designed to be most effective when used with a pointing device such as a *mouse*. Using a mouse, you can execute commands, specify options, display help, or indicate where you want to type in data. Mice can vary considerably in design, but the most common mouse has two buttons and is connected to the computer by a thin cable.

Turn your mouse over and you may see part of a ball protruding through its bottom (not all mice use balls). When you move the mouse across the table surface, this ball spins and sends electrical signals to the computer through the cable. These signals move the *mouse pointer* on the screen. The mouse pointer is usually an arrow, but it changes shape depending on what it is pointing to and what function it is ready to perform. For example, when it is a single-headed arrow, you can click icons or buttons. When it is a two-headed arrow, you can drag a window's border to make the window wider or deeper.

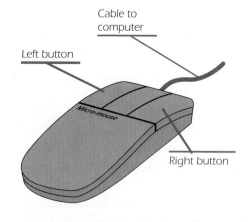

Cable to computer

Left button

Micro-mouse

Right button

Mouse Pointer Shapes

Normal

Pointing to left or right window border

Pointing to window corner

Pointing to top or bottom window border

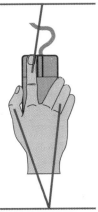

Rest your index finger on the left button.

Grip the sides of the mouse with your thumb and ring finger.

PAUSING FOR PRACTICE

Moving the mouse pointer is one of the most fundamental skills you must master. Pause at this point to practice. At first, it seems hard to point to just the right place. Don't be discouraged; it just takes some practice. Pick out an object on the screen, perhaps one of the letters in an icon's title, and then quickly move the mouse pointer to it. Point to window borders and corners until you can accurately make the pointer change shape. Con tinue practicing until you can move it to any point you want on the first try.

▶▶ **TUTORIAL**

1. With the mouse cable facing away from you, grip the mouse with your thumb and ring finger.

2. Move the mouse about the desk and watch the mouse pointer move about the screen. This is called *pointing*. If you haven't used a mouse before, you'll see that you need practice to make the mouse pointer move in a predictable fashion. If you run out of room on the desk or mouse pad when moving the mouse, lift it and place it in a new position and then continue moving it.

COMMON WRONG TURNS: MOVING THE MOUSE POINTER

When first using a mouse, most people cannot control the mouse pointer on the screen. It seems to move in unpredictable directions. To gain control, hold the mouse exactly perpendicular to the front of the screen. Now when you move it left or right, the pointer on the screen moves left or right on the screen. When you move the mouse forward or backward, the pointer moves up or down on the screen. If you hold the mouse at an angle other than perpendicular to the front of the screen, it's harder to predict the direction in which the pointer will move.

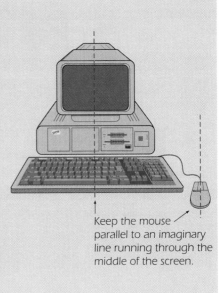

Keep the mouse parallel to an imaginary line running through the middle of the screen.

3. Point to each side of the Program Manager window and you'll see the pointer change shape.

4. Point to each corner of the Program Manager window and you'll see the pointer take other shapes.

CLICKING AND DOUBLE-CLICKING THE MOUSE

Moving the mouse pointer around the screen isn't enough to operate Windows. You must also know how and when to click the mouse buttons. Depending on the situation, you click once or twice.

▶ *Clicking* is quickly pressing and then releasing a mouse button—usually the left one. The finger action is similar to typing a character on the keyboard. (Windows has a command that swaps the functions of the left and right buttons on the mouse. If you are left-handed and having trouble, ask for help.)

▶ *Double-clicking* is quickly pressing a button twice in succession. Double-clicking takes practice.

The first question a new user always asks is "When do I click and when do I double-click?" Generally, you click once to select an item and double-click to execute an action. In other words, clicking an item tells Windows you want to use it. Double-clicking starts an application or executes a command.

▶▶ TUTORIAL

Maximize button

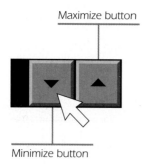

Minimize button

1. With the mouse cable facing away from you, grip the mouse with your thumb and ring finger so that your index finger rests on the left mouse button.

2. Look closely at the title bar labeled *Main* (the smaller of the two windows on the screen), and you'll see two arrowheads, called buttons, to the right of the title. The Minimize button (▼) points down and the Maximize button (▲) points up. Move the mouse until the mouse pointer is pointing to the Main window's Minimize button (▼).

3. Click (the left button) once, and the Main window changes to an icon. It now looks just like the other icons at the bottom of the Program Manager window, but it is labeled *Main* just as the window was.

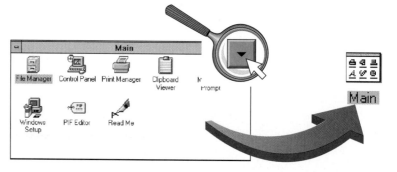

4. Double-click the Main icon to open it up into a window. (If you have problems doing this, see the box "Common Wrong Turns: Double-Clicking.")

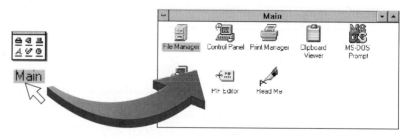

PAUSING FOR PRACTICE

Clicking and double-clicking are fundamental skills for using Windows. Pause here and continue practicing these skills by repeating this Tutorial section until they are second nature. When you are finished, leave the Main group window open.

MINIMIZING, MAXIMIZING, AND RESTORING WINDOWS

A window can be any one of three sizes: maximized so it fills the entire screen or the window that contains it, minimized to an icon, or restored to its original size to occupy only a part of the screen. To change sizes, you use the Maximize, Minimize, and Restore buttons located in the upper-right corner of each window.

▶ Clicking the Minimize button (▼) minimizes the window to an icon. (Double-clicking an icon opens it up into a window of the same size it was before it was minimized.)

Minimize Button
Click to minimize a window to an icon.

▶ Clicking the Maximize button (▲) expands the window to fill the screen or the window that contains it. Once you have clicked the Maximize button, it is replaced by the *Restore button*, which has both an up and a down arrowhead.

Maximize Button
Click to maximize a window to full screen.

Restore Button
Click to restore a window to its original size.

▶ Clicking the Restore button returns the window to its original size.

▶▶ **TUTORIAL**

1. Click Program Manager's Maximize button to enlarge the window to full screen.

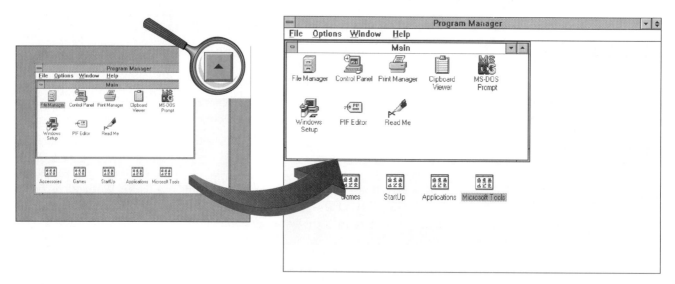

2. Click Program Manager's Restore button to restore the window to its original size.

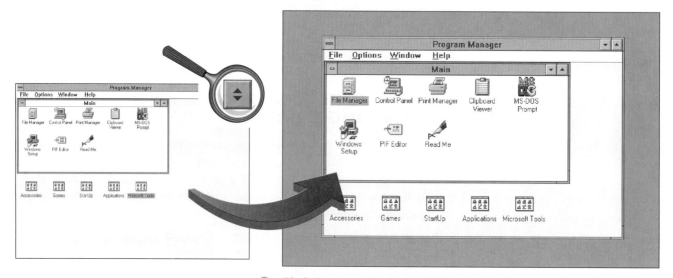

3. Click Program Manager's Minimize button to reduce the window to an icon.

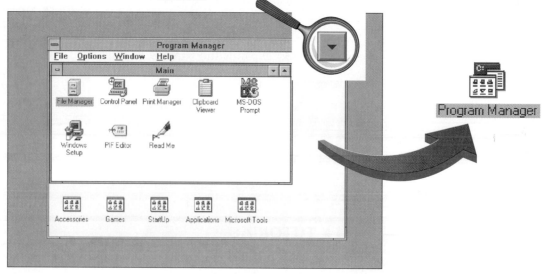

4. Double-click Program Manager's icon to open it back up into a window.

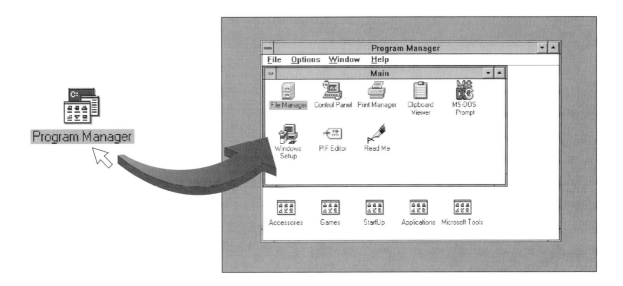

5. Click Program Manager's Maximize button to enlarge the window to full screen.

6. If the Main window is displayed as an icon, double-click the icon to open it back up into a window. Now click the Main window's Maximize button to enlarge it to fill the Program Manager window.

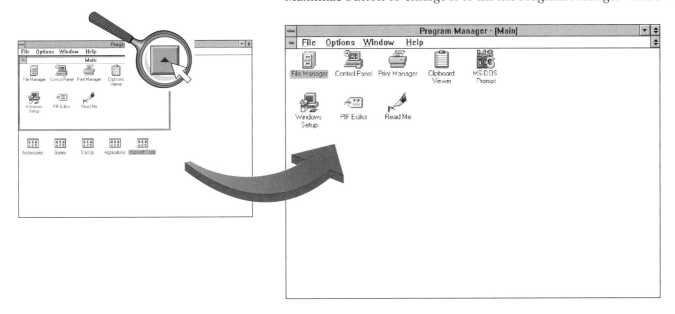

Notice the following about the window:

▶ There appears to be only one window.

▶ There is only one title bar, the one for the Main window, but it contains both names.

▶ There are now two Restore buttons, the upper one for the Program Manager window and the lower one for the Main window.

7. Click the lower Restore button to see what happens.

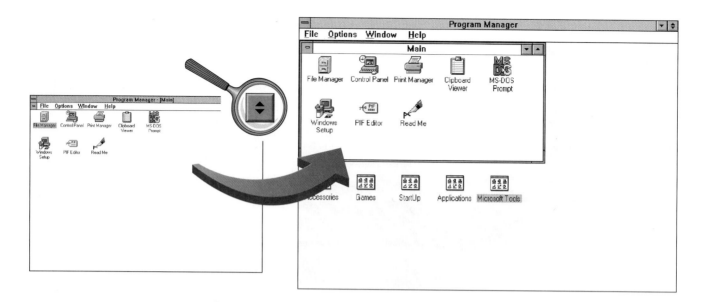

8. Click the remaining Restore button.

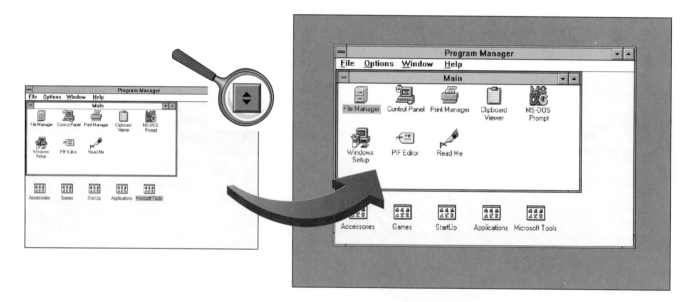

9. Repeat Steps 5 and 6.

10. Repeat Steps 7 and 8 in reverse order to see what happens.

PAUSING FOR PRACTICE

When you work with Windows it's easy to get lost because windows can overlap or hide other windows, making it difficult to find the document or program that you want to work with. You'll only feel at home when you have mastered minimizing, maximizing, and restoring windows. At this point, pause and practice minimizing, maximizing, and restoring the Program Manager window and the Main window until you have mastered the concept and procedures.

EXPLORING PROGRAM MANAGER'S GROUPS

As you work with Windows you will find that there are different kinds of windows and icons. They all work the same, but they are referred to by different names. For example, since Program Manager is an application, its window and icon are referred to as an *application window* and an *application icon*. When Program Manager is displayed as a window, it contains other windows called *group windows* because they contain groups of application icons. When you close one of these group windows to an icon, it is called a *group icon*. Group windows are simply a way to keep related application icons together so the desktop is organized.

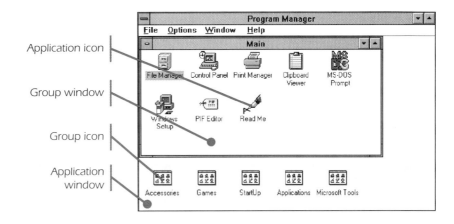

Windows can be easily customized, so group windows and icons vary widely from system to system. However, when Windows is first installed on a computer, its Main, Accessories, and Games group windows are identical on all systems. In addition, there are two group windows that vary widely from system to system. One is the Applications window, which contains icons for the application programs that were on the computer at the time Windows was installed. The other is the StartUp window, which contains icons for the applications you want to run every time Windows is loaded. When Windows is initially installed, the Main group is displayed as a window so you can see its application icons, and other groups are displayed as group icons at the bottom of the Program Manager window.

TIP: DOS 6 AND WINDOWS

Windows runs on top of the DOS operating system, which exists in different versions. DOS 6 is the first version of DOS to be integrated with Windows. It adds a group named Microsoft Tools to Program Manager. This group contains icons that you can use to check for viruses, back up files for security, or undelete files that have been deleted by mistake. You will not see this group window on systems running versions of DOS prior to DOS 6.

▶▶ TUTORIAL

1. Click the Main group's Minimize button to reduce it to an icon.

2. Double-click the group icon labeled *Accessories* to open it into a window.

3. Look carefully at each of the icons it contains.

4. Click the Accessories group's Minimize button to reduce it back to an icon.

5. Double-click the group icon labeled *Games* to open it into a window.

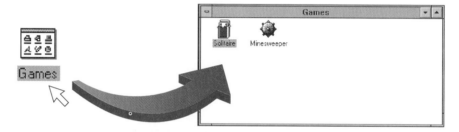

6. Look carefully at each of the icons that it contains.

7. Click the Games group's Minimize button to reduce it back to an icon.

PAUSING FOR PRACTICE

Double-click each of Program Manager's group icons and closely examine the icons it contains. Then click the Minimize button to reduce the window to an icon before opening the next group window. On a separate sheet of paper, write down the names of any icons in the StartUp and Applications groups (and Microsoft Tools if it is on your desktop).

COMMON WRONG TURNS: WHAT TO DO WHEN YOU GET LOST

It's easy to get lost with windows piled on top of windows. If you can't find the data you are looking for, click each window's Minimize button until you find the window you are looking for.

DRAGGING WINDOWS AND ICONS

The desktop can display more than one window at a time. The *active window*, the one you are working in, is always on top of other windows that may overlap it. It may therefore partially or completely hide them. To see one window, you may therefore have to move another. One way to move a window (or an icon) is to drag it with the mouse. *Drag* means to move something on the screen by moving the mouse. To drag an object, you point to it, hold down the left mouse button, and move the mouse to position the object. When you have dragged it to where you want it, you release the mouse button. To cancel a move once you have begun it, you press [Esc] before releasing the mouse button.

▶▶ TUTORIAL

1. Point to Program Manager's title bar.

2. Hold down the left mouse button.

3. Drag the window to where you want it. As you are dragging the window, its outline is displayed.

Outline of window being dragged

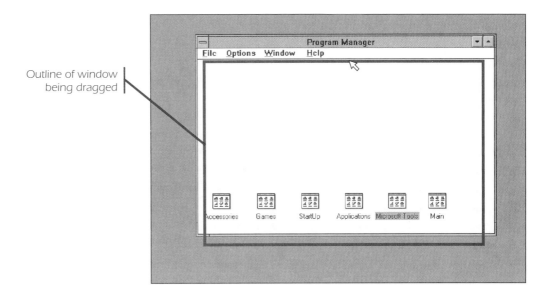

4. Release the left button.

5. If the Main group window is open, click its Minimize button to reduce it to an icon. Now point to the Main icon and hold down the left mouse button.

6. Drag the icon to where you want it and then release the mouse button.

7. Point to the Main icon again, hold down the left mouse button, and drag the icon to a new position but press [Esc] to cancel the move before you release the mouse button.

8. Click Program Manager's Maximize button to open it to full screen.

9. Double-click both the Main and Accessories icons to open both windows. When you do so, the last one you opened overlaps the first.

10. Point to the title bar of the top window, hold down the left mouse button, and drag the window to a new position. When the windows still overlap but you can see the icons in the bottom window, release the mouse button.

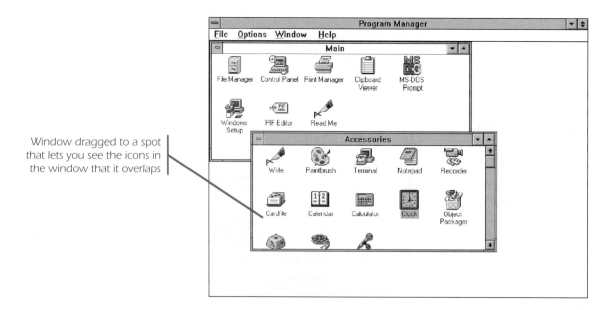

Window dragged to a spot that lets you see the icons in the window that it overlaps

11. Click the visible part of the bottom window to move it to the top and make it the active window. Notice how the title bar of the active window is always highlighted, usually in color on most systems.

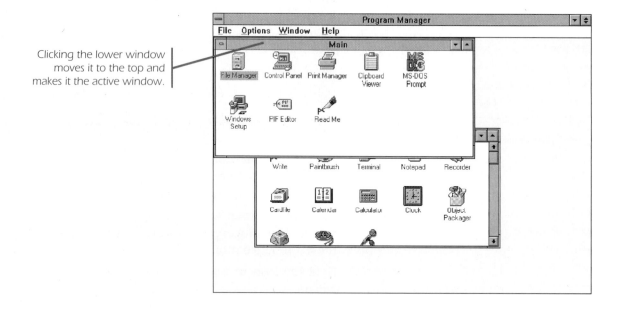

Clicking the lower window moves it to the top and makes it the active window.

PAUSING FOR PRACTICE

Practice dragging windows and icons about the desktop until you feel comfortable with the procedure. Practice pressing Esc in the middle of dragging to cancel the move. With more than one group window open, practice making one after the other the active window.

Dragging the lower (or upper) border makes the window deeper.

Dragging the right (or left) border makes the window wider.

Dragging a corner makes the window both wider and deeper.

CHANGING THE SIZE OF A WINDOW

When you click a window's Restore button, the window returns to its original size. How do you change this original size permanently? You drag one of the window's borders or corners. To do so, point with the mouse to a border or corner so that the mouse pointer turns into a two-headed arrow. Then hold down the left button and drag the border or corner to make the window larger or smaller. When the window is the size you want, release the button.

▶▶ TUTORIAL

1. Point to the right side of any open window until the mouse pointer turns into a horizontal double-headed arrow.

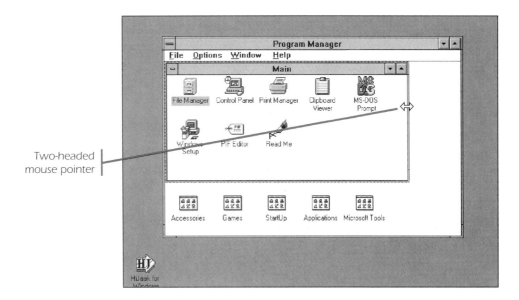

Two-headed mouse pointer

2. Hold down the left mouse button and drag the window wider. As you do so, an outline of the window's new size is displayed.

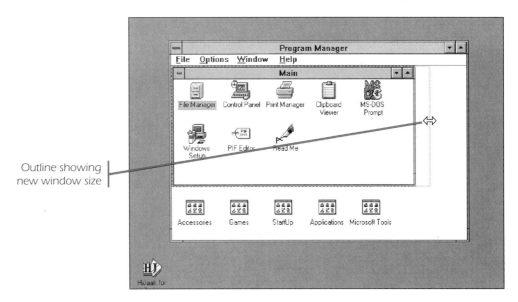

Outline showing new window size

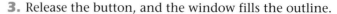

3. Release the button, and the window fills the outline.

4. Point to the bottom of any open window until the mouse pointer turns into a vertical double-headed arrow.

5. Hold down the left mouse button and drag the window deeper and then release the button.

6. Point to the lower-right corner of any open window until the mouse pointer turns into a diagonal double-headed arrow.

7. Hold down the left mouse button and drag the window so it is both narrower and shallower, and then release the button.

PAUSING FOR PRACTICE

Practice changing the size of windows on the screen until you feel comfortable with the procedure. When you make them smaller, some icons may be hidden, but ignore that for now.

EXPLORING SCROLL BARS

Scroll bars are located on the right and bottom edges of many windows so you can use the mouse to scroll through the contents of the window. Program Manager's group windows display these scroll bars only when they are too small to display all of the icons they contain.

The scroll bar you use to move the contents of a window up and down is called the *vertical scroll bar*. The one you use to move the contents side to side is called the *horizontal scroll bar*. Both scroll bars contains three basic elements: the *up* (or left) *scroll arrow*, the *down* (or right) *scroll arrow*, and the *scroll box*. To scroll the contents of the window a line at a time, click one of the scroll arrows. If you point to one of these arrows and hold down the mouse button, the screen scrolls continuously.

The scroll box, which is sometimes referred to as an elevator because of the way it moves up and down the vertical scroll bar, serves two functions. First, its position on the vertical scroll bar tells you where you are in a window's contents. If it is at the top of the scroll bar, you are at the beginning of the contents. If it is halfway between the top and bottom of the scroll bar, you are in the middle of the contents. If it is at the bottom of the scroll bar, you are at the end of the contents.

Second, the scroll box lets you move quickly to any part of a window's contents. To scroll one screen at a time, point to the scroll bar above or below the scroll box and click. To move to a specific part of a window's contents (such as the middle), drag the box to that part of the vertical scroll bar.

The horizontal scroll bar works the same way. Drag the box to the right side of the horizontal scroll bar to see the right edge of the window's contents.

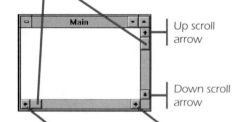

Scroll box

Up scroll arrow

Down scroll arrow

Left scroll arrow   Right scroll arrow

▶▶ **TUTORIAL**

1. With the Program Manager window open, press [F1] to open the Program Manager Help window. Below the menu bar is a row of *command buttons*.

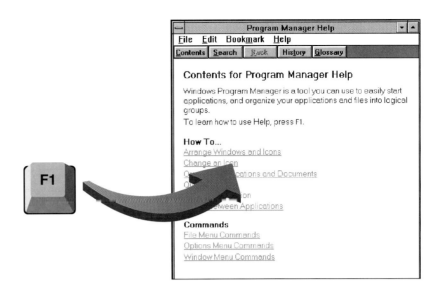

2. Click the **Glossary** command button to display a list of terms.

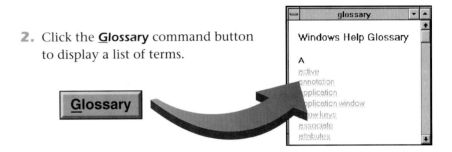

3. Click the Glossary window's Maximize button to enlarge it to full screen. You'll see a vertical scroll bar displayed at the right side of the window.

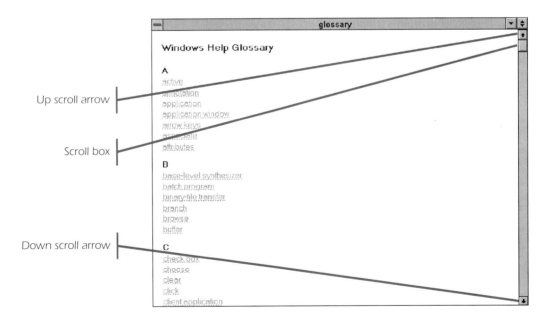

4. Point to the scroll bar's down scroll arrow and hold down the left mouse button until the scroll box reaches the bottom of the scroll bar. This indicates that you are at the end of the document.

5. Point to the up scroll arrow and hold down the left mouse button until the scroll box reaches the top of the scroll bar. This indicates that you are at the beginning of the document.

6. Point to the scroll box, hold down the left mouse button, and drag the scroll box to the bottom of the scroll bar. Then release the mouse button, and you move to the end of the document.

COMMON WRONG TURNS: DRAGGING SCROLL BOX DOESN'T WORK

If you drag the scroll box left or right off the scroll bar when you release the mouse button, the scroll box jumps back to where it was when you started. To be sure the screen scrolls the way you want, release the mouse button only when you can see the outline of the scroll box on the scroll bar.

7. Practice scrolling the window's contents up and down a line at a time by clicking the up and down scroll arrows.

8. Practice clicking the scroll bar above and below the scroll box to scroll a screen at a time.

PAUSING FOR PRACTICE

Practice using the scroll bar until you have mastered the three basic procedures: clicking the arrows and the scroll bar, pointing to the arrows and holding down the left button, and dragging the scroll box.

9. Click the Glossary window's Minimize button to run it as an icon.

10. Click the Program Manager Help window's Minimize button to run it as an icon.

LOOKING AHEAD: RUNNING A PROGRAM AS AN ICON

When you click the Minimize button to reduce an application window to an icon, you do not close the application. It stays open until you issue a command to close it or until you exit Windows.

EXITING WINDOWS

When you have finished for the day, you should always exit Windows to return to the operating system. Windows frequently creates temporary files on the disk. When you exit correctly, these files are closed and all data is stored where it should be.

To exit Windows, click the **File** menu to pull it down, then click the **Exit Windows** command to display a dialog box. Click the **OK** command button to exit or the **Cancel** command button to return to where you were.

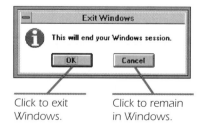

Click to exit Windows.

Click to remain in Windows.

TIP: EXITING WHEN YOU HAVEN'T SAVED YOUR WORK

If you try to exit Windows without first saving your work in an open application, you are prompted to save it and are offered the choices **Yes**, **No**, and **Cancel**. Click the **Yes** command button to save the file and the **No** command button to abandon it. To cancel the exit command and return to where you were, click the **Cancel** command button.

After exiting Windows, always do the following:

1. Remove any disks from the floppy disk drives. This will prevent their loss, increase security, and ensure that no one mistakenly erases them. (It also prevents the disk drives' read/write heads from leaving indentations in the disks' surfaces.) Make sure you take your own disks with you.

2. Turn off the computer or use the display monitor's controls to dim the screen so that an image will not be "burned" into its phosphor surface or so passers-by cannot see what you are working on. (Windows has a built-in *screen saver* that you can turn on to prevent the screen from being damaged when the computer is left on for long periods of time with Windows running, but it is not available after you have exited Windows.)

TIP: TURNING OFF YOUR COMPUTER

You wouldn't think that leaving a computer on was a major environmental issue, but it is. Computers already account for 5% of all the electricity consumed in the United States, and they are the fastest growing users of electric power. Some 30% to 40% of the U.S.'s 35 million computers are left on overnight and on weekends. New technologies are being developed to lower the power consumption of these idling machines. If their energy consumption is reduced by 40%, it will save carbon dioxide emissions equal to those of 5 million automobiles. Many newer systems are labeled with the Environmental Protection Agency's Energy Star logo. These Energy Star systems, also known as "green machines," consume less power than older models. They also go into a sleep mode when not in use. In this mode, everything remains in memory but power is reduced.

▶▶ TUTORIAL

1. Click **File** on Program Manager's menu bar to pull down the menu.

Point to the **File** menu name and click to pull down the menu.

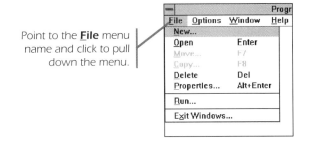

COMMON WRONG TURNS: CLICKING COMMANDS

Many first-time users have trouble choosing commands because they don't point to the right place before clicking. The point of the mouse pointer must be over one of the letters in the command when you click. If it is above or below a letter, even by a little bit, you may execute the wrong command or the menu may disappear.

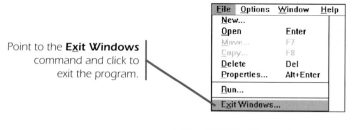

Point to the **Exit Windows** command and click to exit the program.

Click to exit Windows.

2. Click the **Exit Windows** command on the menu.

A dialog box appears telling you that this will end your Windows session.

3. Click the **OK** command button to exit or click the **Cancel** button to return to where you were if you want to continue working.

▶▶ **SKILL-BUILDING EXERCISES**

Exercise 1. Loading Windows on Your Own System

List the steps here that you use to load Windows so that you have them for future reference.

1. _____

_____

2. _____

_____

3. _____

_____

4. _____

_____

5. _____

_____

NOTE: WINDOWS STUDENT RESOURCE DISK

In Exercise 2, you use the *Windows Student Resource disk*. If your copy of the book does not contain this disk inside the back cover, your instructor will make it available to you.

Exercise 2. Booting Your System

When you turn on your system, watch the lights on the disk drives. You will see the light on drive A flash momentarily as the computer looks to that drive for the files that it needs to start up. If it can't find them there, it looks to drive C. However, if there is a disk in drive A without the needed files, the computer stops and displays the error message *Non-System disk* or *disk error* (or a similar message).

Insert your *Windows Student Resource Disk* into drive A and turn on the computer. You will see the error message that your machine gives in this situation. Write down the error message and the instructions it gives to continue.

_____

_____

_____

Follow the instructions that appear on the screen to continue.

Exercise 3. Using the Windows Tutorial to Learn About Your Mouse

1. Load Windows, point to Program Manager's **Help** menu, and click to pull down the **Help** menu.

2. Point to the **Windows Tutorial** command and click to execute the command.

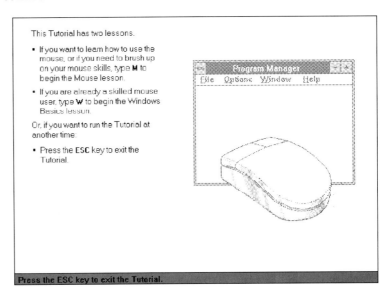

3. Press Ⓜ to begin the mouse lesson.

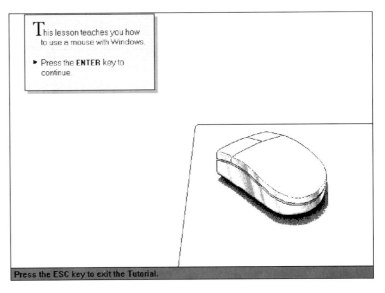

4. Press Enter ↵ to continue, and then follow the instructions that appear on the screen. You can press Esc at any point to end the tutorial.

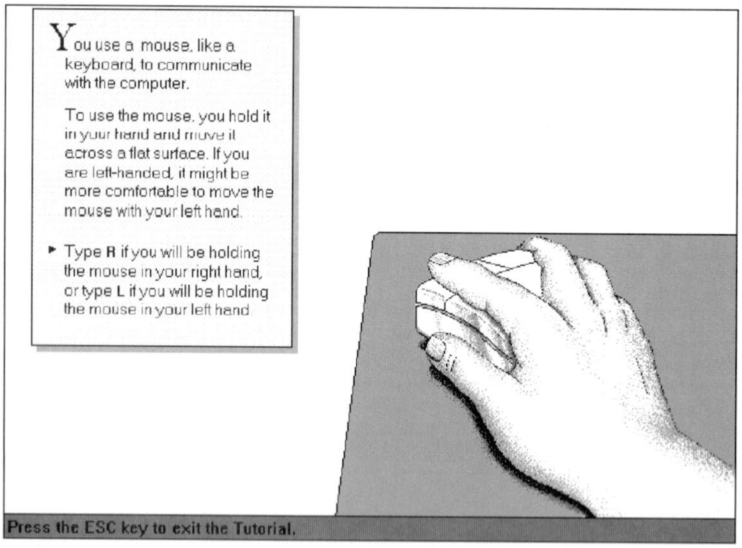

Exercise 4. **Practicing Mouse Skills**

1. Since minimizing, maximizing, and restoring windows is basic to all programs, it is important that you feel comfortable with the procedures. Practice minimizing, maximizing, and restoring Program Manager and its group windows until you feel comfortable. Be sure not to quit until you feel comfortable double-clicking icons to open them.

2. Practice moving and sizing windows by dragging their borders.

3. Maximize all of Program Manager's group icons into windows. Then size and drag them about to lay out the screen as attractively as possible. Drag the icons within the windows into neat arrangements.

PICTORIAL **1** ▶VISUALQUIZ

1. For each of these buttons, write down the name and what happens when you click it.

a
b
c

    a. Name: _minimize_   What happens: _icon_

    b. Name: _maximize_   What happens: _full-screen_

    c. Name: _restore_   What happens: _original_

2. For each of these scroll-bar elements, write down the name and what happens when you click (or drag) it.

a
b
c

d
e
f

    a. Name: _____   What happens: _____

    b. Name: _____   What happens: _____

    c. Name: _____   What happens: _____

    d. Name: _____   What happens: _____

    e. Name: _____   What happens: _____

    f. Name: _____   What happens: _____

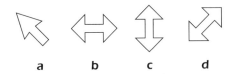

3. Describe the circumstances in which the mouse pointer will take each of the shapes shown here.

a. _____

b. _____

c. _____

d. _____

Program Manager
a

Accessories
b

4. Give the specific name for each of these two icons and describe what each reveals when you double-click it.

a. Name: _____ What's revealed: _____

b. Name: _____ What's revealed: _____

5. Name and briefly describe each of the window parts indicated here.

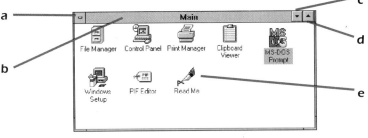

a. *control - menu box* _____

b. *title bar* _____

c. *min* _____

d. *max* _____

e. *application icon* _____

6. Name and briefly describe each of the scroll-bar elements indicated here.

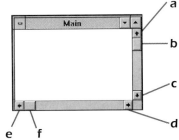

a. _____

b. _____

c. _____

d. _____

e. _____

f. _____

7. Name and briefly describe each of the Program Manager elements indicated here.

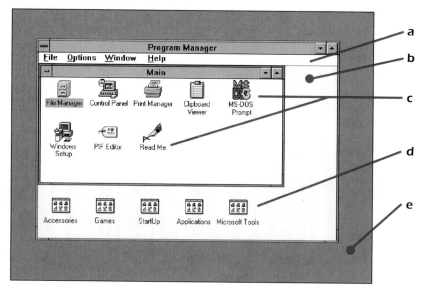

a. ___menu bar___

b. ___application window___

c. ___"   icons___

d. ___group icon___

e. ___desktop___

8. Here is a situation that you frequently encounter when working with Windows.

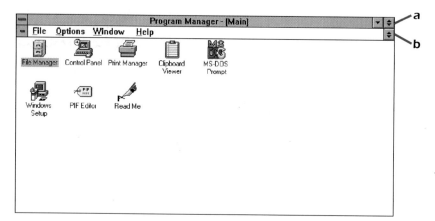

a. Describe what happens when you click the element labeled a.

_____

_____

b. Describe what happens when you click the element labeled b.

_____

_____

_____

9. Name this icon and describe what it reveals when you double-click it.

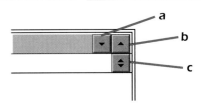

Name: _____   What's revealed: _____

10. Describe what happens when you click each of these buttons.

a. _____

b. _____

c. _____

11. How do you display this dialog box? Write down what happens when you click the buttons labeled a and b.

Exit Windows

This will end your Windows session.

a —   OK   Cancel   — b

How to display box: _File → Exit Windows_

a. _closes_

b. _cancels command_

PicTorial 2

EXECUTING COMMANDS AND GETTING HELP

After completing this PicTorial, you will be able to:

▶ Execute commands from menus

▶ Specify choices in dialog boxes

▶ Get on-screen help on commands

▶ Save any changes you make to Windows' screen layout

▶ Practice your skills by displaying the Clock application

▶ Practice your skills by playing Solitaire

Windows makes it easy to issue commands. It's nearly always just a matter of pulling down a menu from the menu bar and then clicking a command on the menu. Either the command is executed immediately or a dialog box appears asking you to specify options or supply more information. On-screen help is available at any point in most procedures.

USING MENUS

In Windows, there is almost always a menu bar displayed on the screen at the top of the active application window. This menu bar lists the names of the menus that are currently available to you.

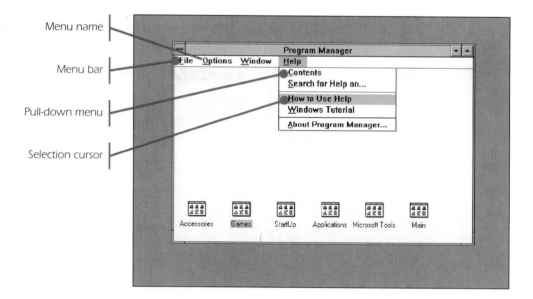

1. To pull down a menu, point to its name with the mouse and click once. (Alternatively, you can hold down [Alt] while you press the underlined letter in the menu's name.)

2. To choose a command from a pulled-down menu, point to the command and click once. (Alternatively, you can press the underlined letter in the command's name.)

If you pull down a menu by mistake, you can click another menu to pull it down or point anywhere outside of the menu or menu bar and click to close the menu without selecting a command.

You can also pull down all the menus in succession and move from one command to another by pointing to a menu, holding down the left mouse button, and dragging the highlight, called the *selection cursor*. Whatever command is highlighted when you release the mouse button is executed. If you decide not to choose a command when dragging the selection cursor like this, point anywhere other than to a menu name or command when you release the mouse button.

▶▶ TUTORIAL

1. Click the **Help** menu name on Program Manager's menu bar to pull down the menu. Notice the following about the menu:

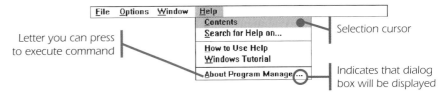

Letter you can press to execute command

Selection cursor

Indicates that dialog box will be displayed

- ▶ The top command is highlighted by the selection cursor.

- ▶ The **A** in the **About Program Manager** command is underlined to indicate you can execute the command by pressing the letter A. The ellipsis (...) that follows the command indicates that choosing the command displays a dialog box.

2. Press ↓ and ↑ to move the selection cursor from command to command. Notice how when the selection cursor is on the last choice pressing ↓ moves it to the top. When it is on the first choice, pressing ↑ moves it around to the bottom.

COMMON WRONG TURNS: PRESSING ↓ AND ↑ ENTERS NUMBERS

If pressing the arrow keys enters numbers instead of moving the selection cursor, either press NumLock to turn off the numeric keypad or use the other set of arrow keys on the keyboard.

3. Click the **About Program Manager** command to choose it. This displays a dialog box telling you the version of Windows that you are using, to whom the copy of the software is registered, and how much memory is available for your system.

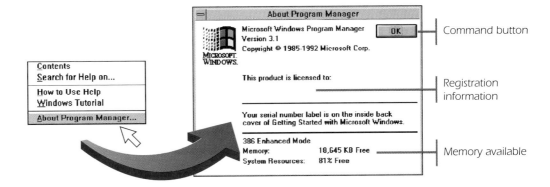

Command button

Registration information

Memory available

4. Notice the **OK** button in the upper-right corner of the dialog box. This is called a *command button*. Point to it and click to close the window.

5. Point to **File** on the menu bar and hold down the left button until told to release it. Notice how some menu commands are followed by a key combination. The listed keys can be used instead of the menu as a shortcut to executing the command that they follow. For this reason they are called *shortcut keys*. You will find shortcut keys listed on many Windows menus.

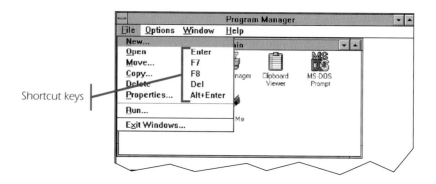

6. Without releasing the button, drag the selection cursor first to the right along the menu bar and then back to the left, pulling down one menu after the other.

7. Still without releasing the button, pull down the **Help** menu and then drag the selection cursor down the menu to highlight the **About Program Manager** command.

8. Release the button to execute the command and again display the About Program Manager dialog box.

9. Click the **OK** command button to close the About Program Manager dialog box.

10. Pull down the **Help** menu. (From here on this is how we tell you what menu to use. You now know that to pull it down, you just click its name on the menu bar.)

11. Point to any place but the menu or menu bar and click again to close the menu without selecting a command.

PAUSING FOR PRACTICE

Pause here to practice pulling down menus and then closing them without selecting a command.

USING CONTROL MENUS

Every window has a Control menu you can use to perform some of the procedures you have already learned to perform in other ways. For example, you can click commands on the Control menu to minimize, maximize, or restore windows. You can also click commands that allow you to move or size windows using the keyboard (although these procedures are not covered in this text). The way you display the Control menu depends on whether the window is open or closed to an icon.

▶ If the window is open, there is a *Control-menu box* in the upper-left corner. To display the Control menu you click this box once.

▶ If an application has been minimized so it is displayed as an icon, you display the Control menu by clicking the icon once.

Double-clicking the Control-menu box also provides you with a shortcut to closing an open window. This procedure has different results depending on where you use it. For example, if you double-click Program Manager's Control-menu box, it ends your Windows session. If you double-click an application's Control-menu box, it closes the application. If you double-click a group window's Control-menu box, it minimizes it to an icon.

TIP: CONTROL-MENU BOXES

If you look carefully at the Control-menu boxes on the screen, you'll see that there are two kinds. One kind is used for application windows and another kind for windows within applications. For example:

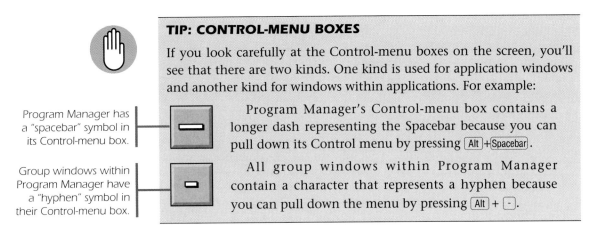

Program Manager has a "spacebar" symbol in its Control-menu box.

Program Manager's Control-menu box contains a longer dash representing the Spacebar because you can pull down its Control menu by pressing [Alt]+[Spacebar].

Group windows within Program Manager have a "hyphen" symbol in their Control-menu box.

All group windows within Program Manager contain a character that represents a hyphen because you can pull down the menu by pressing [Alt]+[-].

▶▶ TUTORIAL

1. Click Program Manager's Control-menu box located in the upper-left corner of its window to pull down the Control menu.

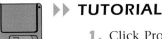

1 When you click the Control-menu box . . .

2 . . . the Control menu is pulled down.

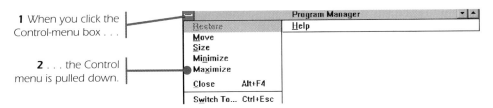

2. Click the **Minimize** command on the Control menu to reduce Program Manager to an icon.

3. Click Program Manager's icon to display its Control menu.

1 When you click the Program Manager icon . . .

2 . . . the Control menu is displayed.

4. Click the Control menu's **Maximize** command to open Program Manager up into a full-screen window.

Pull down the Control menu and click the Maximize command to display Program Manager full screen.

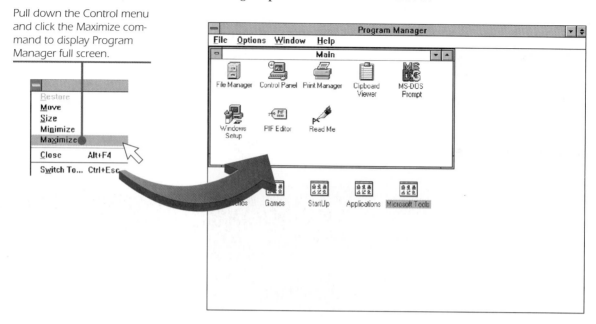

5. Click Program Manager's Control-menu box again to display the Control menu.

6. Click the **Restore** command to restore Program Manager to its original size.

Pull down the Control menu and click the Restore command to restore Program Manager to its original size.

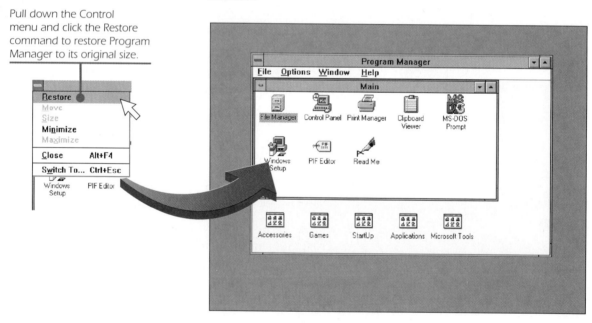

7. Pull down the **Help** menu and click the **About Program Manager** command to display the dialog box.

8. Double-click About Program Manager's Control-menu box to close the dialog box.

Double-click the
Control-menu box
to close the window.

9. If the Main group window is open, double-click its Control-menu box to display the group as an icon.

10. Double-click Program Manager's Control-menu box to display a dialog box warning you that this will end your Windows session.

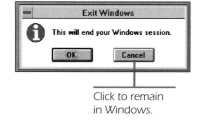

Click to remain
in Windows.

11. Click the **Cancel** command button to cancel the command. If you had clicked the **OK** command button, you would have exited the Windows program.

PAUSING FOR PRACTICE

Using menus is one of the basic skills you must master. Pause here in the PicTorial to continue practicing using the Control menu to minimize, maximize, and restore both the Program Manager window and one of the group windows such as the Main group. Then practice opening the About Program Manager dialog box listed on the **Help** menu and double-clicking the Control-menu box to close the dialog box.

USING ON-LINE HELP

Windows has extensive *on-line help* available from almost anywhere in any application (only the Clock application has no on-line help). To display help, click the **Help** menu name on the menu bar, click a **Help** command button in a dialog box, or press F1 at any time. Once you are in the help system, you can choose topics by clicking items on lists, clicking on command buttons, or making choices from menus.

Lists available Help
topics

Displays a dialog box
so you can search for
a specific Help topic

Explains how to
use Help

Runs a tutorial on
using Windows

Displays version,
registration, and
memory information

If you press F1 or click a **Help** command button, the help displayed depends on where you are in a procedure. Since help is *context sensitive*, the help screen describes the procedure you are using and the options you can choose from.

▶▶ TUTORIAL

1. Pull down the **Help** menu and click the **How to Use Help** command to display a list of topics.

Menu names

Command buttons

Terms with glossary definitions are underscored with dotted lines.

Help topics are underlined.

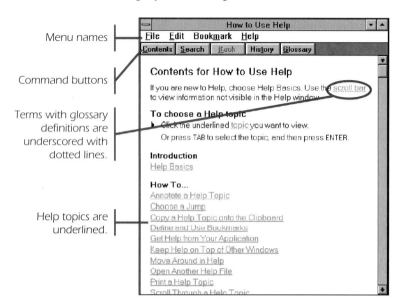

Notice the following parts of the Help window:

▶ A menu bar lists the names of pull-down menus.

▶ Command buttons quickly move you around the help system. Any command button with a dimmed name, such as "**Back**," cannot be executed from where you are in the system.

▶ *Jumps* are underlined words or phrases that jump you to other topics when you click them. Words or phrases underlined with dotted lines display definitions, and those underscored with solid lines jump you to related topics.

2. Hold down ⌈Ctrl⌉ and press ⌈Tab⇆⌉ to highlight all of the topic's jumps. Release the keys to remove the highlights.

Pressing ⌈Ctrl⌉+⌈Tab⇆⌉ highlights all jumps.

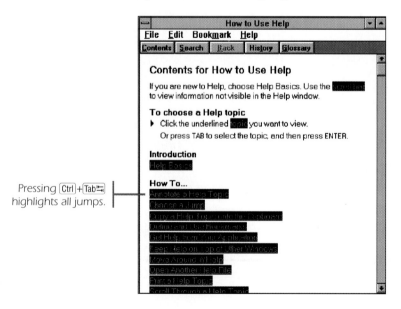

3. Point to the phrase *scroll bar* (a jump) which is underlined with a dotted line, and the mouse pointer turns into a hand with a pointing finger.

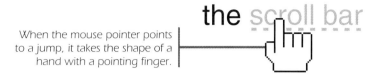

When the mouse pointer points to a jump, it takes the shape of a hand with a pointing finger.

4. Click the phrase *scroll bar* to display a definition of the term.

1 Clicking a word underlined with a dotted line . . .

2 . . . displays a definition of the term in a window.

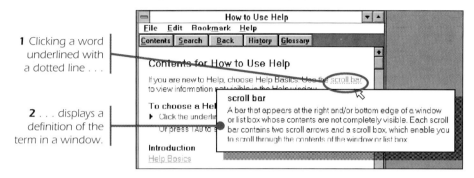

5. Click again to remove the definition. (It's not important where the mouse pointer is when you click.)

6. Click the underlined *Help Basics* to jump to help on that topic.

7. Click the **Back** command button to back up one screen. The **Back** command button becomes dim again because you have backed up as far as you can go.

The **Back** command button dims when you cannot back up any further.

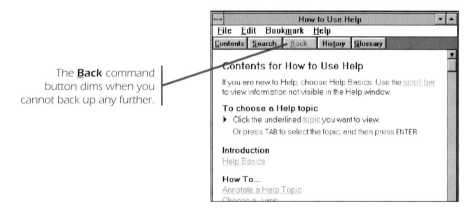

8. Click the underlined *Choose a Jump* to jump to help on that topic.

9. Click the **History** command button for a list of the topics you have viewed since loading Windows in the current session. The topic you viewed most recently is at the top of the list.

Clicking the **History** command button displays a list of the Help screens you have viewed.

10. Double-click any of the listed topics to jump to it. This is a great way to return to a topic you viewed earlier.

11. Click the **Back** command button until you return to the screen titled *Contents for How to Use Help*, and the command button becomes dimmed.

12. Click the **Glossary** command button to display a glossary of terms.

Clicking the **Glossary** command button displays a list of terms for which definitions are available.

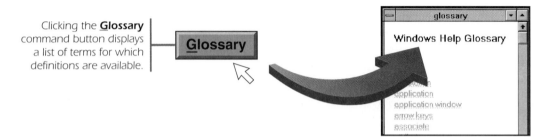

13. Click the Glossary window's Maximize button to enlarge it to full screen.

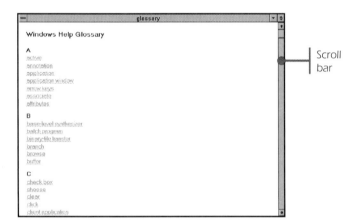

Scroll bar

14. Use the Glossary window's scroll bar to scroll down through the listed terms. You can also press PgDn and PgUp to scroll through the list.

15. Click any term for a definition; then click again to remove it.

16. Double-click the Glossary window's Control-menu box to close the window and return to Help.

17. Double-click the Help window's Control-menu box to close the Help window.

PAUSING FOR PRACTICE

When working with Windows or any of its application programs, help is always available on line. Knowing how to find the information you need is a very useful skill. Pause here to practice using on-line help. For example, you might look for help on printing help topics and navigating help.

USING DIALOG BOXES

When you choose a menu command, a dialog box may appear letting you supply information about available options. There are many different dialog boxes, but each is made up of elements that include boxes into which you enter text, lists from which you can choose items, and check boxes or buttons that you click to turn options on or off.

TEXT BOXES

Text boxes contain space for typing data. When a text box is empty, you click in it to move to it. An *insertion point* (a flashing vertical bar sometimes called a *cursor*) appears at the left edge of the box. As you type characters, the insertion point moves to indicate where the next character you type will appear.

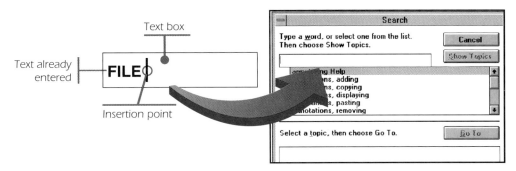

To edit the text in a text box:

▶ If the text box already has an entry, the entire entry will be selected when you press ⎇Tab⎇ to move to the text box or double-click in it. The first character you type deletes this previous entry. To edit the entry instead, click in the box or press one of the arrow keys or ⎇Home⎇ or ⎇End⎇ to remove the highlight and position the insertion point.

▶ To insert characters, click with the mouse or use ⎇←⎇ or ⎇→⎇ to position the insertion point where you want to insert them, and type them in. The characters to the right move aside to make room for the new characters as you type them in.

▶ To delete a character to the left of the insertion point, press ⎇← Bksp⎇. To delete a character to the right of the insertion point, press ⎇Del⎇. Holding down either of these keys deletes characters one after another.

▶ To delete a word and the space that follows it, double-click the word and then press ⎇Del⎇.

▶ To delete adjacent characters or words, move the insertion point to the left of a character, hold down the left mouse button, drag the highlight over adjoining text to select it, and then release the mouse button. (Holding down ⎇⇧Shift⎇ while you press an arrow key also extends the selection.) When the text is selected, press ⎇Del⎇ to delete it.

LIST BOXES

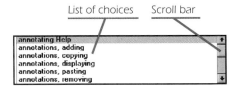

List boxes display a list from which you can choose an item by clicking it. Lists too long to be displayed in the window can be scrolled with the box's scroll bar.

Some list boxes show only a single value and arrows you click to increase or decrease the value.

A *drop-down list box* is displayed as a rectangular box listing only the current selection. To display other choices, click the down scroll arrow to the right of the box.

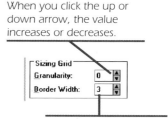

When you click the up or down arrow, the value increases or decreases.

Here the up arrow was clicked three times.

Drop-down lists have a downward-pointing arrow to their right.

When you click the arrow, a list descends along with a scroll bar.

COMMAND BUTTONS

Command buttons execute commands when you click them. If a button is dimmed, it cannot be chosen from where you are in a procedure.

Commands can also be executed by pressing the underlined button letter on the keyboard.

Dimmed buttons cannot be selected.

A few command buttons contain symbols. If the button's name is followed by an ellipsis (...), clicking it displays another dialog box. If the name is followed by greater-than signs (>>), clicking it expands the current dialog box to reveal more choices.

Clicking a command button with greater-than signs expands the current dialog box.

Clicking a command button with an ellipsis displays another dialog box.

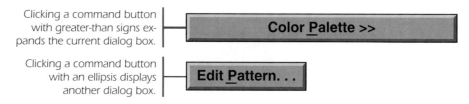

OPTION BUTTONS

Option buttons offer mutually exclusive options (only one can be selected at a time). The one that is on contains a black dot. If you click a button that is off, any other related button that is on automatically turns off.

Only one of these option buttons can be on at a time. If you click **Landscape** to turn it on, **Portrait** will automatically turn off.

CHECK BOXES

Check boxes offer nonexclusive options (one or more of them can be on at the same time). To turn an option on, click it to display an X in its box. To turn the option off, click the box to remove the X. If the name of one of the check boxes is dimmed, it can't be chosen from where you are in a procedure.

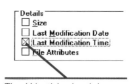

The X in this check box indicates that this option is turned on.

CANCELING COMMANDS

To cancel a command that you have begun but not yet completed, click the **Cancel** command button or double-click the dialog box's Control-menu box.

 ▶▶ **TUTORIAL**

1. Pull down Program Manager's **Help** menu and click the **Search for Help on** command to display the Search dialog box.

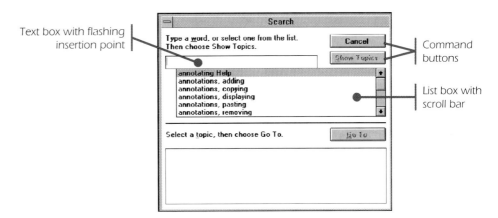

Text box with flashing insertion point

Command buttons

List box with scroll bar

Notice this about the dialog box:

▶ There is a text box with a vertical line, called the insertion point or cursor, flashing in it.

▶ There is a list of topics in a box with a vertical scroll bar. This is called a list box.

▶ There are command buttons you can use to complete or cancel the command.

2. Click *applications, starting* in the list box, and it is automatically entered into the text box.

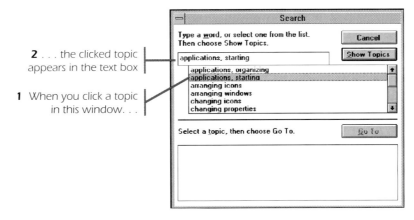

2 . . . the clicked topic appears in the text box

1 When you click a topic in this window. . .

3. Click the **Show Topics** command button to display a list of topics on starting applications in the lower box.

4. Click *Starting an Application from a Group* in the lower box to select it.

5. Click the **Go To** command button to display help on that topic.

6. Double-click the Program Manager Help window's Control-menu box to close the window.

7. Pull down the **Help** menu and click the **Search for Help on** command on to display the Search dialog box again.

8. Click *applications, starting* again to enter it into the text box.

9. Point to the text box, and you'll see the mouse pointer change into an I-beam shape.

10. Click anywhere in the box to the right of the word *starting*.

11. Press ⎡← Bksp⎤ repeatedly until you have deleted the word *starting*.

"starting" is deleted.

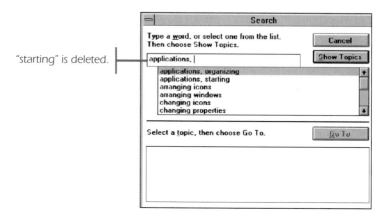

12. Type **organizing** and click the **Show Topics** command button to list the topics available on organizing your applications.

1 Edit the search text.

2 Click the command button.

3 Related topics are listed.

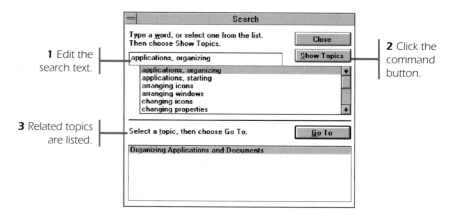

13. Point to the Search window's title bar, hold down the left button, and drag the window to a new position before releasing the button. You'll find that occasionally dialog boxes cover up information you want to see in other windows. When this happens, you can drag them out of the way.

14. Double-click the Search window's Control-menu box to close the window. (Be sure not to click Program Manager's.)

ARRANGING WINDOWS AND ICONS ON THE DESKTOP

When you have a number of windows and icons displayed on the desktop, they can overlap and hide one another. It may even be hard to find what you are looking for. When this happens, you can use commands on the **Window** menu to jump directly to another window or rearrange items on the desktop. When you rearrange windows, you can have them cascaded or tiled. *Cascaded* windows overlap one another.

Cascaded windows overlap one another.

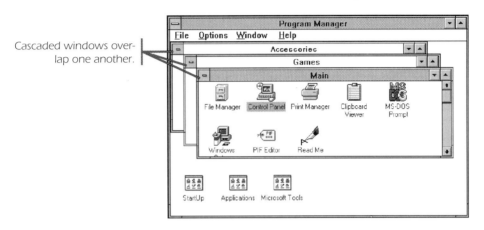

Tiled windows are arranged side by side, much like the tiles on a floor.

Tiled windows are arranged side by side or above one another.

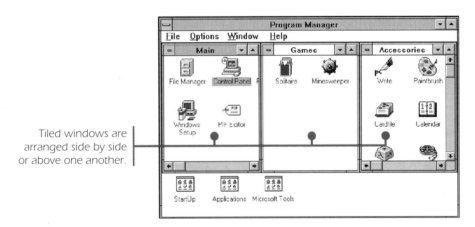

Once you have organized the windows or icons to your liking, you can save the layout. To do so, use one of the following procedures.

▶ Pull down the **Options** menu and click the **Save Settings on Exit** command to remove the check mark (✔) from in front of it. Then press Alt + ⇧ Shift + F4 to save the settings.

▶ Pull down the **Options** menu and click the **Save Settings on Exit** command to place a check mark (✔) in front of it. When you exit Windows, the current settings will be saved. Be sure to remove the check mark the next time you load Windows or subsequent changes will also be saved whether you intended them to be or not.

▶▶ TUTORIAL

1. Maximize the Program Manager window.

2. If the Main, Accessories, and Games windows are not open, double-click each of their icons to open them.

3. Pull down Program Manager's **Window** menu and click the **Tile** command to rearrange group windows side by side. (Your windows may not be in the order shown here.)

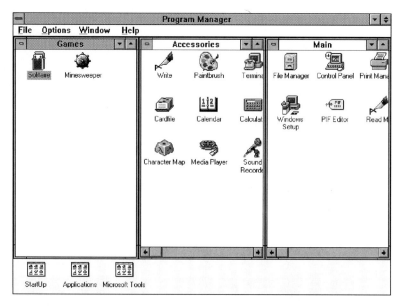

4. Click the Main window to make it the active window. It may have a scroll bar indicating that all of its icons are not displayed.

5. Pull down Program Manager's **Window** menu and click the **Arrange Icons** command to rearrange the icons within the Main window.

6. Pull down Program Manager's **Window** menu and click the **Cascade** command to rearrange group windows so they overlap with their title bars displayed. (Your windows may not be in the order shown here.)

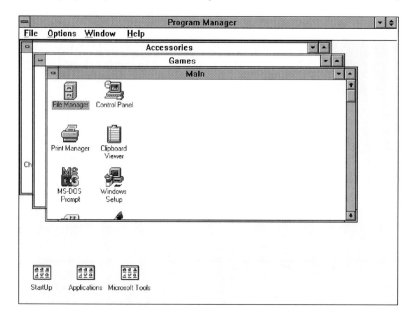

PAUSING FOR PRACTICE

Continue practicing arranging the windows on your desktop. For example, experiment with making different windows active when you execute the **Tile** command. What effect does this have on the position of the active window?

7. Click one of the windows in back to move it to the front of the cascade and make it the active window.

8. Click the Minimize buttons on the Main, Accessories, and Games windows to reduce them all to icons.

9. Drag the icons about on the desk to scatter them in a random arrangement.

10. Click one of the icons to select it and then click the desktop to close its Control menu. The icon's title remains highlighted.

11. Pull down Program Manager's **Window** menu and click the **Arrange Icons** command to space application icons evenly along the lower portion of the Program Manager window.

13. Pull down the **Options** menu. If there is a check mark (✔) in front of the **Save Settings on Exit** command, click the command to remove it. If there isn't a check mark in front of the command, click anywhere but in the menu to cancel the command.

PRACTICING YOUR SKILLS WITH THE CLOCK APPLICATION

One of the application programs in the Accessories group is a clock that can display the time and date based on the computer's built-in clock. If that clock is not set correctly, then the time and date will not be displayed correctly by the clock.

 ▶▶ **TUTORIAL**

1. Open the Accessories group window and double-click the Clock icon to display the Clock on the screen. The time is displayed in analog or digital style.

Analog clock display

Digital clock (and date) display

2. Pull down the **Settings** menu and click the **Digital** or **Analog** command to change the display.

3. If you just set the clock to analog, repeat Step 2 to reset it to digital.

4. With the digital clock displayed, pull down the **Settings** menu and click the **Set Font** command. Write down the name of the font listed in the Font text box.

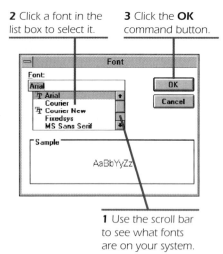

2 Click a font in the list box to select it.

3 Click the **OK** command button.

1 Use the scroll bar to see what fonts are on your system.

5. Scroll the list box to see what fonts are available on your system, click one to select it, and then click the **OK** command button. The Clock is now displayed in the font you selected.

6. Pull down the **Settings** menu and click the **Set Font** command. Change the font back to the original font that was active when you first loaded the Clock.

7. Click the Clock's Maximize button to display it full screen.

8. Click the Clock's Restore command button in the upper-right corner of the screen to display the Clock small.

9. Pull down the **Settings** menu and click the **No Title** command to remove the title bar and menu.

10. Make the Clock as small as possible and drag it around the desktop.

11. Press Esc and then click the Maximize button to display the title bar and menu again.

12. Double-click the Clock's Control-menu box to close the application.

TIP: CHEATING?

When you can't find the card you want, hold down Ctrl + Alt + ⇧ Shift in Solitaire and when you click the deck, only one card turns over.

BUILDING YOUR SKILLS PLAYING SOLITAIRE

Windows comes with two games, *Solitaire* and *Minesweeper*. Although they are enjoyable to play, the primary purpose for including them here is to let you practice pointing and clicking.

The game of Solitaire is normally played by one person using a deck of cards. Using Windows, you play the game electronically. As you do so, you are able to build your skills in pointing and clicking with the mouse, selecting commands from menus, responding to options presented to you in dialog boxes, and using on-line help.

▶▶ **TUTORIAL**

Opening Solitaire

1. Double-click the Games group icon to display the Solitaire and Minesweeper application icons.

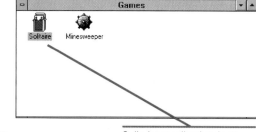

2. Double-click the Solitaire application icon to open up the Solitaire game.

Solitaire application icon

Printing the Rules of the Game

3. To find how to play Solitaire, pull down the **Help** menu and click the **Contents** command.

4. Now click the underlined *Rules of the Game* to display a screen listing the rules of Solitaire.

5. Pull down the **File** menu and click the **Print Topic** command to print the rules of the game.

6. Pull down the **File** menu again and click the **Exit** command to exit help.

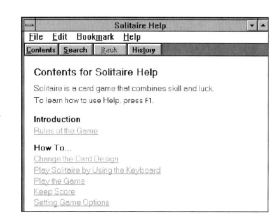

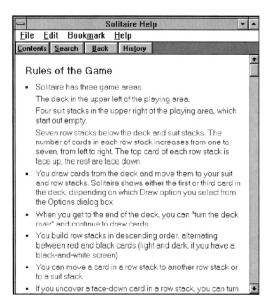

Playing Solitaire

7. To play the game:

▶ Drag any playable card to where it belongs. To do so, point to the card, hold down the left mouse button, and move the mouse. When you have the card positioned where you want it (you don't have to place it perfectly), release the mouse button, and the card jumps to the new position. (Try dragging a card to an illegal position and see what happens when you release the mouse button.)

▶ Turn over additional cards from the deck by clicking the deck once. When all cards have been dealt, click the circle where the deck was, and the deck is ready to deal from again.

▶ To deal a new game, pull down the **Game** menu and click the **Deal** command.

Modifying Solitaire

8. Modify the game following these simple procedures:

▶ To change the design on the back of the cards, pull down the **Game** menu and click the **Deck** command to display various designs. Click the one you want to use to select it, then click the **OK** command button.

▶ To change from turning over three cards at a time to turning over one, pull down the **Game** menu and click the **Options** command to display a dialog box. Click the **Draw One** option button to turn it on. Then click the **OK** command button to return to the game.

Exiting Solitaire

9. Pull down the **Game** menu and click the **Exit** command to close the Solitaire window and display it as an icon.

10. Click the Minimize button to close the Games window and display it as an icon.

▶▶ SKILL-BUILDING EXERCISES

1. Exploring Help

1. Pull down Program Manager's **Help** menu and click the **Contents** command to display a list of help topics.

2. Display help on the three menus listed on the screen under the heading *Commands*. After reading each screen, click the **Back** command button to return to the page headed "Contents for Program Manager Help," and then display the next topic.

3. Display help on quitting windows.

4. Close the Help window.

2. Adding Bookmarks to Help Topics

1. Pull down Program Manager's **Help** menu and click the **How to Use Help** command to display a list of help topics.

2. Display help on defining and using bookmarks and take notes or make a printout so you can add bookmarks on your own.

3. Add some bookmarks to various Help screens, move between them, and then delete them.

4. Close the Help window.

3. Annotating Help Topics

1. Pull down Program Manager's **Help** menu and click the **How to Use Help** command to display a list of help topics.

2. Display the various Help screens on annotating a help topic and take notes or make printouts so you can add annotations on your own.

3. Add an annotation to one of the Help screens.

4. Close the Help window.

4. Using the Windows Tutorial to Review What You've Learned

1. Pull down Program Manager's **Help** menu and click the **Windows Tutorial** command.

2. Press Ⓦ to begin the Windows Basics lesson.

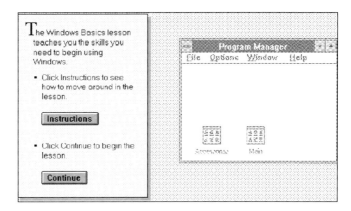

3. Follow the instructions that appear on the screen. Click the **Instructions** command button for advice on how to use the tutorial.

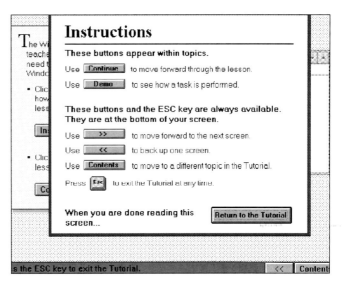

You can press Esc at any point to end the tutorial. To resume later, or to jump to another topic, click the **Contents** command at the bottom of the screen. Then click the button in front of the topic you want to learn about.

5. Playing Minesweeper

1. Open the Minesweeper game. (Its icon is in the Games group.)

2. To find how to play Minesweeper, pull down the **Help** menu and click the **Contents** command button. Then click the underlined phrase *What is Minesweeper?* to display a screen listing the rules of the game. Read the information displayed on the screen or make a printout for reference.

3. Play the game following these simple procedures.

   ▶ To mark a square as a mine, point to it and click the **right** mouse button once.

   ▶ To uncover a square that isn't a mine, point to it and click the **left** mouse button once.

   ▶ To mark a square as a question mark, point to it and double-click the **right** mouse button.

▶ To change a square marked as a mine into a question mark, point to it and click the **right** mouse button once.

▶ To clear a square marked as a mine, point to it and double-click the **right** mouse button.

▶ To start a new game, pull down the **Game** menu and click the **New** command.

▶ To change the level of the game, pull down the **Game** menu and click the **Beginner, Intermediate,** or **Expert** command.

PicTorial 2 ▶ VISualQuiz

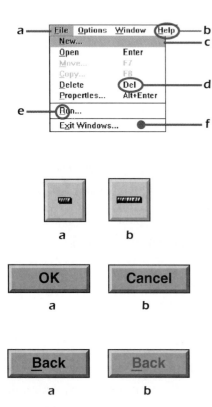

1. The menu shown here has a number of elements or features that you will see on many Windows menus. Write down the name of each of these elements or describe what it is used for.

a. _____

b. _____

c. _____

d. _____

e. _____

f. _____

2. Write down the name of each of these elements and what the symbol on each represents.

a. Name: _____ What symbol represents: _____

b. Name: _____ What symbol represents: _____

3. Write down the name of each of these elements and describe what happens when you click each.

a. Name: _____ What happens: _____

b. Name: _____ What happens: _____

4. Describe the difference between these two buttons.

a. _____

b. _____

5. The ellipsis and greater-than signs on these command buttons indicate something that will happen when you click them. Describe what each symbol indicates.

Edit Pattern. . .	**Color Palette >>**
a	b

a. _____

b. _____

6. Give the name of this menu and describe how to display it like this.

_____

_____

_____

7. Describe where you see this icon and what happens when you click it.

_____

_____

_____

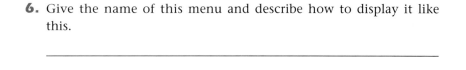

8. Give the name of these buttons and describe how to turn them on or off. Also describe what happens to the one that is currently on when you turn the other one on.

_____

_____

_____

9. Give the name of the boxes in front of each of these items and tell how to know if one is turned on or off. Describe how to turn them on or off.

_____

_____

_____

10. These illustrations show windows arranged in two different ways. Write down the name of each type of arrangement and describe how to arrange windows in these ways.

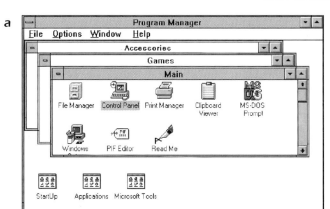

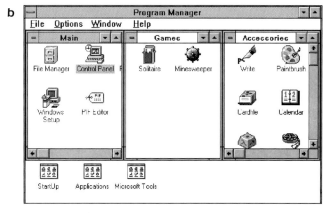

a. Name: _~~the~~ cascade_ How you arrange like this: _____

_____

b. Name: _tile_ How you arrange like this: _____

_____

11. These illustrations show two types of underscoring that you encounter when using on-line help. Describe what is displayed when you click each.

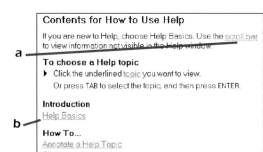

a. _____

b. _____

12. Give the name of each of the items specified in this figure and describe how you use it.

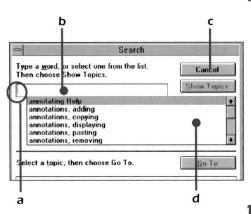

a. Name: _____ How to use: _____
_____

b. Name: _____ How to use: _____
_____

c. Name: _____ How to use: _____
_____

d. Name: _____ How to use: _____
_____

13. Give the name of each of the items specified in this figure and describe each of them.

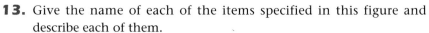
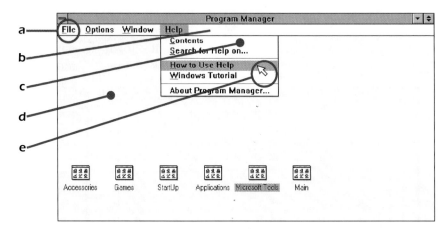

a. Name: _____ Description: _____

b. Name: _____ Description: _____

c. Name: _____ Description: _____

d. Name: _____ Description: _____

e. Name: _____ Description: _____

14. Describe what happens when you click each of the items specified in this figure.

a. _____

b. _____

True-False (Circle T if the statement is true or F if it is false.)

(T) F **1.** To work on a specific type of application, you use an application program.

T (F) **2.** To be computer literate, you must be able to design and build a computer.

T (F) **3.** To boot a computer, you give it a stiff kick in the side.

T (F) **4.** The drive the computer looks to first when you turn it on is called the startup drive. This drive is always drive A.

T (F) **5.** When you boot a computer, Windows is always loaded automatically.

(T) F **6.** Normally, when you boot a computer that has a hard disk drive, there must not be a disk in drive A.

T (F) **7.** The main function of Program Manager is to make the screen look pretty.

(T) F **8.** Program Manager is always in memory when Windows is loaded.

(T) F **9.** The Windows desktop is the screen area where windows and icons can be displayed.

T (F) **10.** Icons are things that Windows users worship.

(T) F **11.** Group windows contain one or more application icons.

(T) F **12.** The Maximize and Minimize buttons display the window at full screen or reduce it to an icon.

T (F) **13.** The Restore button is displayed only after you have clicked the Minimize button.

(T) F **14.** Only one window can be active at a time, and it is always the one on top of other windows when they overlap.

(T) F **15.** To scroll through a document with the scroll bar, you can drag the scroll box to a new position and then release it.

(T) F **16.** To change the size of a window, you drag the borders.

T (F) **17.** To drag a window to a new position, you point to the Control-menu box, hold down the left mouse button, and move the mouse.

T (F) **18.** The mouse pointer is always the same shape, so it is easy to identify.

T (F) **19.** When you double-click the mouse button, the pause between clicks isn't important.

T (F) **20.** The only way to pull down a menu from the menu bar is to click it.

(T) F **21.** To choose a menu command, you double-click it.

(T) F **22.** The highlight that you can move along the menu bar or up and down menu commands is called the selection cursor.

T F **23.** To close a menu without making a choice, you click it again.

(T) F **24.** To choose a command button, you just click it.

(T) F **25.** To display the Control menu, you click the Control-menu box.

(T) F **26.** To close a window, you double-click the Control-menu box.

T (F) **27.** The only way to display help is to press F1.

(T) F **28.** To display help in the middle of a command, press F1.

SMILE

T (F) **29.** Some words and phrases on Help screens are underlined only to make them stand out.

(T) F **30.** When the mouse pointer turns into a pointing finger on a Help screen, clicking the mouse takes you to another screen or displays a definition.

T (F) **31.** To force you to buy books on Windows, Microsoft designed it so you cannot print out help screens.

(T) F **32.** The flashing vertical line in a text box indicates where the next character that you type will appear.

(T) F **33.** List boxes list choices you can make by clicking them.

(T) F **34.** You turn check boxes and option buttons on and off by clicking them.

(T) F **35.** Only one option button can be on at a time. When you turn one on, the other automatically turns off.

T (F) **36.** Tiled windows overlap one another on the screen. Cascaded windows don't.

 Multiple Choice (Circle the correct answer.)

1. When you first turn on your computer, it always looks first to ___ for the operating system files that it needs to run.
(a.) Drive A
b. Drive B
c. Drive C
d. The drive on the bottom

2. A typical application program is __.
a. Windows
b. DOS
(c.) Microsoft Word
d. On-line help

3. If Windows stops working (it "freezes up"), you press __ to perform a local reboot.
a. [Esc]
b. [Enter ←]
(c.) [Ctrl]+[Alt]+[Del]
d. [⇧ Shift]+[Tab ⇆]

4. The sole function of Program Manager is to __.
a. Provide menus from which you can choose
(b.) Launch application programs
c. Manage the help system for all applications
d. Manage the memory in your computer

5. The windows containing application icons are called ___.
a. Application windows
(b.) Group windows
c. Program Manager windows
d. Document windows

6. When you click a window's Maximize button, the __ appears.

    a. Control menu

    b. Minimize button

    c. Restore button

    d. Icon

7. To close a window down to an icon, you click the ___.

    a. Menu bar

    b. Minimize button

    c. Restore button

    d. Icon

8. To *drag*, you __.

    a. Double-click an object to select it, then click where you want it moved to

    b. Point to an object, hold down both buttons, and move the mouse

    c. Point to an object, hold down the left button, and move the mouse

    d. Point to an object, hold down the right button, and move the mouse

9. To pull down a menu from the menu bar, you __.

    a. Press Ctrl and the underlined letter in the menu's name

    b. Click it with the left mouse button

    c. Double-click it

    d. Press Tab to highlight it, and then press Enter

10. To obtain context-sensitive help in the middle of a procedure, you can always ___.

    a. Click the **Help** command button

    b. Press F1

    c. Click the **Help** menu

    d. Ask your lab instructor

11. Dialog boxes provide __ so you can supply information on a command.

    a. Text boxes, list boxes, option buttons, and check lists

    b. Menus and screens of text describing options

    c. Page numbers in the reference manual

    d. A Maximize and Minimize button

Fill In the Blank (Enter your answer in the space provided.)

1. To work on an application, you use a(n) _____ program.

2. If you understand how to use a computer and application software to do useful work, you can consider yourself _____.

3. Windows has what is known as a graphical _____.

4. Turning on your computer is referred to as _____ it.

5. The drive the computer looks to when you first turn it on is called the _____ .

6. If your system freezes up when using Windows, you press _____+_____+_____ to perform a local reboot.

7. To exit Windows, you pull down the _____ menu and click the _____ command.

8. The sole function of Program Manager is to _____.

9. Clicking the Minimize button makes the window into a(n) _____.

10. To quickly close a window, you can double-click the _____ .

11. The windows that contain application icons are called _____ windows.

12. When you minimize a group window, it is displayed as a(n) _____.

13. To open an application, you _____ the application's icon.

14. When windows overlap, the one on top is the _____.

15. To scroll through a document one screen at a time, you click above or below the _____.

16. To scroll continuously through a document, you point to one of the _____ and hold down the left mouse button.

17. When you point to one of the borders of a window, the mouse pointer changes shape into _____.

18. When you click the mouse button once, it is called clicking; and when you click it twice, it's called _____.

19. You can pull down a menu by holding down _____ when you press the underlined character in its name.

20. The highlight that you can move about the menu bar and menus to highlight commands is called the _____ .

21. To close a menu without making a choice, point _____ and click.

22. If a command button is dimmed, you _____ use it from where you are in the program.

23. If a command button displays an ellipsis, clicking it will display _____.

24. If a command button displays greater-than signs (>>), clicking it will display _____.

25. The Control-menu box is located in the _____ corner of every window.

26. If you click the Control-menu box, you _____.

27. If you double-click the Control-menu box, you _____.

28. There are two different symbols in Control-menu boxes. One is like a hyphen and the other a longer dash. The hyphen represents the _____ and the dash represents the _____ because you can pull down the Control menu by holding down [Alt] while you press these keys.

29. You can display help at any time by pressing _____.

30. If you click a word or phrase on a Help screen that is underlined with a dotted line, you display _____ .

31. If you click a word or phrase on a Help screen that is underlined with a solid line, you display _____ .

32. When the mouse pointer changes to a pointing finger on a Help screen, it indicates that you can _____.

33. To edit the entry in a text box, you move the _____ to indicate where you want to insert or delete characters.

34. When you click an option button that was previously off, any other related option button automatically turns _____.

35. If windows are displayed side by side without overlapping, they are _____. If they overlap one another, they are _____.

36. To save any layout changes you make to the desktop, you can press _____+_____+_____.

 Projects

Project 1. Describing the Anatomy of the Windows Opening Display

This illustration shows the Windows display that appears when you first load the program. In the spaces provided, write down the name of each of the lettered elements.

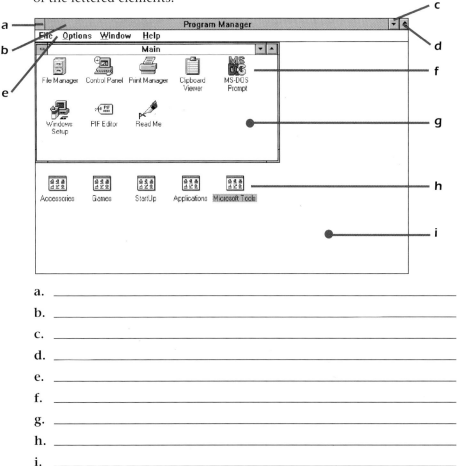

a. _____

b. _____

c. _____

d. _____

e. _____

f. _____

g. _____

h. _____

i. _____

Project 2. Describing the Dynamics of a Windows Display

In this illustration, each of the active elements of the Windows display is lettered. In the spaces provided, indicate whether you click or double-click the element and describe what happens when you do so. (Items a, g, and h actually each have two answers, either of which is correct.)

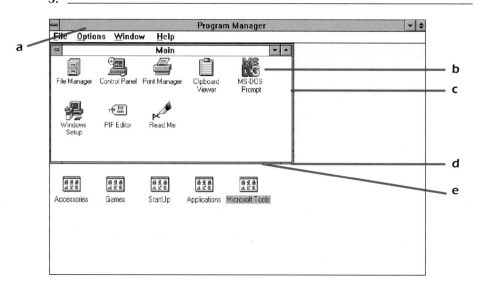

a. ☐ Click ☐ Double-click _____

b. ☐ Click ☐ Double-click _____

c. ☐ Click ☐ Double-click _____

d. ☐ Click ☐ Double-click _____

e. ☐ Click ☐ Double-click _____

f. ☐ Click ☐ Double-click _____

g. ☐ Click ☐ Double-click _____

h. ☐ Click ☐ Double-click _____

Project 3. Describing More Dynamics of a Windows Display

In this illustration, each of the elements of the Windows display that you can drag is lettered. In the spaces provided below, first list the steps you follow to drag an item and then describe what happens when you drag each of the lettered items.

Steps to Drag

1. _____

2. _____

3. _____

Effects of Dragging Lettered Item

a. _____

b. _____

c. _____

d. _____

e. _____

Project 4. Describing the Dynamics of Help

In this illustration, each of the command buttons on the How to Use Help screen is lettered. In the spaces provided below, describe what happens when you click each of them.

a. _____

b. _____

c. _____

d. _____

e. _____

Project 5. Describing the Dynamics of a Scroll Bar

In this illustration, various parts of a scroll bar are lettered. In the spaces provided below, describe what happens when you click (or drag) each of them.

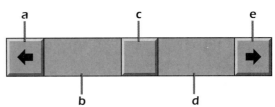

a. _____

b. _____

c. _____

d. _____

e. _____

Chapter 2
WORKING WITH FILE MANAGER

PicTorial 3

FILE MANAGER – AN INTRODUCTION

After completing this topic, you will be able to:

▸ Open and close the File Manager application

▸ Change the selected drive and directory

▸ Describe file icons used to represent types of files

▸ Control the information displayed about files

▸ Display and change a file's attributes

All the data and programs in a computer are stored in files. When you save these files to a disk, you name them so you and the computer can tell one from another. A disk can easily have hundreds or even thousands of files stored in it. To make these files easier to find, you divide the disk into directories so related files can be stored together. File Manager is the Windows application that you use to manage your files and directories.

OPENING AND CLOSING FILE MANAGER

To open the File Manager application, you double-click its icon in Program Manager's Main group. When you do so, File Manager displays a *directory window*.

THE ANATOMY OF THE DIRECTORY WINDOW

The directory window is normally split into two parts. The left half displays a *tree* of the directories on the disk. The right half displays the contents of the selected directory. You can size or move the directory window about the File Manager's workspace or minimize it to an icon.

Current directory and path

Menu bar

Drive icons

Volume label or network name

Directory list

Contents list

Status bar

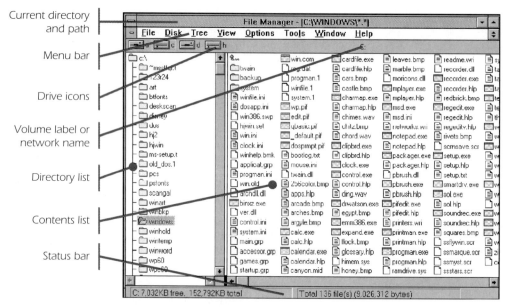

File Manager's directory window has the following elements:

▶ A *directory path* indicates the name of the selected directory (and the path to it, if any).

▶ The *menu bar* lists commands you can use to manage your disks and files. (If your system is using a version of DOS earlier than 6, the menu name **Tools** will not appear on the bar.)

▶ *Drive icons* represent each of the drives on the system.

▶ A *volume label* indicates the name of the disk if one was assigned to it when it was formatted. The name of your network-drive connection (if you have one) is displayed in place of the volume name.

▶ The *directory tree* displays a graphic illustration of how your disk is organized into directories and makes it easy to move between directories or create and delete them. The selected directory is highlighted. The directories are identified by labeled icons that resemble file folders because directories are like folders into which you can place documents to keep your disk well organized. Scroll bars are provided so you can scroll the directory tree if it is longer than the window.

LOOKING AHEAD: DIRECTORIES AND PATHS

Disks can store a lot of files. To keep them organized, you divide the disk into directories that are like file folders in which related documents can be stored. These directories can then be subdivided into subdirectories. Knowing which directory a document is in is important since you may not be able to locate or open a document unless you do. For now, think of a directory as an address. Just as you may live in San Francisco in the state of California, a file may be stored in a directory named DOS on a drive named C.

A path specifies exactly where a directory is on a drive. The elements of the path are separated by backslashes (\), as in *c:\dos*.

▶ The *contents list* displays the files in the selected (highlighted) directory. Scroll bars are used to scroll the contents list.

▶ The *status bar* displays information about the selected drive and selected files. It tells you how many bytes are available on the disk, the number of files in the selected directory and the number of bytes they occupy, and the number and size of selected files (if any). You can turn the display of this bar on and off with the **Status Bar** command on the **Options** menu.

CLOSING FILE MANAGER

When you are finished with File Manager, you can close it. This removes it from the computer's memory and removes its window or icon from the desktop (although the icon remains in the group window). To close, or exit, File Manager, do any of the following:

▶ Pull down the **File** menu and click the **Exit** command.

▶ Click the Control-menu box to display the Control menu, and then click the **Close** command.

▶ Double-click File Manager's Control-menu box.

▶ Press Alt + F4 when File Manager is the active window.

▶▶ TUTORIAL

1. Open the Main group window and double-click the File Manager icon to open the application. (If necessary, click File Manager's Maximize button to enlarge it to full screen.)

File Manager

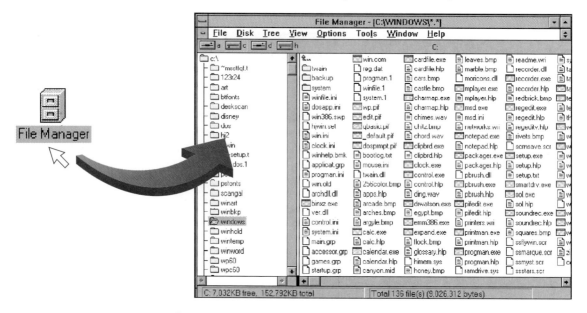

2. Compare your screen with the illustration on page 58 that has parts labeled. (The files and directories listed on your screen will be different from those in the illustration, but the elements of the screen will be the same.) Locate each of the following items on your screen:

▶ Drive icons   ▶ The path to the selected directory

▶ The volume label   ▶ The directory tree

▶ The contents list   ▶ The status bar

Double-click here to close File Manager.

3. Double-click File Manager's Control-menu box to close the application. (Click the upper Control-menu box. The lower one is for the directory window.)

4. Double-click the File Manager icon to open the application again.

TIP: IF PROGRAM MANAGER REDUCES TO AN ICON

If you find that Program Manager has been reduced to an icon when you exit an application, just double-click the Program Manager icon to open it back up into a window. Then, if you want to stop Program Manager from reducing to an icon, pull down the **Options** menu and click the **Minimize on Use** command to turn it off.

CHANGING THE SELECTED DRIVE

The directory tree and contents list always display the tree and contents of the selected drive, the drive whose icon is outlined by the selection cursor. Different icons are used to represent floppy disk, hard disks, CD-ROM drives, RAM drives, and network drives. One of the drive icons is always selected.

Floppy disk drive icons (also used for other removable media)   Local hard disk icon   Network drive icon   CD-ROM drive icon

The disk drive is outlined when you select it.

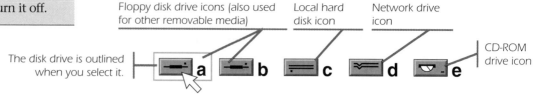

To change the selected drive, do any of the following:

▶ Click the drive icon.

▶ Hold down Ctrl while you press the drive letter. For example, to change to drive C, press Ctrl+C.

▶ Press Tab to move the selection cursor to the drive icons, use the arrow keys to highlight the desired drive, and then press Enter↵.

▶ Pull down the **Disk** menu and click the **Select Drive** command to display a dialog box listing all of the drives on your system. (You can also display the dialog box by double-clicking the background area of the bar where the drive icons are displayed.) Select the drive you want to change to, and then click the **OK** command button.

When you change drives, File Manager reads the names of the directories and files on that drive and then displays them in the directory window. If the drive has a lot of directories and files on it, this can take a few moments. (While it is happening, the Windows hourglass is displayed.) You can press Esc at any point to stop the process and display a partial tree.

1 Click the desired drive.

2 Click to change to the selected drive.

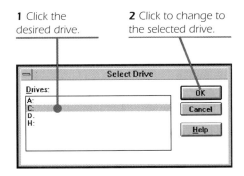

COMMON WRONG TURN: NO DISK IN DRIVE

If you click the icon for a drive that doesn't contain a disk, a dialog box is displayed. Insert a disk and click the **Retry** command button, or click the **Cancel** command button to cancel the command.

TIP: NETWORK DRIVES

You can access any drive on a network if you know its location and password (if any). File Manager displays icons for network drives, and the design of these icons is different from those used to represent other drives. This allows you to distinguish drives shared by other users on the network from those accessible only from your own computer. The procedures you follow to use network drives vary from system to system. However, to begin, pull down the **Disk** menu and click the **Network Connections** command (or a similar command such as **Connect Network Drive**). Enter the drive's path and password in the dialog box that is displayed, and click the **Connect** or **Disconnect** command button.

▶▶ **TUTORIAL**

1. Open the Main group window and double-click the File Manager icon to open the application. (In all of the following tutorials, this step is assumed.)

2. Insert the *Windows Student Resource Disk* into drive A.

NOTE: WINDOWS STUDENT RESOURCE DISK

In this tutorial, you use the *Windows Student Resource Disk*. If your copy of the book does not contain this disk inside the back cover, your instructor will make it available to you.

NOTE: QUITTING

If you have to quit at any point, finish any tutorial you have started, then be sure to remove your disk from drive A. Later you can resume where you left off if you:

1. Double-click the File Manager icon to open it.

2. Insert the *Windows Student Resource Disk* into drive A.

3. Click the drive A icon to make that the selected drive.

3. Click the drive A icon to select drive A. When you do so, the drive's icon is highlighted by the selection cursor. The contents list lists the directories and files on the disk in drive A.

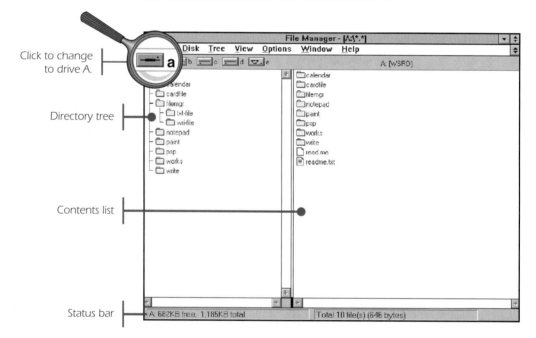

Click to change to drive A.

Directory tree

Contents list

Status bar

COMMON WRONG TURN:
OPENING A NEW DIRECTORY WINDOW

If you double-click a drive icon instead of clicking it, File Manager opens a new directory window for the drive on top of the old one. The first window is still open, but it is hidden. To see if more than one window is open, pull down the **Window** menu. All open windows are listed at the bottom of the menu. To close any unwanted extra windows, click the **Tile** command to display them all, then double-click each window's Control-menu box until only one window remains open. (You cannot close the last window, since one window must always be open.)

PAUSING FOR PRACTICE

Selecting different drives is one of the Windows skills that you must master. Pause here to practice changing to each of the drives listed for your system and looking carefully at the listings that result.

4. Click the drive C icon to list its files and directories. (Depending on the speed of your computer and the contents of drive C, this may take a few moments. On some systems you may not be able to select drive C, but there may be another drive available for you to look at.)

5. Look at the status bar to see the disk's free space and total capacity.

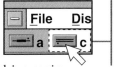

The selected drive is highlighted by the selection cursor.

6. Click the drive A icon to select that drive again.

7. Look at the status bar again to see how much free space is on the disk in drive A and the disk's total capacity.

CHANGING DIRECTORIES

Dividing a disk into directories helps you organize your files better. A disk is like an empty drawer in a new filing cabinet: It provides storage space but no organization. To make it easier to find items in a file drawer, you divide it into categories with hanging folders. You can file documents directly into the hanging folders, or you divide the hanging folders into finer categories with manila folders. A directory is like a hanging folder, and a subdirectory is like a manila folder within a hanging folder. A file in a directory or subdirectory is like a letter, report, or other document within either a hanging folder or a manila folder.

A new hard disk is like an empty file drawer. It has lots of room for files but no organization.

You can divide the hard disk into directories, which is like dividing the file drawer with hanging folders.

If you want, you can then subdivide the directories into smaller subdirectories, which is like dividing the hanging folders with manila folders

You can save files in any of these directories or subdirectories the same way you would file a document in one of the hanging or manila folders.

Directories on a hard disk drive are organized in a hierarchy. The main directory, the one not below any other directory, is the *root directory*. Below it, directories can be created on one or more levels. These directories can hold files or subdirectories. The terms *directory* and *subdirectory* are used somewhat loosely. Strictly speaking, there is only one directory—the root directory—and all others are subdirectories. In most discussions, however, any directory above another is called a directory, and those below it are called its subdirectories.

File Manager's tree lists directories starting at the top of the window with the root directory. All other directories (if any) branch from this topmost directory. When the directory tree is displayed, one and only

TIP: SELECTING DIRECTORIES BEFORE CHANGING DRIVES

When you select a directory on a drive and then select another drive, the directory on the first drive remains selected. When you switch back to that drive, you return to that directory.

one directory may be selected at a time, and it is always indicated by the selection cursor. Most directory and file management commands work only within the selected directory. For example, you can only select a file to be renamed, copied, moved, or deleted from the list of files in the selected directory. If you want to work with a file in another directory, you first have to select the directory in which it is stored. To select a directory, click its name or icon on the directory tree.

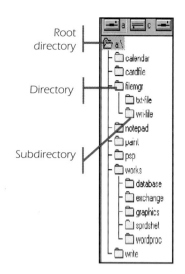

Root directory

Directory

Subdirectory

▶▶ TUTORIAL

1. Insert the *Windows Student Resource* Disk into drive A. If necessary, click the drive A icon to select that drive.

Click to display a directory window for drive A.

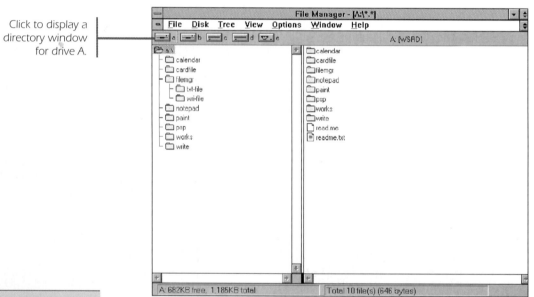

PAUSING FOR PRACTICE

Selecting directories is an essential Windows skill that you must master. Pause here to practice selecting each of the directories listed for the *Windows Student Resource Disk* in drive A.

2. Click each of the directories listed on the directory tree. As you click each directory to select it, notice that:

▶ It is highlighted and its file-folder-shaped icon opens.

▶ The directory's name is listed on the directory window's title bar.

▶ The contents of the directory, if any, are listed in the contents list.

▶ The *filemgr* and *works* directories display file folders on the contents list. These are subdirectories.

▶ The number of files in the directory (counting each subdirectory as 1 file) and their total size are listed on the status bar. (The size of the files in the subdirectories is not included.)

EXPANDING AND COLLAPSING DIRECTORY LEVELS

When you display a directory window, normally only the root directory and first level of directories are displayed; any subdirectories are hidden. You can, however, expand all levels on a entire branch, one more level on a branch, or all levels on all branches in the tree.

To display the subdirectories under a directory, double-click the directory's name or icon on the directory tree. To use menu commands to specify which subdirectories are displayed, pull down the **Tree** menu and choose one of the commands.

Expands selected directory one level

Expands all levels of selected directory

Expands all directories on the tree

Collapses/expands

Marks all expandable directory icons with a plus sign

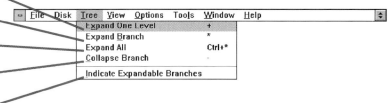

Some commands on the **Tree** menu work only with the selected directory; others work with all directories on the tree. For example, to know which directories on the tree contain subdirectories that haven't been expanded, pull down the **Tree** menu and select the **Indicate Expandable Branches** command. Branches that contain unexpanded subdirectories display a plus sign (+) in their icon. After they have been expanded, this changes to a minus sign (–) indicating that the branch can be collapsed.

Once you have moved down one or more levels in a directory tree, you can also move back up by double-clicking the Up icon—the arrow-shaped icon above the first filename on the contents list.

Up icon at the top of the contents list

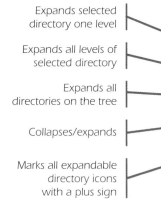

▶▶ **TUTORIAL**

Getting Ready

1. Insert the *Windows Student Resource Disk* into drive A and select that drive.

Indicating Expandable Branches

2. Pull down the **Tree** menu and click the **Indicate Expandable Branches** command to turn it on. (If it is already checked, click anywhere but in the menu to close the menu.)

  ▶ Directory icons with a minus sign (–) contain expanded subdirectories.

  ▶ Directory icons with a plus sign (+) contain unexpanded subdirectories.

  ▶ Directory icons without a plus or minus sign contain no subdirectories.

Opening and Closing Directories by Clicking

3. Double-click any directory icon marked with a plus sign (+) to expand it. When you do so, its folder-shaped icon opens, its symbol changes to a minus sign, and its subdirectories are displayed.

4. Double-click each of the directory icons marked with a minus sign (–), including the root directory, *a:*. When you do so, its folder-shaped icon closes, its symbol changes to a plus sign, and its subdirectories are hidden.

PAUSING FOR PRACTICE

Double-clicking to open and close directories is a basic skill. Pause here to continue practicing double-clicking directory icons with plus and minus signs until you are sure you understand the principles involved.

Opening and Closing Directories Using the <u>T</u>ree menu

4. Double-click the root directory, *a:*, to select it and display its directories.

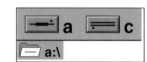

5. Pull down the **<u>T</u>ree** menu and click the **<u>C</u>ollapse Branch** command to hide all directories.

6. Pull down the **<u>T</u>ree** menu and click the **Expand <u>A</u>ll** command to display all directories and subdirectories on the disk. Notice how there are no directory icons with plus signs because the command expanded all directories.

7. Click the *filemgr* directory icon to select it.

8. Pull down the **<u>T</u>ree** menu and click the **<u>C</u>ollapse Branch** command to hide all subdirectories under the selected directory.

9. Pull down the **<u>T</u>ree** menu and click the **Expand <u>B</u>ranch** command to display all subdirectories under the selected directory.

Using the Up Icon

10. Click the *txt-file* directory to select it.

11. Double-click the Up icon at the top of the contents list (it is shaped like an arrow), and you move up one level to the *filemgr* directory. That directory is outlined on the directory tree, and its folder icon is open.

Click the Up icon to move up a directory level.

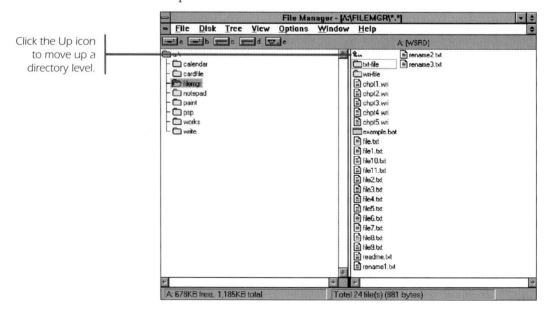

12. Double-click the Up icon again (you may have to scroll it into view), and you move up another level to the root directory. The root directory, *a:*, is now outlined on the directory tree, and its icon folder is open.

PAUSING FOR PRACTICE

Expanding and collapsing the directory tree are basic skills. Pause here to continue practicing expanding and collapsing them by double-clicking and using menu commands until you are sure you understand the principles involved.

EXPLORING THE CONTENTS LIST

The contents list displays the names of files and subdirectories stored in the selected directory so you can locate and manage your files. In order to understand the list, you should know something about Windows filenames. Windows uses the DOS file-naming conventions. You can assign names to files and directories that have up to eight characters and an extension of up to three characters separated from the name by a period.

The file's name can have up to eight characters.

FILENAME . EXT

The file's extension must begin with a period and can have up to three characters.

The characters that you can use in a filename are called *legal characters*. Using any other character results in a name the computer will not accept.

Legal Character	Example
Letters	A–Z
Letters	a–z
Numbers	0–9
Underscore	_
Caret	^
Dollar sign	$
Tilde	~
Exclamatioin point	!
Number sign	#
Percent sign	%
Ampersand	&
Hyphen	-
Braces	{ }
Parentheses	( )
At sign	@
Grave accent	`
Apostrophe	'

Filenames that you use should be unique. If you assign a file the same name and extension as a file that is already on the disk in the same directory, the new file can overwrite the previous file and erase it. However, you can use the same name with different extensions—for example, *letter.doc* and *letter.bak*. You can also use the same extension with different names.

Many applications automatically add unique extensions to files that they create. For example, Windows Notepad adds the extension *.txt*, Write adds *.wri*, Paintbrush adds *.bmp*, and the Clipboard Viewer adds *.clp*. Conventions also dictate that some extensions are to be used only in specific situations. For instance, *.exe* and *.com* are normally used for program files, and *.bat* is used for batch files. The extension *.sys* is used for files containing information about your system's hardware, and *.ini* for Windows files describing your system's setup. In many cases, if you don't use the extension the application automatically adds, the application may not be able to identify the file as its own. This can cause problems when you want to open a file later.

Each filename on the contents list is preceded by an icon that indicates its type. For example, program files have a different icon from document files.

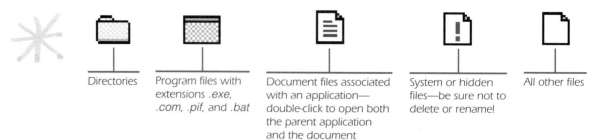

| Directories | Program files with extensions .exe, .com, .pif, and .bat | Document files associated with an application— double-click to open both the parent application and the document | System or hidden files—be sure not to delete or rename! | All other files |

 ▶▶ **TUTORIAL**

1. Insert the *Windows Student Resource Disk* into drive A and select that drive.

2. Click the *filemgr* directory to select it and list its files in the contents list on the right side of the screen.

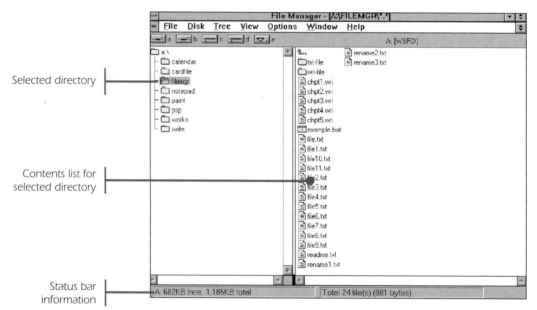

Selected directory

Contents list for selected directory

Status bar information

3. Pull down the **View** menu and click the **By File Type** command to display a dialog box.

4. Click all of the check boxes including the **Show Hidden/System Files** check box to turn them all on. (An X in the box indicates that a box is on.)

5. Click the **OK** command button to return to the directory window.

6. Search the icons on the contents list for an example of each of the following types:

▶ Directory

▶ Document file associated with an application

▶ Program file

▶ System or hidden file

▶ All other files

SPECIFYING FILE INFORMATION TO BE DISPLAYED

Normally just the names of all files (except those that are hidden) are displayed in the contents list. There are times, however, when it is helpful to display more information about the files. For example, you may want to know their size or the date they were created.

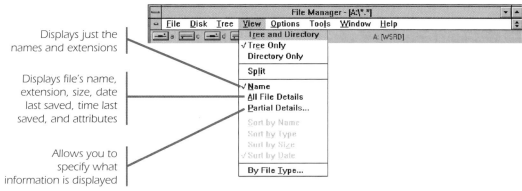

Displays just the names and extensions

Displays file's name, extension, size, date last saved, time last saved, and attributes

Allows you to specify what information is displayed

When you first load File Manager, the **Name** command on the **View** menu has a check mark in front of it to indicate it has been chosen and that just filenames will be displayed in the contents list. This is most useful when the active directory has a large number of files since it displays more filenames at one time than any other command.

When you want more information about a file than just its name, you can use the **All File Details** command to display all of the available information about the file.

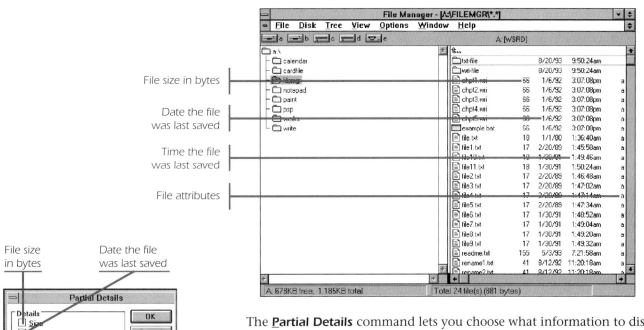

File size in bytes

Date the file was last saved

Time the file was last saved

File attributes

File size in bytes

Date the file was last saved

Time the file was last saved

r (read-only), h (hidden), s (system), or a (archive)

The **Partial Details** command lets you choose what information to display about the files. To display size, date, time, or file attribute information, click the appropriate check boxes to turn them on (X) or off (no X).

When you use the **View** menu's **All File Details** command, the contents list displays the attributes of each file. These attributes are indicated by letters. A file's attributes tell you if the file is a read-only file

(R), a hidden file (H), or a system file (S) and whether the file has been changed since a backup copy was last made with the Windows/DOS Backup command (A for "archive"). You can display a file's attributes, and change them if you like, using the **File** menu's **Properties** command.

▶▶ **TUTORIAL**

1. Insert the *Windows Student Resource Disk* into drive A and select that drive.

2. Click the *filemgr* directory to select it.

3. Pull down the **View** menu and click the **All File Details** command to display filenames, the size of each file, the date and time it was last saved, and its file attributes.

4. Pull down the **View** menu and click the **Partial Details** command to display a dialog box. All of the check boxes have an X because they have been turned on.

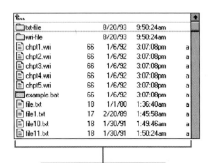

The file's name, size, date, time, and attributes

All check boxes are initially on.

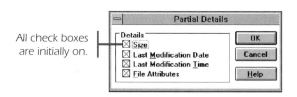

5. Click all check boxes with an X other than **Size** to turn them off. Only **Size** should have an X so it's turned on.

6. Click the **OK** command button, and the contents list displays only filenames and sizes.

7. Pull down the **View** menu and click the **Partial Details** command to display a dialog box.

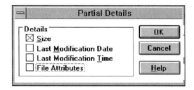

8. Click the **Last Modification Date** check box to turn it on.

9. Click the **OK** command button, and the contents list displays the file's name, size, and last modification date.

10. Pull down the **View** menu and click the **Name** command to display just filenames again.

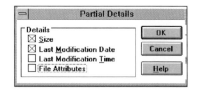

11. Pull down the **View** menu and click the **By File Type** command to display a dialog box.

12. If the **Show Hidden/System Files** command isn't on, turn it on, then click the **OK** command button. Otherwise, click the **Cancel** command button to close the menu without making a choice.

13. Click the *hidden.txt* filename in the contents list to select it.

14. Pull down **File** and click the **Properties** command to display a dialog box listing the file's attributes. Notice that the **Hidden** check box is on.

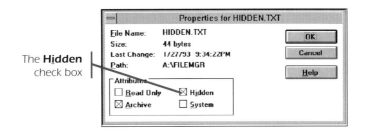

The **Hidden**
check box

15. Click the **Hidden** check box to turn it off.

16. Click the **OK** command button to return to the directory window. Notice how the icon for the *hidden.txt* file changes from an exclamation point that indicates it's a hidden or system file to an icon that indicates it is an associated file.

17. Pull down **File** and click the **Properties** command to display the dialog box again.

18. Click the **Hidden** check box to turn it back on, then click the **OK** command button to return to the directory window. The icon for the *hidden.txt* file again has an exclamation point to indicate it's a hidden or system file.

19. To finish the tutorial, pull down the **View** menu and click **By File Type**, then turn off **Show Hidden/System Files** and click the **OK** command button.

SORTING FILES

Normally, files in the contents list are sorted in ascending alphabetical order by name. There are times, however, when it's helpful to sort them in another order. For example, you may want to delete all files ending with the extension *.bak*. Doing so would be easier if the files were arranged by extension so all *.bak* files were together on the list. At other times, you may want to know which are the largest files on the disk. Sorting the list by file size would be helpful in this situation.

Arranges files in ascending alphabetical order (a, b, c) by name

Arranges files in ascending alphabetical order by extension

Arranges files with largest at top and smallest at bottom

Arranges files with most recent at top and oldest at bottom

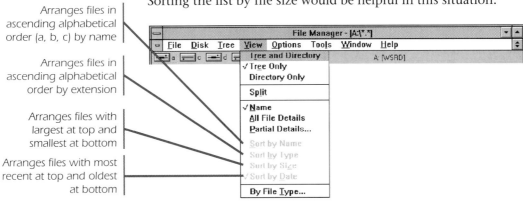

▶▶ **TUTORIAL**

1. Insert the *Windows Student Resource Disk* into drive A and select that drive.

2. Click the *filemgr* directory to select it.

3. Pull down the **View** menu and click the **All File Details** command to turn it on. The files are all listed on the contents list in ascending alphabetical order by name.

4. Pull down the **View** menu and click the **Sort by Type** command to list the files in ascending order by extension. For example, a file with the extension *.bat* is listed before a file with the extension *.wri*. However, directories are always listed first, before filenames.

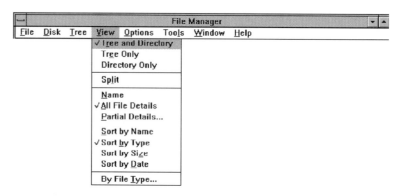

5. Pull down the **View** menu and click the **Sort by Size** command to list files in descending order by file size. Larger files are listed first.

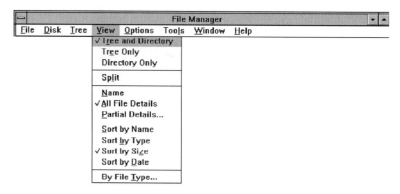

6. Pull down the **View** menu and click the **Sort by Date** command to list files in descending order by date. Those last modified on the same date are subsorted in descending order by time.

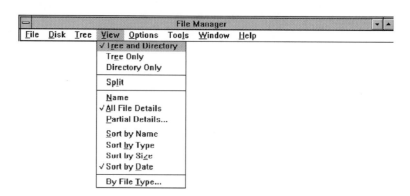

7. Pull down the **View** menu and click the **Sort by Name** command to return the list to its original order.

8. Pull down the **View** menu and click the **Name** command to display just filenames again.

DISPLAYING ONLY SELECTED FILES

When you first open File Manager, the contents list displays the names of all directories and all files in the selected directory (except for system or hidden files). However, you can specify which kinds of files are displayed. To do so, pull down the **View** menu and click the **By File Type** command to display a dialog box. Enter a *filename specification* in the **Name** text box to specify the types of files you want displayed. The phrase *filename specification* refers to any combination of text and wildcards that you enter to control which filenames are displayed. The default filename specification, ***.***, displays all files. When you have finished, click the **OK** command button to display filenames based on the choices you have made.

The filename specification entered here determines which files are displayed.

Displays subdirectories in the current directory

Displays files with extensions *.exe*, *.com*, *.pif*, and *.bat*

Displays documents associated with applications

Displays all other files not displayed by Programs or Documents options

Displays hidden and system files

To take advantage of the **Name** text box, you need to understand DOS and Windows conventions for filenames and wildcards. The filename specification you enter into the **Name** text box can contain both text and wildcards. For example, if you want to display only the file named *myfile.txt*, you enter that filename. However, you can also use the **?** and ***** wildcards to specify groups of files. The term *wildcard* comes from card games where a designated card, say a jack, can substitute for any other card in the deck. For example, in the card sequence 4-5-J-7-8, the jack stands for the 6 card.

The wildcard

THE QUESTION MARK

The question mark substitutes for any single character. For example, to display all filenames that begin with *chpt* followed by one or two other characters (such as *chpt1* or *chpt10*) and the extension *.doc*, pull down the **View** menu and click the **By File Type** command, type **chpt??.doc** in the **Name** text box, and click the **OK** command button. The filename

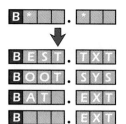

specification *chpt??.doc* will display filenames such as *chpt10.doc*, but not *chtp100.doc* because there is no third question mark.

THE ASTERISK

The asterisk represents any character in a given position and all following characters in the part of the filename (either the name or extension) where it is used. For example, to display all filenames that begin with a *c* and have the extension *.doc*, pull down the **View** menu and click the **By File Type** command, type **c*.doc** in the **Name** text box, and click the **OK** command button.

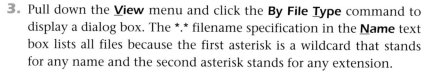

▶▶ TUTORIAL

Getting Ready

1. Insert the *Windows Student Resource Disk* into drive A and select that drive.

2. Click the *filemgr* directory to select it.

Using the Asterisk Wildcard

3. Pull down the **View** menu and click the **By File Type** command to display a dialog box. The ***.*** filename specification in the **Name** text box lists all files because the first asterisk is a wildcard that stands for any name and the second asterisk stands for any extension.

4. Type ***.txt** in the **Name** text box and click the **OK** command button to list all the files with the extension *.txt*. Notice how the filename specification is listed in the directory window's title bar.

5. Pull down the **View** menu and click the **By File Type** command to display the dialog box again.

6. Type ***.wri** in the **Name** text box and click the **OK** command button to list all files with the extension *.wri*.

Using the Question Mark Wildcard

7. Pull down the **View** menu and click the **By File Type** command to display a dialog box.

8. Type **file?.txt** in the **Name** text box and click the **OK** command button to list all files that begin with *file*, have up to one additional character, and have the extension *.txt*. (Note that files with the names *file10.txt* and *file11.txt* are not listed.)

9. Pull down the **View** menu and click the **By File Type** command to display a dialog box.

10. Type **file??.txt** in the **Name** text box and click the **OK** command button to list all files that begin with *file*, have up to two additional characters, and have the extension *.txt*. Now the files with the names *file10.txt* and *file11.txt* are listed.

Finishing Up

11. Pull down the **View** menu and click the **By File Type** command to display a dialog box.

12. Type ***.*** in the **Name** text box and click the **OK** command button to list all files in the directory.

COMMON WRONG TURNS:
ALL FILES NOT LISTED IN CONTENTS LIST

When you enter anything other than *.* when using the **By File Type** command, you should reenter that filename specification before continuing or files you look for later may not be listed. If the **Options** menu's **Save Settings on Exit** command is on, the filename specification you enter is remembered, even when you close File Manager and then reopen it.

CHANGING THE DISPLAY

Commands that control what is displayed

When you first load File Manager, the directory window displays both the directory tree and the contents list. However, you can pull down the **View** menu and choose one of the commands **Tree and Directory**, **Tree Only**, or **Directory Only**. You can switch back and forth between any of these views at any time. When you do so, you display the tree of directories on the disk, the contents of the active directory, or both.

Initially, the directory window allocates the same space for the directory tree and the contents list. If your disk has a lot of levels in its tree or directories have a lot of files, you can drag the *split bar* that divides the windows to make more room in one window or the other. The split bar is located to the right of the scroll bar in the middle of the screen. When you point to the bar, the mouse pointer turns into a double-headed arrow. When this arrow appears, hold down the left mouse button while you drag the bar to where you want it and then release it.

Mouse pointer on the split bar

Split bar

You can also change the font used to display files and directories. To do so, pull down the **Options** menu and click the **Font** command to display a dialog box. Select a font, a font style, and a font size. As you do so, a sample of the font is displayed in the Sample window. When you have selected the font you want to use, click the **OK** command button.

Any changes you make using the **Options** menu are saved automatically when you exit File Manager. However, to save your File Manager screen layout and the settings that you have made on the **View** menu, use one of the following approaches:

▶ Pull down the **Options** menu and click the **Save Settings on Exit** command to place a check mark (✔) in front of the command. When you exit Windows, the current settings will be saved. Be sure to remove the check mark the next time you load Windows or subsequent changes will also be saved whether or not you intended them to be.

▶ Pull down the **Options** menu and click the **Save Settings on Exit** command to remove the check mark (✔) from in front of the command. Then press [Alt]+[⇧ Shift]+[F4] to save the settings.

►► TUTORIAL

Getting Started

1. Insert the *Windows Student Resource Disk* into drive A and select that drive.

2. Click the *filemgr* directory to select it.

Changing the Directory Window Display

3. Pull down the **V̲iew** menu and click the **Tr̲ee Only** command to display just the directory tree. This tree lists the directories into which the disk has been divided.

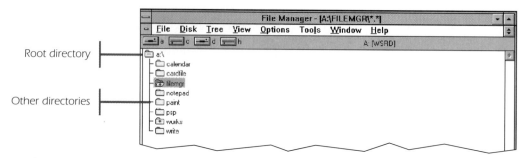

Root directory

Other directories

4. Pull down the **V̲iew** menu and click the **Directory O̲nly** command to display just the files in the selected directory.

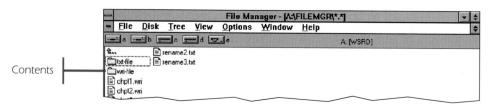

Contents

5. Pull down the **V̲iew** menu and click the **Tr̲ee and Directory** command to display a split screen.

6. Pull down the **O̲ptions** menu and change any of the following settings. (A check mark in front of the command indicates that it is on.) You'll have to pull the menu down again for each change:

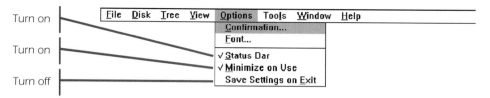

Turn on

Turn on

Turn off

▶ Turn off the **Save Settings on E̲xit** command if it is on. When it is off, any changes you make to the positions of directory windows are not saved.

▶ Turn on the **S̲tatus Bar** command if it is off. When on, a status bar at the bottom of the screen lists disk and file sizes when you work with files.

▶ Turn on the **M̲inimize on Use** command if it is off. When it is on, File Manager minimizes to an icon when you open another application.

Dividing the Screen Differently

7. Point to the split bar in the middle of the directory window so the mouse pointer takes on the shape of a line with arrows pointing left and right.

Mouse pointer on the split bar

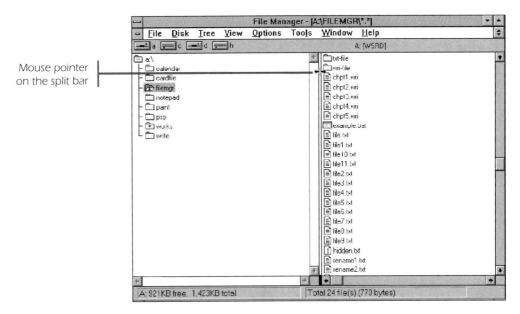

8. Hold down the left button and drag the split bar to the left so there isn't a lot of empty space in the directory tree window.

9. Release the mouse button.

Changing the Font

10. Pull down the **Options** menu and click the **Font** command to display a dialog box listing fonts on your system. The current font, style, and size are highlighted on the three list boxes. Jot down the font's name, style, and size because you'll want to select them again later.

Your font: _____

Your style: _____

Your size: _____

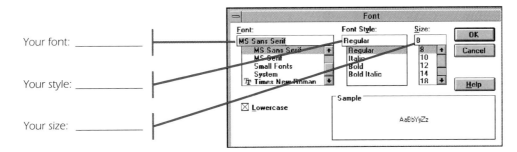

11. Use the scroll arrows to scroll the list of fonts in the **Font** list box and click a different font to select it. When you do so, the Sample box displays the new font.

12. Scroll the **Size** list box and click any font size between *12* and *20* to select it. When you do so, the Sample box displays the new size. (If your system does not list such a size, change the font.)

13. Click the **OK** command button, and the directory window changes to display all text in the new font. What differences do you notice between the original selection and the new one?

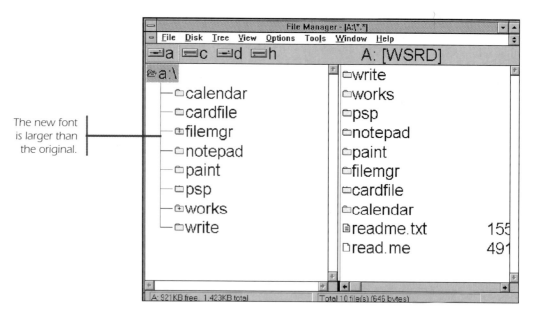

The new font is larger than the original.

14. Repeat Steps 10 through 13 but select the original font and the original size before clicking the **OK** command button.

DISPLAYING, ARRANGING, AND CLOSING MULTIPLE DIRECTORY WINDOWS

To compare the files on different drives or in different directories, you display more than one directory window. This is useful when copying or moving files from one drive or directory to another and especially so when you are dragging and dropping them, as you will see in a later PicTorial.

DISPLAYING MORE THAN ONE DIRECTORY WINDOW

You open another directory window without closing the current one by double-clicking a second drive icon. You can also pull down the **Window** menu and click the **New Window** command to open a window identical to the current one. To display a listing of the files in any directory displayed on the directory tree, hold down ⬆Shift while double-clicking its directory icon. This opens a new directory window, listing just the files in that directory.

When you open a second directory window that shows the same information as the one you opened it from, the windows are numbered. For example, the first may be *C:*.*:1* and the second *C:*.*:2*. Whenever you open one window from another, the new window has the same settings as the one you opened it from. For example, if the directory tree is displayed in the original window, it is displayed in the new one.

Once you have more than one directory window displayed, only one of them can be active. To make a directory window active, do any of the following:

▶ Click anywhere on the window.

▶ Press Ctrl+Tab⇆ or Ctrl+F6 to cycle through the available windows.

▶ Pull down the **W̲indow** menu and choose the window's name from the list displayed at the bottom of the menu to move directly to that window.

ARRANGING DIRECTORY WINDOWS AND DIRECTORY ICONS

To rearrange directory windows, pull down the **W̲indow** menu, then click the **C̲ascade** command to arrange the windows so they overlap with their title bars displayed or **T̲ile** to fit all of the directory windows into File Manager's workspace. Normally, tiled windows are displayed one above another. To display the windows side by side, hold down ⌖ Shift when you click the **T̲ile** command. The currently selected window will always be displayed on top or to the left when you tile windows. To change their order, first select the window you want on top or to the left before you click the **T̲ile** command.

You can also minimize directory windows to icons. To rearrange icons, you can drag them about on File Manager's workspace. To line them up automatically along the lower portion of the File Manager window, select the File Manager window, then pull down the **W̲indow** menu, and click the **A̲rrange Icons** command.

CLOSING DIRECTORY WINDOWS

One directory window must always be open, but you can close others by selecting them and then double-clicking their Control-menu box.

TIP: QUICKLY CLEARING EXTRA DIRECTORY WINDOWS

Since double-clicking a drive's icon can create a new directory window, you may find many such windows on your screen. To quickly clear them, pull down the **W̲indow** menu and click the **T̲ile** command. Then double-click the Control-menu boxes on the windows you want to close.

▶▶ **TUTORIAL**

Getting Ready

1. Insert the Windows Student Resource Disk into drive A and select that drive.

2. Click the root directory, *a:*, to select that directory.

Opening a New Directory Window

3. Double-click the icon for drive C to open a second window for drive C. (You may not be able to tell immediately that it is a second window.)

Moving Between Windows

4. Pull down the **W̲indow** menu; names of the two directory windows should be listed at the bottom of the menu.

5. Click *A:*.** to make it the current window.

Tiling Windows

6. Pull down the **Window** menu and click the **Tile** command to display the two directory windows one above the other. Note that the window for drive A is on top since it was the active window when you executed the **Tile** command.

Directory windows above one another

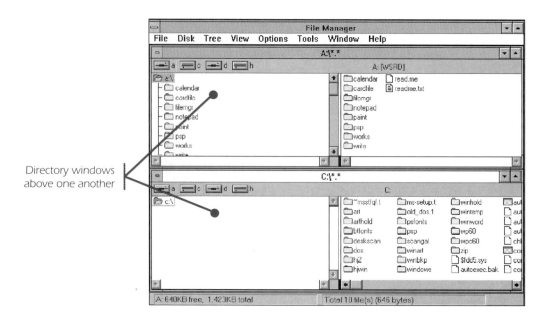

7. Pull down the **Window** menu and hold down ⟨⇧ Shift⟩ when you click the **Tile** command to display the two directory windows side by side. Note that the window for drive A is on the left since it was the active window when you executed the **Tile** command.

Directory windows arranged side by side

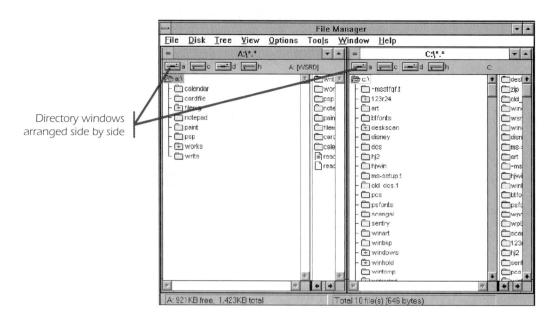

Cascading Windows

8. Pull down the **Window** menu and click the **Cascade** command to display the two directory windows overlapping.

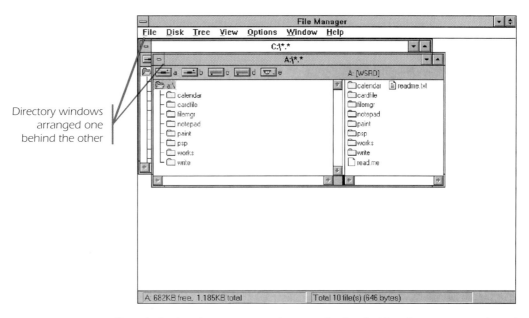

Directory windows arranged one behind the other

9. Click the directory window in the back (the directory window for drive C) to bring it to the front and make it the active window.

Closing a Directory Window

10. Double-click the Control-menu box for drive C's directory window to close the window.

PAUSING FOR PRACTICE

Displaying and arranging directory windows is one of the Windows skills that you must master. Pause here to open directory windows for each of the drives on your system that contains a disk. Practice arranging, moving between, and closing the windows.

▶▶ **SKILL-BUILDING EXERCISES**

1. Exploring a Useless but Interesting File Manager Feature

1. Open the File Manager application.

2. Pull down the **Help** menu and click the **About File Manager** command.

3. Hold down Ctrl+⇧ Shift while double-clicking the Microsoft Windows flag icon in the upper-left corner.

4. Click the **OK** command button to close the dialog box.

5. Repeat Steps 2 and 3 to display a dedication with a waving flag.

6. Click the **OK** command button to close the dialog box.

7. Repeat Steps 2 and 3 to display a list of credits, presented by a caricature of Bill Gates or one of the other key people behind the development of Windows. The bear stands for the bear that bonks people who introduced bugs into the program during development. If you repeat the series of commands, four different presenters appear in random order.

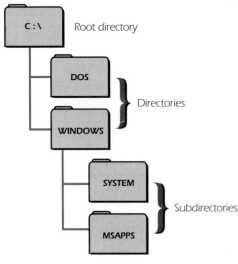

C:\ — Root directory

DOS
WINDOWS — Directories

SYSTEM
MSAPPS — Subdirectories

Extension	Number of Files
bat	_____
txt	_____
writ	_____

8. When you get bored, just click the **OK** command button to quit.

2. Exploring the Directory Tree

Use File Manager to explore the directory tree of the hard disk on your system where Windows is stored. You should be able to locate a tree similar to the one shown at the left.

3. Calculating File Sizes

1. Insert your *Windows Student Resource Disk* into drive A.

2. Display the directory window for the *Windows Student Resource Disk*. Can you calculate how much space on the disk is occupied by files?

3. Display the directory window for drive C or any other drive on your system that contains a disk. How much space on the disk is occupied by files?

4. Using Wildcards

1. With your *Windows Student Resource Disk* still in drive A, select that drive.

2. Change to the *filemgr* directory.

3. Using the *.<ext>* filename specifications, list in the spaces below the number of files there are with each extension. For example, to complete the first entry, use the filename specification ***.bat**. Then list in the table the number of filenames displayed.

4. Be sure to reset the filename specification to *.** when you are finished so all filenames are displayed.

PICTORIAL 3 ▶ VISUAL QUIZ

1. This illustration shows File Manager's directory window. Write down the name of each of the labeled parts in the space provided.

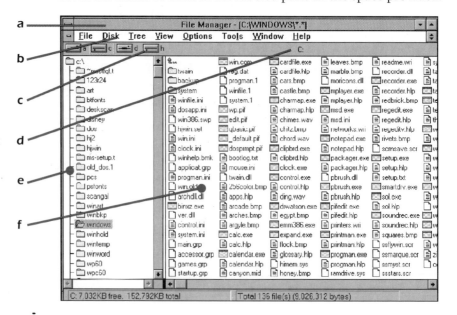

a. _current dir & path_
b. _menu bar_
c. _drive icons_
d. _volume label/network name_
e. _dir. list_
f. _contents list_

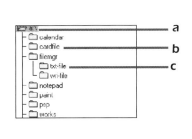

2x This directory tree shows three levels of directories. In the space provided, write down the name of each of the labeled levels.

a. _root dir_
b. _dir._
c. _subdir._

3x The three folders shown here are from the directory tree. In the space provided, describe what each indicates.

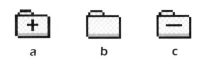

a. _____
b. _____
c. _____

What command do you use to turn these symbols on and off and what menu is it on? _____

4x This illustration shows some typical drive icons. (a) What is the name of the outline around drive A, and (b) what is the major difference between drives A and C?

a. _____
b. _____

5x What is the name of the element shown here? _____
What do you use it for? _____

⬆..

6x Name the two parts of the filename shown here and indicate how many characters can be in each part.

CHAP-10.WRL

a. _filename 8_
b. _extension 3_

7x You may see the icons shown here on File Manager's contents list. Describe the type of file that each icon indicates.

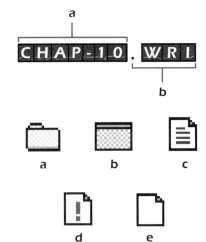

a. _dir_
b. _program file w/ ext._
c. _document files associated w/ applications_
d. _system or hidden files_
e. _all other files_

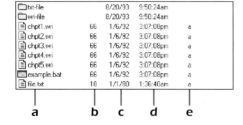

txt-file		8/20/93	9:50:24am	
wri-file		8/20/93	9:50:24am	
chpt1.wri	66	1/6/92	3:07:08pm	a
chpt2.wri	66	1/6/92	3:07:08pm	a
chpt3.wri	66	1/6/92	3:07:08pm	a
chpt4.wri	66	1/6/92	3:07:08pm	a
chpt5.wri	66	1/6/92	3:07:08pm	a
example.bat	66	1/6/92	3:07:08pm	a
file.txt	18	1/1/80	1:36:40am	a

a   b   c   d   e

8. There is one major difference between the two contents lists shown here. Explain what the difference is and how you accomplish it.

_____

_____

_____

For the second contents list, explain what information is shown in each of the columns.

a. _name_____

b. _size_____

c. _date_____

d. _time_____

e. _attributes_____

9. Which filenames shown in the left column would be displayed by the filename specifications on the top row? Put a check mark in every box that applies.

Filename	f*.wri	*.*	*.w*
chpt.wri		✔	✔
file.wri	✔	✔	✔
file.doc		✔	
new.wrt		✔	✔

10. Which filenames shown in the left column would be displayed by the filename specifications on the top row? Put a check mark in every box that applies.

Filename	f*.w??	f???.*	n??.w*
chpt.wri			
file.wri	✔	✔	
file.doc		✔	
new.wrt	✔		✔

11. These two screens show tiled directory windows. Explain how each was tiled.

a. _____

b. _____

a

b

PicTorial 4

Managing Your Disks and Files

After completing this PicTorial, you will be able to:

▶ Format data and system disks and explain the difference between the two

▶ Copy a disk

▶ Label a disk

▶ Organize your files on a disk

▶ Turn confirmation on and off

▶ Search files listed in the contents list

▶ Move and copy files and directories using menu commands

▶ Move and copy files and directories by dragging and dropping

▶ Make directories and subdirectories

▶ Delete and rename files and directories

Some of the operations you perform with File Manager affect the entire disk. The commands for these operations are located on the **Disk** menu. They include commands to format, copy, and label disks.

Makes an exact duplicate of a disk

Adds a label to a disk

Formats a disk

Transfers the DOS system files to a formatted disk

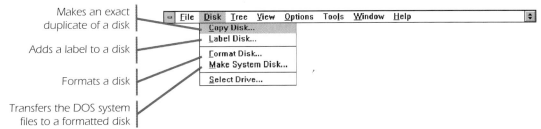

Other operations affect one of more files. For example, you make backup copies of important files in case something goes wrong and delete files when they are no longer needed. At times, you may also want to copy or move files to another disk or change the name of a file or directory. All of these tasks, and many others, can be performed by commands listed on the **File** menu.

Moves selected files

Copies selected files

Deletes selected files

Renames selected files

Changes the properties of a file

Creates a new directory

Selects files

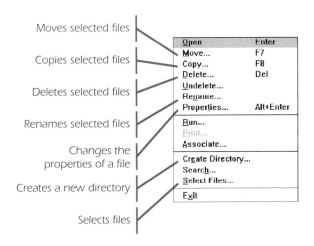

FORMATTING DISKS

A computer cannot store data on a disk until the disk has been formatted for the type of system you are using. Some new disks come already formatted for use with Windows and DOS, but others have to be formatted before you can use them.

Formatting a disk effectively erases any data that may already have been saved on it. You therefore have to be careful with this command. You should never format a previously used disk unless you are sure you will not need any of the files on it. Moreover, you should never format a hard disk drive unless you are willing to lose every file on the disk. (However, since no one is perfect and mistakes do happen, DOS 5 and later versions have an *unformat* command that helps you recover files should you format a disk by mistake.)

Formatting checks the disk surface for unusable spots, divides the disk into tracks and sectors, and creates a directory in which to store a map of the files on the disk. Tracks and sectors are an invisible magnetic pattern on the disk that looks something like the pattern on a dart board. On a formatted disk, tracks run in circles around the disk. Because tracks can store a great deal of data, the computer needs to divide them into sectors, which makes it easier to find a location on the disk. These sectors are like pie-shaped wedges that divide each track into the same number of sectors.

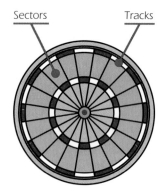

Sectors   Tracks

To store more data, the tracks on some disks are placed closer together. The spacing of these tracks is measured as *tracks per inch* (TPI). The number of TPI determines the density of the disk and the amount of data that can be stored on it. A *high-density disk* (also called a high-capacity or quad-density disk) has more tracks per inch than a *double-density disk* and can therefore store more data—1.2MB as opposed to 360KB for 5¼-inch disks. The maximum density that can be used to store data on a disk is indicated on the disk label and box.

The most common versions of the smaller 3½-inch floppy disks can store 720KB or 1.44MB. These disks can store more data than the larger 5¼-inch disks because they have more tracks per inch than the larger disks. You can tell the two types of 3½-inch disks apart because a 720KB disk has a single square cutout and a 1.44MB disk has two square cutouts.

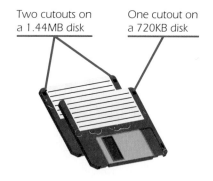

Two cutouts on   One cutout on
a 1.44MB disk   a 720KB disk

To format a data disk, you pull down the **Disk** menu and click the **Format Disk** command. When you do so, a dialog box is displayed offering a number of options.

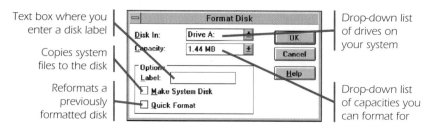

Text box where you enter a disk label

Copies system files to the disk

Reformats a previously formatted disk

Drop-down list of drives on your system

Drop-down list of capacities you can format for

The **Disk In** drop-down list box lists the floppy disk drives on your system. You choose the drive that contains the disk you want to format.

The **Capacity** drop-down list box displays a list of the formats from which you can choose for the selected floppy disk drive. Unless you specify otherwise, Windows formats a disk to match the drive it is being formatted in. However, at times you may want to change the selection to format a 360KB 5¼-inch disk in a 1.2MB drive or a 720KB 3½-inch disk in a 1.44MB drive.

The **Label** text box is where you enter a label for the disk up to 11 characters long. This label is always displayed at the top of File Manager's contents list when you select the drive containing the disk. (You can also add or change a volume label at any time with the **Label Disk** command on the **Disk** menu.)

Turning on the **Make System Disk** check box copies three files needed to make the floppy disk a self-booting system disk for drive A. Disks with these files are called *system disks* because they can be used to boot the system. When you boot the computer with a system disk in that drive, the operating system is loaded from that disk instead of from drive C.

COMMON WRONG TURNS: BOOTING FROM THE DISK IN DRIVE A

Even if a floppy disk is formatted as a system disk, it may not be wise to boot your system from it. The hard disk contains two files that set up your system for you. These are the *autoexec.bat* and *config.sys* files. If you don't copy these two files to the floppy disk, your system will not run the same way when you boot from drive A as when you boot from drive C.

Checking the **Quick Format** check box formats a previously formatted disk. This form of formatting is faster than a normal format because it does not check the disk for bad sectors. When DOS formats a disk, bad or defective sectors are normally marked so data isn't stored on them. Since the quick format doesn't check for them, don't use this command unless you know the disk is in good shape.

 ▶▶ **TUTORIAL**

1. Load Windows and double-click the File Manager icon to open it.

2. Label a blank floppy disk for drive A of your computer, using as a guide the label shown here. **Be sure the disk does not contain any data that you want to save because formatting it will erase the data!**

3. Insert your newly labeled disk into drive A.

4. Pull down the **Disk** menu and click the **Format Disk** command to display a dialog box. The command automatically selects drive A to format, but your **Capacity** setting may be different from the one illustrated here, depending on what type of drive A your system has.

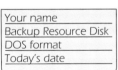

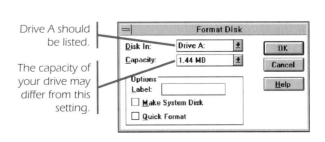

Drive A should be listed.

The capacity of your drive may differ from this setting.

5. Click in the **Label** text box to move the insertion point there, then type your first name (abbreviating it to 11 characters if necessary).

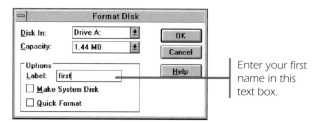

Enter your first name in this text box.

6. Click the **OK** command button to display the Confirm Format Disk dialog box.

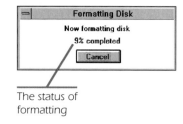

The status of formatting

7. Click the **Yes** command button, and the drive spins and its light comes on as the disk is formatted. A box displays the status of the formatting procedure.

When the disk has been formatted, the Format Complete box appears. This box tells you how much total space is on the disk and how much is available for your files. A prompt asks you if you want to format another disk.

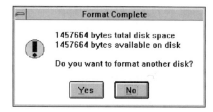

8. Click the **No** command button, and you return to File Manager. Your first name, which you entered as the disk's label, should be displayed at the top of the contents list. If it isn't, pull down the **Window** menu and click the **Refresh** command.

COPYING DISKS

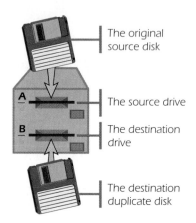

The original source disk

The source drive

The destination drive

The destination duplicate disk

To make an exact copy of a disk, you use the **Copy Disk** command on File Manager's **Disk** menu. When you choose this command, a dialog box appears if your system has more than one floppy disk drive. The dialog box contains two drop-down list boxes you use to specify the source and destination drives. When using this command, keep the following points in mind:

▶ The destination disk will be formatted as part of the process, if necessary, before files are copied to it.

▶ If you use this command to copy files to a disk that already contains files, the existing files will be erased.

▸ You can only use the **Copy Disk** command to copy files between disks with identical storage capacities. For example, you cannot use **Copy Disk** between a high-density 5¼-inch disk and a disk in a 360KB drive. And you cannot use this command between 5¼-inch and 3½-inch drives.

▸ The command copies not only files but also directories and sub-directories.

TIP: WRITE-PROTECTING YOUR DISKS

When you work with files and disks, you can lose work if you make a mistake. To protect important files, write-protect the disk. If a disk is write-protected, you can read files on the disk, but you cannot save files on it, format it, or erase files from it.

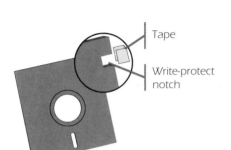

Tape

Write-protect notch

Write-protected when window is open

Not write-protected when closed

▸ To write-protect a 5¼-inch floppy disk, cover the write-protect notch with a piece of tape. You must use a write-protect tape that light cannot shine through since some drives use a light to determine whether the notch is covered. If you use a transparent tape, the light will shine through the notch just as if it were not covered, and the drive will assume it is not write-protected.

▸ To write-protect a 3½-inch floppy disk, open the sliding tab in the write-protect window.

Why do you write-protect one type of disk by *covering* the notch and the other by *uncovering* the window? If you are paranoid and believe in conspiracies, this may be evidence you need to prove that there is a plot to make computers as difficult as possible!

▸▸ TUTORIAL

1. Insert the **write-protected** original *Windows Student Resource Disk* into drive A and select that drive.

2. Pull down the **Disk** menu and click the **Copy Disk** command. What then happens depends on your system:

Original

▸ If your system has only one floppy disk drive, the Confirm Copy Disk dialog box appears. Proceed to Step 3.

▸ If your system has two floppy disk drives, a dialog box is displayed with two drop-down list boxes showing the source and destination drives. The source is the drive you are copying from (drive A) and the destination is the drive you are copying the disk to.

The drive with your original disk

The drive with the disk you are copying to

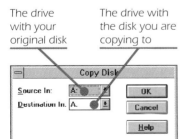

▸ If your system has two drives but they don't match, leave both drives set to A. Click the **OK** command button, and the Confirm Copy Disk dialog box appears.

With the original Windows Student Resource Disk in drive A, click to continue.

▶ If your system has more than one drive of the same type, pull down the **Destination In** list box and select the drive you are copying to (usually drive B). Click the **OK** command button, and the Confirm Copy Disk dialog box appears.

3. Click the **Yes** command button, and the dialog box asks you to insert the source disk.

4. You have already done so, so click the **OK** command button to begin copying. A Copying Disk dialog box keeps you posted on the copying progress. If you left both source and destination drives set to drive A, dialog boxes may periodically appear asking you to swap disks:

▶ When the prompt *Insert destination disk* appears, insert the *Backup Resource Disk* you formatted in the preceding tutorial and click the **OK** command button to continue.

▶ When the prompt *Insert source disk* appears, insert the original *Windows Student Resource Disk* and click the **OK** command button to continue. When the dialog box disappears, the disk has been copied and is identical to the original disk. However, note that the disk's label above the contents list still shows your first name as the disk's label. This is because the directory window has not been updated.

5. Pull down the **Window** menu and click the **Refresh** command to update the directory window. The disk's label changes to *[WSRD]*.

6. **Save this disk to use throughout the rest of this text. It is your *Backup Resource Disk*. From this point on, you should use this disk when the tutorials specify the *Windows Student Resource Disk*.**

TIP: STORE YOUR WINDOWS STUDENT RESOURCE DISK NOW!

Now is the time to store your original *Windows Student Resource Disk* in a safe place. If anything happens to your *Backup Resource Disk*, you can make another copy if you have your original *Windows Student Resource Disk*, following the steps shown in this tutorial.

2 Click to label the disk.

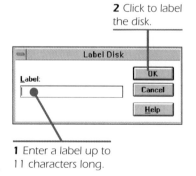

1 Enter a label up to 11 characters long.

LABELING DISKS

You can label each of your disks so its name appears above the contents list when you are using File Manager. To change a disk's label or add a label to a disk that hasn't already been labeled, pull down the **Disk** menu and click the **Label Disk** command to display a dialog box. Type the name of the disk into the **Label** text box (up to 11 characters) and then click the **OK** command button.

1. Insert the backup *Windows Student Resource Disk* into drive A and select that drive.

2. Pull down the **D**isk menu and click the **Label Disk** command to display a dialog box; the label *WSRD* is highlighted. Although you labeled the disk with your first name when you formatted it, the **Copy Disk** command changed the label to the same one used on the original *Windows Student Resource Disk*.

3. Type your last name (abbreviating it to 11 characters if necessary); as you do so, the first character you type deletes the entire previous entry.

4. Click the **OK** command button. Your last name is now the disk's label, and it is displayed at the top of the contents list.

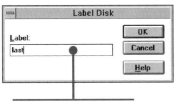

The text box displays the current name of the disk.

Type your last name into the text box.

SELECTING FILES IN THE CONTENTS LIST

To perform operations on files such as copying, renaming, or deleting, you must first select the files to be affected. When you select files, the number selected and their total size is indicated on the status bar. (You can turn the display of this bar on and off with the **S**tatus Bar command on the **O**ptions menu.)

POINTING AND CLICKING TO SELECT FILES

You can select any single file by clicking it. However, at times you want to *extend the selection* to more than one item in the contents list.

▶ To extend the selection over sequential files, click the first filename to select it, and then either hold down [⇧ Shift] while you click the last filename or hold down [⇧ Shift] and use the arrow keys to extend the highlight over sequential items in the list.

▶ To select nonsequential items, hold down [Ctrl] while you click each item. To cancel a selection, hold down [Ctrl] and click the item again.

▶ To select more than one sequential group, click the first filename to select it, and then hold down [⇧ Shift] while you either click the last filename or use the arrow keys to extend the highlight over sequential items in the list. To select the next group, hold down [Ctrl] while you click the first item. Then hold down [Ctrl]+[⇧ Shift] while you click the last item.

▶ To select all files in the contents list window, click any filename, then press [/]. If you then want to unselect some files, hold down [Ctrl] and click each of them.

USING THE SELECT FILES COMMAND

To select files, pull down the **F**ile menu and click the **S**elect Files command to display a dialog box. Enter a filename specification and click the **S**elect command button to select the files or the **D**eselect command button to unselect them. Rectangular boxes in the contents list surround each of the files that match the filename specification you entered. Click the **C**lose command button to return to the directory, and the selected files are highlighted.

1 Enter a filename specification.

2 Click to select files that match the filename specification in the **F**ile(s) text box.

3 Click to deselect any previously selected files.

▸▸ TUTORIAL

Getting Ready

1. Insert the *Windows Student Resource Disk* into drive A and select that drive.

2. Double-click the *filemgr* directory on the directory tree to expand it and display its contents in the contents list.

Selecting All Files by Clicking

3. Click any filename in the contents list to select it.

4. Press ⌷ to select all of the files.

TIP: "MY SCREEN DOESN'T MATCH THE BOOK'S."

The default settings for File Manager display just the names of nonhidden files sorted by name. If your contents list is not displayed this way, your screen will not match the illustrations throughout this PicTorial. To make your screen match ours, pull down the **V̲iew** menu and:

▸ Click **By File T̲ype**, then turn off **Show Hidden/S̲ystem Files** and click the **OK** button

▸ Turn on the **N̲ame** command

▸ Turn on the **S̲ort by Name** command

You will have to pull down the menu once for each setting you change.

1 Click any filename to select it.

2 Press ⌷ to select all files on the contents list.

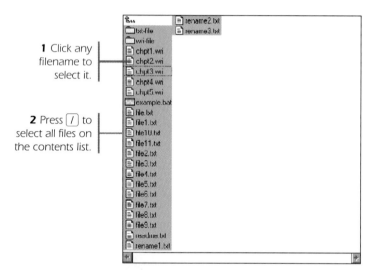

5. Hold down Ctrl and click the two subdirectories *txt-file* and *wri-file* (in the contents list) to unselect them.

Hold down Ctrl when you click the two directories to unselect them.

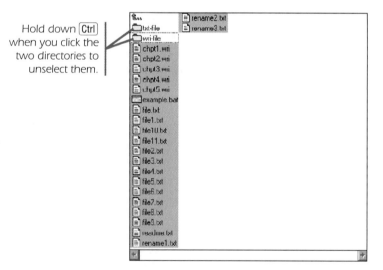

6. Click any filename to remove the highlight from all of the other files and select just the file you click.

Selecting Adjacent Files by Clicking

7. Click *chtp1.wri* to select it. Then hold down ⇧Shift and click *chpt5.wri* to select all adjacent files between it and the first file you selected.

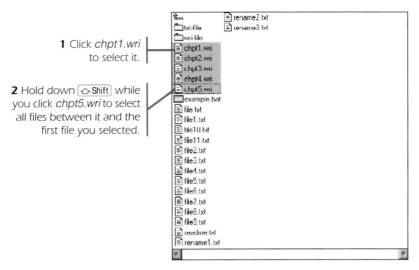

1 Click *chpt1.wri* to select it.

2 Hold down [⇧ Shift] while you click *chpt5.wri* to select all files between it and the first file you selected.

Selecting Nonadjacent Files by Clicking

8. Click *chpt1.wri* to select just it again. Then hold down [Ctrl] while you click *file1.txt* and *rename1.txt* to select these nonadjacent files.

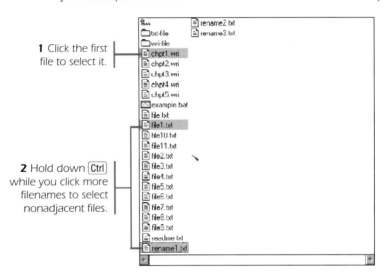

1 Click the first file to select it.

2 Hold down [Ctrl] while you click more filenames to select nonadjacent files.

9. Click the Up icon at the top of the contents list to remove the selection highlight from all of the files. (You may have to scroll it into view.)

Selecting All Files with the Menu

10. Pull down the **File** menu and click the **Select Files** command to display a dialog box. The *.* filename specification in the **Files(s)** text box means that all files will be selected.

11. Click the **Select** command button and then the **Close** command button to select all of the files.

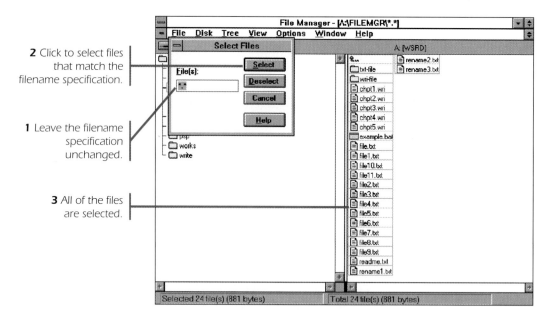

2 Click to select files that match the filename specification.

1 Leave the filename specification unchanged.

3 All of the files are selected.

Selecting Specific Files with the Menu

12. Pull down the **File** menu and click the **Select Files** command to display a dialog box. Click the **Deselect** command button to deselect all of the files on the contents list.

13. Type ***.txt** into the **File(s)** text box and click the **Select** command button to select all files with the *.txt* extension. The selected files are outlined on the contents list.

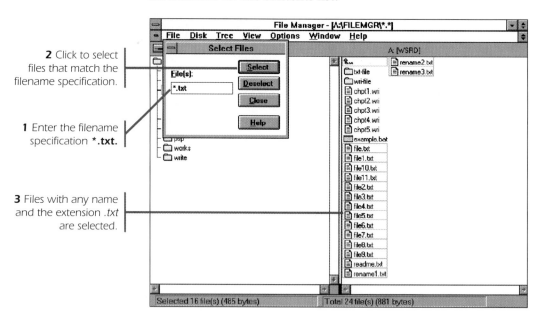

2 Click to select files that match the filename specification.

1 Enter the filename specification ***.txt.**

3 Files with any name and the extension *.txt* are selected.

14. Click the **Close** command button to close the dialog box. The selected files are highlighted.

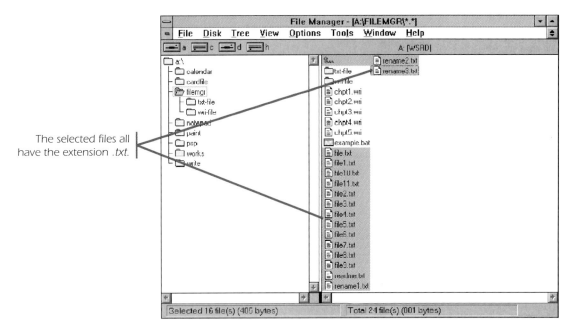

The selected files all have the extension *.txt*.

Finishing Up

15. Click the Up icon at the top of the contents list to remove the selection highlight from the files.

> **PAUSING FOR PRACTICE**
>
> Selecting files is a basic procedure that you must master to use File Manager. Pause here to continue selecting files on the contents list until you have mastered all of the selection procedures discussed in this section.

TURNING CONFIRMATION ON AND OFF

When you copy, move, and delete files, it's easy to accidentally overwrite an existing file of the same name or delete a file by mistake. To prevent such accidents, you can turn confirmation on. Then if the destination has a file of the same name, you are prompted to confirm that you want to replace it. If you are copying or moving a number of files, you can turn the prompt off for all files at once by choosing the **Yes To All** command button when the confirmation box appears.

To turn confirmation on, pull down the **Options** menu and click the **Confirmation** command to display a dialog box. Turn check boxes on for those actions where you want Windows to prompt you for confirmation. It is a good idea to leave all of these options on until you become an experienced Windows user.

Prompts when you delete a file

Prompts when you delete a directory

Prompts when you drag and drop a file

Prompts when you format or copy a disk

Prompts when you copy or move a file into a directory where a file already has the same name

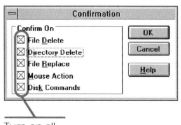

Turn on all confirmation options.

▶▶ TUTORIAL

1. Pull down the **Options** menu and click the **Confirmation** command to display a dialog box.

2. Turn on all confirmation options if they are not already on and then click the **OK** command button to return to the directory window. (If all the options are already on, click the **Cancel** command button.)

COPYING AND MOVING FILES WITH MENU COMMANDS

You can copy or move files or directories between drives or between directories. To copy or move more than one file or directory in a single procedure, select them first. The location you copy or move them from is called the *source*, and the location you copy or move them to is called the *destination*.

To copy or move files using menu commands, you first select them on the contents list, then pull down the **File** menu and click the **Copy** command. When the dialog box appears, you specify the *path* to where you want the file copied in the **To** text box. For example, to copy a file from drive B to drive A, you would enter the path **a:** or **a:** in the **To** text box. However, when a disk is divided into directories, you must specify not only a drive but also a directory. Specifying the drive and directories is called specifying a path.

Name of the selected file(s)

Enter the path to copy the files to.

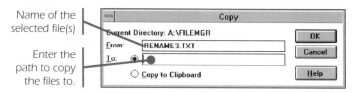

Paths are simply a listing of the directories and subdirectories that specify exactly where a file is to be copied to. It is like telling someone to "file the letter to ACME Hardware in the manila folder labeled *ACME* in the hanging folder labeled *Hardware* in the third file cabinet from the right." These precise instructions make it easy to locate the file's destination.

To specify a path, you indicate the drive, then the name of all subdirectories leading to the destination. All elements must be separated from one another by backslashes (\)—for example, *a:\reports\markets*.

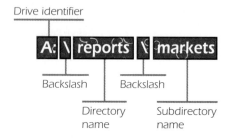

Let's assume your disk has the directories and files shown here:

Specify the path **a:** to copy or move files here.

Specify the path **a:\\cardfile** to copy or move files here.

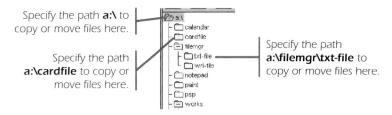

Specify the path **a:\filemgr\txt-file** to copy or move files here.

▶▶ TUTORIAL

Getting Ready

1. Insert the *Windows Student Resource* Disk into drive A and select that drive.

Copying Files

2. Click the *filemgr* directory on the directory tree to select it.

3. Click the file named *chpt1.wri* to select it on the contents list. Then hold down ⟨⇧ Shift⟩ while you click the file named *chpt5.wri*. Release ⟨⇧ Shift⟩, and all of the files between *chpt1.wri* and *chpt5.wri* are selected.

All files with the extension *.wri* should be selected.

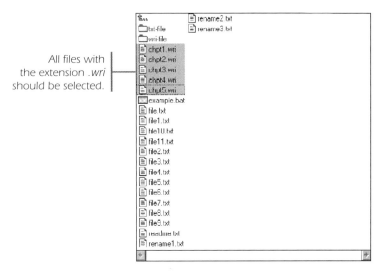

4. Pull down the **File** menu and click the **Copy** command to display a dialog box with the selected filenames displayed in the **From** text box.

All selected files are listed.

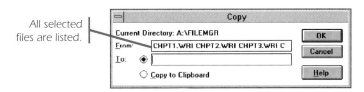

5. Type **a:\write** in the **To** text box.

Enter the path to copy the files to.

6. Click the **OK** command button to copy the files to the *write* directory. When copying is completed, the dialog box disappears.

7. Click the *write* directory on the directory tree to select it and see that the *chpt1.wri* through *chpt5.wri* files are now also listed in this directory.

Moving Files

8. Without changing directories, click the filename *chpt1.wri* in the contents list. Hold down ⇧Shift while you click the filename *chpt5.wri*, then release ⇧Shift. All of the files between *chpt1.wri* and *chpt5.wri* are selected.

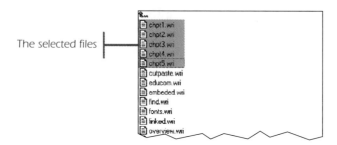

The selected files

9. Pull down the **File** menu and click the **Move** command to display a dialog box with the selected files' names displayed in the **From** text box.

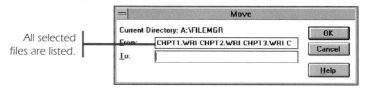

All selected files are listed.

10. Type **a:\filemgr** in the **To** text box.

Enter the path to move the files to.

11. Click the **OK** command button to move the files to the *filemgr* directory. Since a copy already exists in the *filemgr* directory, the Confirm File Replace dialog box appears. Notice how information is supplied for both files so you can tell one from the other. In this case they are identical.

Information on the file you will replace

Information on the file you will replace it with

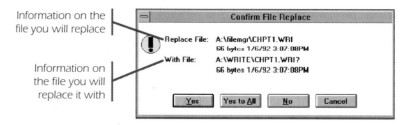

12. Click the **Yes** command button to move the file anyway. After it has been moved, the Confirm File Replace dialog box appears again, listing the next file.

13. Click the **Yes to All** command button to move all of the files into the directory. After the files have been moved, notice how they are no longer listed in the contents list for the *write* directory.

The *chpt1.wri* through *chpt5.wri* files are no longer listed because they have been moved to the *filemgr* directory.

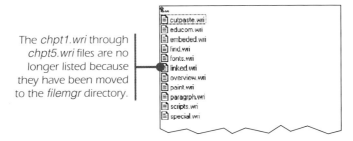

14. Click the *filemgr* directory on the directory tree to see the files listed in this directory. The files you moved overwrote the previous versions in the directory.

COPYING AND MOVING FILES BY DRAGGING AND DROPPING

Instead of using the menu to copy or move files, you can drag their file icons from one place to another with the mouse and then release them. This is called *dragging and dropping* and is a quick way to copy or move files.

As you drag files and directories, the mouse pointer assumes the shape of a file icon. If you drop the files onto a drive icon, they are copied or moved into the currently selected directory on that drive. To copy or move files into a specific directory, drop them onto the desired directory on the directory tree.

To drag and drop files and directories, follow these procedures:

1. Make sure both the source and destination are visible in the directory window or windows. (You can use the **Window** menu's **Cascade** or **Tile** command to do this.)

2. Select the files to be copied or moved.

3. Drag the files or directories to the destination's drive icon, directory window, or directory icon as follows:

   ▶ To move them to another location on the same disk, drag them there and release the mouse button to drop them.

   ▶ To move them to another disk, hold down ⌂ Shift while dragging them. To drop them, release the mouse button and then release ⌂ Shift.

   ▶ To copy them to another location on the same disk, hold down Ctrl while dragging them. To drop them, release the mouse button and then release Ctrl.

   ▶ To copy them to another disk, drag them there and release the mouse button to drop them.

4. If a confirmation box appears, read it and choose the appropriate option.

COMMON WRONG TURNS:
RELEASING ⇧Shift **OR** Ctrl **TOO EARLY**

Be careful when using the ⇧Shift or Ctrl keys while dragging. If you release these keys before you release the mouse button, the file will be copied instead of moved or moved instead of copied. If you have turned confirmation on for mouse actions, a dialog box will ask you to confirm the action and tell you whether the files are being copied or moved. If you released the key by mistake, just click the **Cancel** command button and try again.

▶▶ **TUTORIAL**

Getting Ready

1. Insert the *Windows Student Resource Disk* Disk into drive A and select that drive.

2. Click the *filemgr* directory on the directory tree to select it.

Selecting Files

3. Click the filename *file.txt* to select it.

4. Hold down ⇧Shift while you click the filename *rename3.txt*.

5. Release ⇧Shift, and all of the files between *file.txt* and *rename3.txt* are selected.

Copying Files

6. Hold down Ctrl, point anywhere in the selected files, and hold down the left mouse button. Drag the files (they are represented by a file icon) to the directory *notepad* on the directory tree.

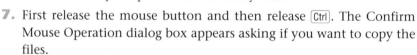

Adjacent files are selected.

7. First release the mouse button and then release Ctrl. The Confirm Mouse Operation dialog box appears asking if you want to copy the files.

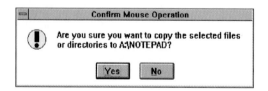

8. Click the **Yes** command button to copy the files. After the files have been copied, the dialog box disappears.

9. Click the *notepad* directory on the directory tree to see that the files have been copied there.

The notepad directory is selected when you drag the file icon near it.

Selecting Files

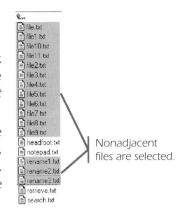

10. Click the filename *file.txt* to select it.

11. Hold down ⬆Shift while you click the filename *file9.txt*, and then release ⬆Shift. All of the files between *file.txt* and *file9.txt* are selected.

12. Hold down Ctrl while you click the filenames *rename1.txt*, *rename2.txt*, and *rename3.txt*, and then release Ctrl. This selects the nonadjacent file while leaving the first group selected.

Nonadjacent files are selected.

Moving Files

The *filemgr* directory is selected when you drag the file icon near it.

13. Hold down the left mouse button and drag the files to the directory *filemgr* on the directory tree.

14. Release the mouse button, and the Confirm Mouse Operation dialog box appears asking if you want to move the files.

15. Click the **Yes** command button to move the files. Since a copy already exists in the *filemgr* directory, the Confirm File Replace dialog box appears. Notice how information is supplied for both files so you can tell one from the other. In this case they are identical.

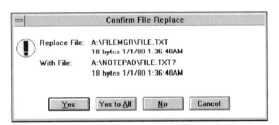

16. Click the **Yes** command button to move the file anyway. After it has been moved, the Confirm File Replace dialog box appears again, listing the next file.

17. Click the **Yes to All** command button to move all of the files into the *filemgr* directory. The files are no longer listed in the *notepad* directory.

CREATING DIRECTORIES

To organize your work on a hard disk drive, you create directories. When the directories are no longer needed, you remove them. When creating directories, you should have some kind of plan.

▶ Keep only essential files in the root directory.

▶ Store all program files related to a program in their own directory. For example, you might want separate directories for word processing, spreadsheet, and database applications.

▶ Do not store the data files that you create in the same directory as the program files. For example, the Microsoft Write program files might be in the Windows directory but you might store its document files in a directory named *write*.

▶ Keep all related data files in their own directories. For example, you might have separate directories for memos, letters, reports, financial documents, and name and address lists.

▶ Do not create too many levels of directories, since it takes time to specify them. Most disks can be well organized with no more than three levels, including the root directory.

When you first begin using a computer, directories may not seem important. However, after a while you will have so many files that if they aren't organized into directories, you'll have trouble knowing which file is which.

To copy or move files into a directory that does not exist, you first have to create the directory. To do so, select the directory in which you want the new directory to appear. For example, if you select the root directory, the new directory will be created one level below it. If you select an existing directory such as *letters*, the new directory will be a subdirectory of that directory. For example, to create the directories shown here: you would follow these procedures:

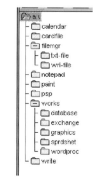

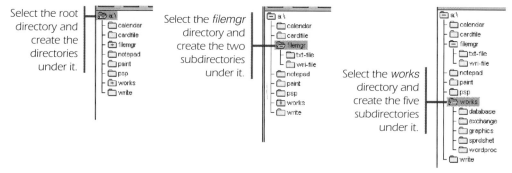

Select the root directory and create the directories under it.

Select the *filemgr* directory and create the two subdirectories under it.

Select the *works* directory and create the five subdirectories under it.

1. Select the root directory and create the first level of directories.

2. Select the *filemgr* directory and create the two subdirectories named *txt-file* and *wri-file*.

3. Select the *works* directory and create the five subdirectories named *database*, *exchange*, *graphics*, *sprdshet*, and *wordproc*.

Once you have selected the directory in which you want to create a subdirectory, pull down the **File** menu and click the **Create Directory** command to display a dialog box. Type the name of the new directory into the **Name** text box and then click the **OK** command button. Directory names follow the same conventions that you use for filenames. However, you should not use a period and extension, or you might confuse directories with filenames at some later date. Files and

The directory in which the new directory will be created

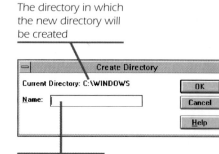

Enter the name of the directory here.

subdirectories in one directory can have the same names as files and subdirectories in other directories. If you want to create the new directory elsewhere on the disk, you can type a path in front of it. For example, to create a subdirectory named *new* in the directory named letters, type **c:\letters\new** into the **N**ame text box.

▶▶ TUTORIAL

Getting Ready

1. Insert the *Windows Student Resource Disk* into drive A and select that drive.

Creating a Directory

2. Click the root directory, *a:*, on the directory tree to select it.

3. Pull down the **F**ile menu and click the **Cr**e**ate Directory** command to display a dialog box.

4. Type **backups** in the **N**ame text box.

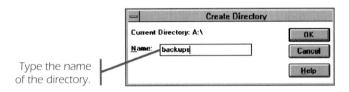

Type the name of the directory.

5. Click the **OK** command button to create a directory named *backups*. The new directory is now listed on the directory tree.

Creating Subdirectories

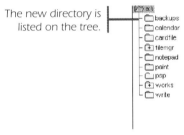

The new directory is listed on the tree.

6. Click the *backups* directory on the directory tree to select it.

7. Pull down the **F**ile menu and click the **Cr**e**ate Directory** command to display a dialog box.

8. Type **chpts** in the **N**ame text box.

Type the name of the new subdirectory.

9. Click the **OK** command button to create a subdirectory named *chpts* in the directory named *backups*.

10. Pull down the **F**ile menu and click the **Cr**e**ate Directory** command to display a dialog box.

11. Type **others** in the **N**ame text box.

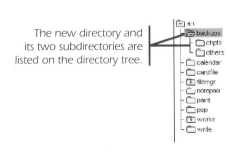

The new directory and its two subdirectories are listed on the directory tree.

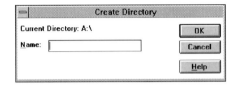

Type the name of the new subdirectory.

12. Click the **OK** command button to create a subdirectory named *others* in the directory named *backups*. Your directory tree should now look like the illustration at the left.

Moving Files into the New Chpts Subdirectory

13. Click the *filemgr* directory on the directory tree to select it.

14. Select all of the files in the contents list that have the name *chpt*.

15. Drag the files to the new subdirectory *chpts* on the directory tree and release the mouse button. The Confirm Mouse Operation dialog box appears asking if you want to move the files.

16. Click the **Yes** command button to move the files.

17. Click the *chpts* subdirectory on the directory tree to see that the files have been moved there.

Moving Files into the New Others Subdirectory

18. Click the *filemgr* directory on the directory tree to select it.

19. Select the remaining file(s) in the contents list but don't select the subdirectories *wri-file* and *txt-file*.

20. Drag the file(s) to the subdirectory *others* on the directory tree and release the mouse button. The Confirm Mouse Operation dialog box appears asking if you want to move the files.

21. Click the **Yes** command button to move the files. When the move operation is completed, the *filemgr* directory contains only the subdirectories *wri-file* and *txt-file* and the file *hidden.txt*, which is not displayed.

22. Click the *others* subdirectory on the directory tree to see that the files have been copied there.

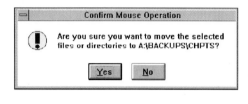

DELETING FILES AND DIRECTORIES

To delete unneeded files or directories from your disk, you first select them and then use **Delete** command on the **File** menu. To remove a directory, first select it on the directory tree. Then pull down the **File** menu and click the **Delete** command to display a confirmation box.

The name of the directory or subdirectory to be deleted

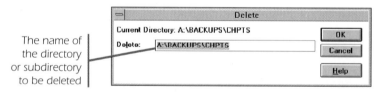

If the directory you are deleting contains files, a second directory box appears.

The name of the file to be deleted

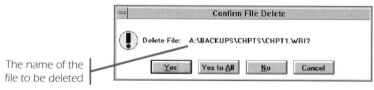

When deleting files and directories, you should always have **File Delete** and **Directory Delete** confirmations turned on so you are prompted to confirm any deletions. Once the confirmation box appears, if you are deleting a number of files and directories, you can turn the prompt off for each deletion by choosing the **Yes To All** command button.

TIP: UNDELETING FILES

If you are using DOS 5 or later versions, you can often recover or "undelete" files should you delete them by mistake. With DOS 5 you use the *undelete* command from the DOS command prompt. With DOS 6, you open the Microsoft Tools group window and double-click the Undelete application icon. There are also programs available from other publishers that will recover many lost files for you.

 ▶▶ **TUTORIAL**

Getting Ready

1. Insert the *Windows Student Resource Disk* into drive A and select that drive.

Deleting a Directory

2. Click the subdirectory *chpts* on the directory tree (under the new *backups* directory) to select it.

3. Pull down the **File** menu and click the **Delete** command to display a dialog box listing the path to the current directory in the Delete text box.

Name of the subdirectory to be deleted

4. Click the **OK** command button to begin deleting, and the Confirm Directory Delete dialog box is displayed.

The subdirectory about to be deleted

5. Click the **Yes** command button to confirm that you want to delete the directory, and the Confirm File Delete box appears and lists the first file in the directory to be deleted.

The name of the first file to be deleted

Click to delete all without further confirmation.

6. Click the **Yes to All** command button to confirm that you want to delete all of the files in the directory. In a moment, the subdirectory *chpts* is no longer listed on the directory tree.

Deleting a File

7. Click the *others* directory on the directory tree to select it.

8. Click the filename *example.bat* on the contents list to select it.

9. Pull down the **File** menu and click the **Delete** command to display the Delete dialog box listing the selected file.

10. Click the **OK** command button to delete the file, and the Confirm File Delete dialog box appears listing the selected file.

11. Click the **Yes** command button to delete the listed file, and it is no longer listed on the contents list.

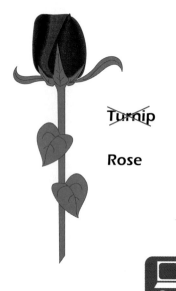

Turnip

Rose

RENAMING FILES AND DIRECTORIES

To rename files or directories, you use the **Rename** command on the **File** menu. Don't rename any of the directories or files associated with Windows and its applications. If you do so, the application may not be able to find the files that it needs to run correctly.

When you click the **Rename** command, a dialog box appears with the current name listed in the **From** text box. Type the new name into the **To** text box and click the **OK** command button.

To rename groups of files, you can use wildcards. For example, to rename all *.bak* files to *.doc*, you would enter **.bak* in the **From** box and **.doc* in the **To** box.

TIP: CONTENTS LIST ISN'T ACCURATE

When you change disks in a drive or when you copy, move, rename, or delete files, the contents list is not always updated. To be sure the current files are listed, always pull down the **Window** menu and click the **Refresh** command to update the directory of the disk.

▶▶ **TUTORIAL**

Getting Ready

1. Insert the *Windows Student Resource Disk* into drive A and select that drive.

Renaming a Directory

2. Click the *backups* directory on the directory tree to select it.

3. Pull down the **File** menu and click the **Rename** command to display a dialog box. The current name is displayed in the **From** text box.

The name of the selected directory

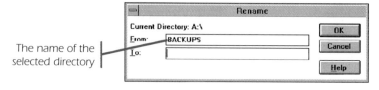

4. Type **newfiles** into the **To** text box.

The new name for the directory

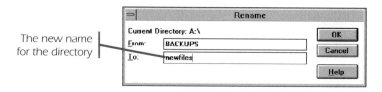

5. Click the **OK** command button to rename the directory. The new name is now listed on the directory tree.

Renaming a File

6. Click the *notepad* directory on the directory tree to select it.

7. Click the *retrieve.txt* file on the contents list to select it.

8. Pull down the **File** menu and click the **Rename** command to display a dialog box. The current name is displayed in the **From** text box.

The name of the selected file

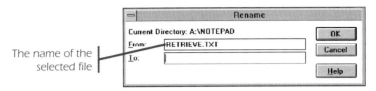

9. Type **newfile.txt** into the **To** text box.

The new name for the file

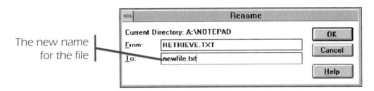

10. Click the **OK** command button to rename the file.

SEARCHING FOR A FILE OR DIRECTORY

You pull down the **File** menu and click the **Search** command to locate files and directories on a disk. When you choose this command, the Search dialog box is displayed with the wildcards *.* in the **Search** For box and the current directory in the **Start From** box.

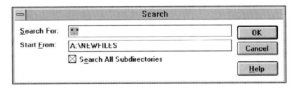

To locate files or directories, enter a filename specification in the **Search For** box. For example, to find all back copies of documents, you might enter *.*bak*.

To search all subdirectories in the current directory, turn on the **Search All Subdirectories** check box. If you want to search only the current directory, turn the check box off.

To begin the search, click the **OK** command button. (You can press [Esc] at any point to stop the search.) When the search is completed, the Search Results box is displayed listing all of the files and directories that matched your filename specification.

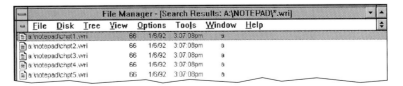

▶▶ TUTORIAL

1. Insert the *Windows Student Resource Disk* into drive A and select that drive.

2. Pull down the **Window** menu and click the **Refresh** command to update the directory window.

3. Click the *a:* directory on the directory tree to select it.

4. Pull down the **File** menu and click the **Search** command to display a dialog box.

   ▶ The filename specification **.** is listed in the **Search For** text box.

   ▶ *A:* is the directory listed in the **Start From** text box.

   ▶ The **Search All Subdirectories** check box is turned on.

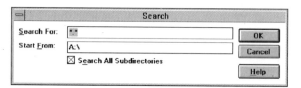

5. Type **newfile.txt** into the **Search For** text box and click the **OK** command button. The Search Results screen is displayed, showing *a:\notepad\newfile.txt*.

6. Double-click the Search window's Control-menu box to close the window.

▶▶ SKILL-BUILDING EXERCISES

1. Formatting Additional Data Disks

Format any additional data disks that you might need for your own work.

2. Checking Disk Labels

Use the File Manager to display the disk label for each of your floppy disks. If you find any disk with a name, write it down.

3. Specifying Your System's Disks

List the specifications for the disks your system requires in the spaces below. You will find this information in the manual that accompanies the computer. Look up "*disks*"

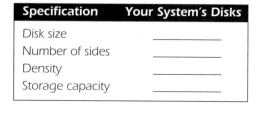

Specification	Your System's Disks
Disk size	_____
Number of sides	_____
Density	_____
Storage capacity	_____

or "*disk drives*" in the index, and refer to the listed sections. If you cannot find the information in the manual, refer to the specifications printed on the box that your disks came in.

4. Searching for Files and Directories

Use the **Search** command on **File** menu to locate the files listed below. Next to each file that you find, list the path displayed on the Search Results screen.

Filename	Path
search.txt	_____
educom.wri	_____
doorway.bmp	_____
setup.exe	_____
phonelst.crd	_____
classes.cal	_____
building.bmp	_____

PicTorial 4 ▶ VISualQuiz

1. This illustration shows two 3½-inch floppy disks. Describe what the cutouts on each tell you about the disks.

a. _HD_

b. _low density_

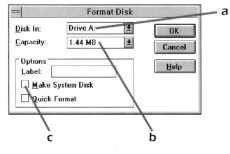

2. This illustration shows the dialog box that appears when you select the **Format Disk** command from the **Disk** menu. Explain when you would change the settings for a and b and when you would turn on the check box c.

a. _____

b. _____

c. _____

3. Describe two ways you would select the files shown selected in this illustration of the contents list.

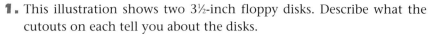

_____

_____

4. Describe how you would select the files shown selected in this illustration of the contents list.

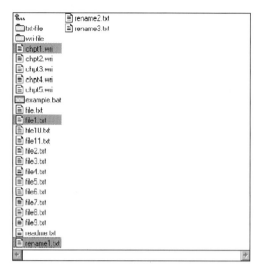

_____

_____

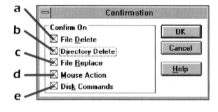

5. Describe what happens when each of these check boxes is turned on.

a. _____

b. _____

c. _____

d. _____

e. _____

6. List the name of each of the labeled parts of this path.

a. _____

b. _____

c. _____

d. _____

e. _____

Where would a file be copied to if you specified this path in the **To** text box of the dialog box that is displayed when copying a file?

_____

7. Indicate the path that you would enter into the **To** text box to copy a file to the labeled directories.

a. _A:_____

b. _A:\filemgr_____

c. _A:\filemgr\wri-file_____

d. _A:\works_____

e. _A:\works\exchange_____

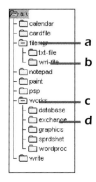

8. List the directories you would select before creating each of the labeled directories or subdirectories.

a. _____

b. _____

c. _____

d. _____

9. This illustration shows the box that appears when you are deleting files if confirmation is on. Describe what happens if you click each of the labeled buttons when the first file is listed.

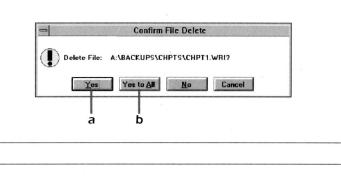

a. _____

b. _____

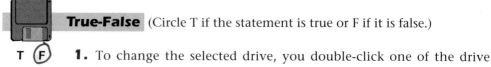

True-False (Circle T if the statement is true or F if it is false.)

T (F) **1.** To change the selected drive, you double-click one of the drive icons.

(T) F **2.** You can drag the split bar the separates the directory tree from the contents list so one window has more space.

(T) F **3.** The topmost directory on the directory tree is called the *root directory*.

(T) F **4.** To select a directory, you just click its name or icon on the directory tree.

(T) F **5.** To expand a directory, you double-click its name or icon on the directory tree.

(T) F **6.** To display only selected files, you pull down the **View** menu and click the **By File Type** command to display a dialog box.

(T) F **7.** The filename specification **.doc* will display files with any name as long as they have the extension *.doc*.

(T) F **8.** The filename specification *c??t.txt* will display the files named *coot* and *coat* if they have the extension *.txt*.

(T) F **9.** If you have more than one directory window open, you can tile or cascade them.

(T) F **10.** Tiled directory windows don't overlap and cascaded windows do.

(T) F **11.** When formatting a data disk, Windows automatically formats the disk in drive A to the capacity of that drive unless you specify otherwise.

T (F) **12.** When formatting 3½-inch floppy disks, you can tell a disk's capacity by its cutouts. For example, a 1.44MB disk has one cutout.

(T) F **13.** When formatting a disk, you turn on the **Make System Disk** check box only if you want to be able to boot the computer from the disk you are formatting.

T (F) **14.** As long as the disk in drive A is a system disk, it doesn't matter whether you boot from drive A or drive C.

T (F) **15.** To make a duplicate copy of a disk, you can use either the **Copy** command on the **File** menu or the **Copy Disk** command on the **Disk** menu.

T (F) **16.** The best thing about the **Copy Disk** command on the **Disk** menu is that you can use it to copy between dissimilar disks or drives. For example, it works well between 3½- and 5¼-inch drives.

(T) F **17.** When you use the **Copy Disk** command on the **Disk** menu, the disk you are copying to doesn't need to be formatted.

T (F) **18.** You can only select files that are next to each other on the contents list.

T (F) **19.** To select all of the files on the contents list, you have to be patient and click them one at a time.

T F **20.** Turning confirmation on is a good way to help you avoid mistakes when deleting and copying files.

T F **21.** To copy a file named *john.doc* to the *letters* directory on drive C, you would enter the path *c:\letters* into the **To** text box when the dialog box appears.

T F **22.** When dragging a file to the same disk, hold down Ctrl or the file will be moved.

T F **23.** When dragging a file to a different disk, hold down Ctrl or the file will be copied.

T F **24.** When holding down Ctrl while dragging a file, you release Ctrl before the mouse button to drop the file.

T F **25.** When you create a new directory, you begin by selecting the directory on the directory tree under which you want the new directory to appear.

T F **26.** Before you can delete a directory, you must first delete all of the files that it contains.

T F **27.** Once you have deleted files or directories, it's impossible to recover them.

T F **28.** Sometimes the contents list isn't accurate—it doesn't list all of the files that it contains.

 Multiple Choice (Circle the correct answer.)

1. File Manager's directory window is normally divided into halves so the ___ can be displayed at the same time.
   a. Contents of two different drives
   b. Filenames and sizes
   c. Directory tree and contents list
   d. Directories and subdirectories

2. To display just the files on a disk, pull down the **View** menu and click the ___ command.
   a. **Tree and Directory**
   b. **Tree Only**
   c. **Directory Only**
   d. None of the above

3. To save any changes you make to File Manager's layout so they are in effect the next time you use the application, ___.
   a. Press Esc
   b. Pull down the **File** menu and click the **Save** command
   c. Press Alt + ⇧ Shift + F4
   d. None of the above

4. To change the selected drive, you click the drive's icon or ___.
   a. Hold down Ctrl while you press the drive's letter
   b. Press Tab⇆ to move the selection cursor to the drive icons, use the arrow keys to highlight the desired drive, and then press Enter ←

c. Pull down the **Disk** menu and click the **Select Drive** command to display a dialog box listing all of the drives on your system, then select the drive you want to change to and click the **OK** command button

d. Any of the above

5. To expand a directory without creating a new directory window, you ___.

a. Double-click the directory

b. Click the directory

c. Drag the directory to the contents list

d. Pull down the **File** menu and click the **Open** command

6. To list just the filename and size on the contents list, you pull down the View menu and click the ___ command.

a. **Sort by Si__z__e**

b. **__N__ame**

c. **Partial Details**

d. **All File Details**

7. To display all files that begin with the letter *c* and have an extension that begins with the letter *t*, you would pull down the **View** menu, click the **By File __T__ype** command, end enter ___ into the **__N__ame** text box.

a. c?.t?

b. c.txt

c. c*.t*

d. None of the above

8. To open an existing file with an application program, you must know ___.

a. The drive it's on, the directory it's in, and its filename

b. What characters are legal in filenames

c. The date and time it was created

d. All of the above

9. To save a file the first time with an application program, you must specify ___.

a. Its filename

b. The drive it's to be stored on

c. The directory it's to be saved in

d. All of the above

10. When more than one directory window is open, you can switch among them by ___.

a. Clicking anywhere on a window

b. Pressing Ctrl + Tab⇆ or Ctrl + F6

c. Pulling down the **__W__indow** menu and clicking the window's name

d. Any of the above

11. To select adjacent files on the contents list, you ___.

a. Click the first filename to select it, and then hold down ⇧ Shift while you click the last filename

b. Hold down ⌂Shift and use the arrow keys to extend the high-light

c. Hold down Ctrl while you click each filename

d. Any of the above

12. You can turn confirmation on so you are asked to confirm ___.

a. Deleting files

b. Deleting directories

c. Replacing a file by another with the same name

(d.) All of the above

13. To copy a file to the same disk by dragging and dropping, you must hold down ___ while dragging it.

(a.) Ctrl

b. Alt

c. No key

d. None of the above

14. To move a file to another disk by dragging and dropping, you must hold down ___ while dragging it.

a. Ctrl

b. Alt

c. No key

(d.) None of the above

15. To create a new subdirectory, you begin by selecting the directory ___ where you want the new one.

a. Immediately below

(b.) Immediately above

c. On the same level as

d. None of the above

Fill in the Blank (Enter your answer in the space provided.)

1. When you open File Manager, it displays the _____ which is divided into two parts. On the left is the _____ and on the right is the _____.

2. To change the selected drive you _____ one of the _____.

3. To save changes you make to File Manager, you can press _____.

4. The topmost directory is called the _____ directory.

5. When a directory contains other directories, they are called _____.

6. To arrange directory windows side by side so they don't overlap, you _____ them. To arrange them so they overlap one another, you _____.

7. To tile directory windows side by side, hold down _____ when you click/ the **T̲ile** command on the **W̲indow** menu.

8. You can tell a 3½-inch floppy disk's capacity by its _____ since a 1.44MB disk has _____ and a 720KB disk has _____.

9. To make a duplicate copy of a disk, use the _____ command on the _____ menu.

10. To select a series of adjacent files on the contents list, you can click the first name and then hold down _____ while you click the last.

11. To select nonadjacent files on the contents list, you hold down _____ while you click each file.

12. To select all of the files on the contents list, you select one then press _____.

13 To copy a file named *john.doc* to the *letters* directory on drive C, you would enter the path _____ into the **To** text box when the dialog box appears.

14. To ensure that the contents list lists all of the files that it contains, you should pull down the Window menu and click the _____ command.

15. When dragging a file to another location on the same disk, it is normally _____. When dragging it to another disk, it is normally _____.

16. When dragging a file to another location on the same disk, hold down _____ to copy it. When dragging it to another disk, hold down _____ to move it.

17. When copying a file to another location on the same drive, be sure to release _____ before releasing _____.

18. When moving a file to another location on a different disk, be sure to release _____ before releasing _____.

19. To tile or cascade directory windows, you pull down the _____ menu and click the _____ or _____ commands.

 Projects

Project 1. Exploring the Directory Tree

Use File Manager to explore the directory tree of the hard disk on your system where Windows is stored. You should be able to locate a tree similar to the one shown in the figure shown here.

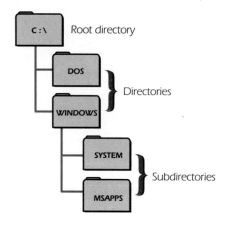

Project 2. Identifying File Icons

Display the contents list for the *Windows Student Resource Disk*, search the icons for an example of each type listed below, and write in its file-name:

File Type	Filename
Directory	_____
Program file	_____
Document file associated with an application	_____
System or hidden file	_____
All other files	_____

Project 3. Creating and Deleting Directories

1. Insert the *Windows Student Resource Disk* into one of the disk drives and select that drive.

2. Create a directory named *1994*.

3. Create two subdirectories in the *1994* directory named *sales* and *budgets*.

4. Delete all the new directories and subdirectories from the disk.

Chapter 3
WORKING WITH APPLICATION PROGRAMS

After completing this PicTorial, you will be able to:

▶ Start applications from Program Manager

▶ Exit applications and return to Program Manager

▶ Open existing documents

▶ Enter and edit text

▶ Save documents and clear the screen

▶ Print documents and manage print jobs with Print Manager

▶ Copy and move text and view data on the Clipboard

The primary purpose of Windows is to make it easy to open and operate applications, including those supplied with Windows. Windows-supplied applications include those in the Main group such as File Manager and Control Panel and those in the Accessories group such as Write, Paintbrush, and Notepad. When you work with many applications such as these, you create *documents*—the generic term that Windows uses for any file of data. Using menu commands, you can also *save* these documents on a disk for later use and *open*, or retrieve, previously saved documents. If you want to file a document or distribute it to others, you can print it.

In this PicTorial you'll use the Notepad application to open, edit, save, and print documents, and to copy and move data. You'll also be introduced to two other essential Windows applications—Print Manager, which you use to manage print jobs; and the Clipboard, which you use to cut and paste data within or between applications. We're using Notepad to introduce basic concepts because it is one of the simplest Windows applications and won't confuse you while you learn procedures and techniques that apply to all other Windows applications.

STARTING AND EXITING APPLICATIONS

Starting (or opening or *launching*) a Windows application is as easy as double-clicking its icon. When you are finished with an application, you can close or quit or exit it. This removes it from the computer's memory and removes its window or icon from the desktop (although its icon remains in the group window). To close, or exit, an open application, do one of the following:

▶ Pull down the application's **File** menu and click the **Exit** command.

▶ Click the application's Control-menu box to display the Control menu and then click the **Close** command.

▶ Double-click the application's Control-menu box.

▶ Make it the active window and press Alt + F4 .

If you try to close an application without saving changes to your document, a dialog box asks if you want to save the current changes. Click the **Yes** command button to save the document or the **No** command button to abandon it. To return to the application instead of closing it, click the **Cancel** command button.

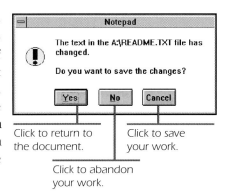

Click to return to the document.

Click to save your work.

Click to abandon your work.

TIP: APPLICATIONS RUNNING AS ICONS

Windows allows you to specify whether an application runs in a window or as an icon when you first open it. If the application is set up to run as an icon, double-clicking its icon in a group window loads it into the computer's memory and then displays it as an icon on the desktop. (You can also display an application this way at any time by clicking its Minimize button.) To open an application that is running as an icon, double-click its icon on the desktop.

▶▶ TUTORIAL

1. Load Windows so that Program Manager is displayed.
2. Open the Accessories group window.

3. Double-click Notepad's icon to open the application.

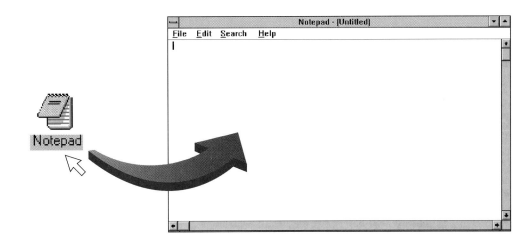

4. Pull down the **File** menu and click the **Exit** command to close the application.

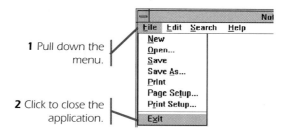

1 Pull down the menu.

2 Click to close the application.

5. Double-click Notepad's icon to open the application again.

6. Click Notepad's Control-menu box to display the Control menu, and then click the **Close** command to close the application.

1 Click to display the Control menu.

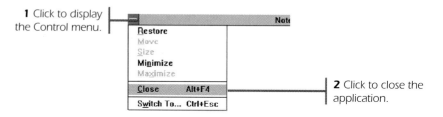

2 Click to close the application.

7. Double-click Notepad's icon to open the application again.

8. Double-click Notepad's Control-menu box to close the application.

9. Double-click Notepad's icon to open the application again.

10. Press ⟨Alt⟩+⟨F4⟩ to close the application.

11. Double-click Notepad's icon to open the application again.

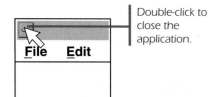

Double-click to close the application.

PAUSING FOR PRACTICE

Opening and closing applications is a basic skill and is the same for all applications. Pause here and continue practicing the various ways you can close an application until you have mastered them.

UNDERSTANDING THE NOTEPAD SCREEN

When you first load Notepad, its document screen is empty except for a flashing vertical line called the insertion point. Look closely at the window and you'll see many of the elements you have already learned about.

▶ The Control-menu box is in the upper-left corner.

▶ The title bar lists the application's name (Notepad) and the document's name (Untitled until you save it).

▶ The Minimize and Maximize buttons are in the upper-right corner.

▶ The menu bar lists the names of Notepad's menus.

▶ Scroll bars are on the right and bottom sides of the window.

▶ The insertion point is a flashing vertical line.

▶ The mouse pointer takes on the shape of an I-beam in the large open area that contains the insertion point. As you'll soon see, this narrow shape allows you to accurately position the pointer between characters of text.

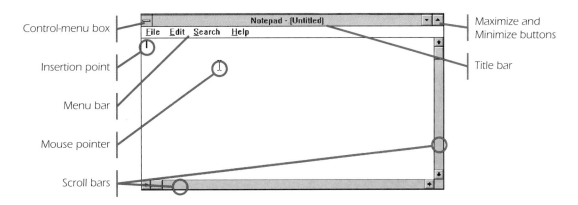

Control-menu box

Insertion point

Menu bar

Mouse pointer

Scroll bars

Maximize and Minimize buttons

Title bar

OPENING EXISTING DOCUMENTS

Notepad is a simple word processing application, called a text editor, that you can use to work with short documents. Notepad can only create and edit a special kind of document called a *text file* or *ASCII text file*. These documents contain just printable ASCII characters with little or no formatting information so they are easily exchanged between applications. Text files are normally identified by their *.txt* extension. This extension isn't essential, but it is a convention that is frequently followed.

To open an existing document, pull down the **File** menu and click the **Open** command. The Open dialog box that appears has four settings that you can select—the drive, the directory, the filename, and the file type.

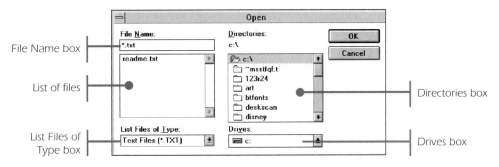

File Name box

List of files

List Files of Type box

Directories box

Drives box

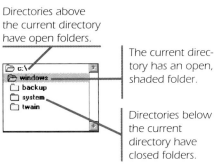

Directories above the current directory have open folders.

The current directory has an open, shaded folder.

Directories below the current directory have closed folders.

The currently selected drive is listed in the **Drives** drop-down list box. To change the drive, click the down arrow on the box to display a list of the drives on your system. Scroll the drive you want into view and click it to select it. When you do so, the listed directories and files change.

To list the document you want, it may also be necessary to change the directory. To do so, you need to understand the **Directories** list box.

Directories all have icons that look like file folders. The current directory, the one that is selected, has its folder open and shaded. The directory above the current one, if any, has an open, unshaded folder. The current directory's subdirectories, if any, have closed file folders. Slight indents also show which directory is above the current directory and which subdirectories are below it. Also, the current directory and the path to it are listed just below the heading **Directories.**

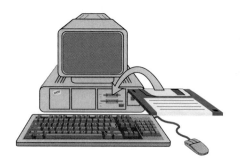

To select a new directory, double-click its name in the **Directories** list box. Doing so allows you to quickly move up or down levels.

When you change drives or directories, the list of documents displayed in the list of files box changes. If no documents are displayed there, it doesn't mean there are none; it just means that the list box displays only documents with the extension *.txt*. This is because the filename specification in the **File Name** text box is **.txt*. To list all documents, you could type ***.*** and press Enter↵ or you could display the **List Files of Type** drop-down list box and click the **All Files [*.*]** command.

When you click a filename in the list of files to select it, its name is displayed in the **File Name** text box. You then click the **OK** command button, and the computer copies the document from the disk into the computer's memory so that it can be displayed on the screen and edited. The copy of the document on the disk remains unchanged until you save the document again.

COMMON WRONG TURNS: DIRECTORY ISN'T LISTED

If the directory you want to select isn't listed in the **Directories** list box, the chances are you have to move up one or more levels to see it. Double-click the first directory above the current one to display its directories. If the one you want still isn't listed, double-click the first directory above the current one and so on until you find the directory you are looking for.

▶▶ TUTORIAL

Getting Ready

1. If Notepad isn't open, open the Accessories group and double-click the Notepad icon. Click Notepad's Maximize button to display the application at full screen.

2. Insert your *Windows Student Resource Disk* into drive A.

3. Pull down Notepad's **File** menu and click the **Open** command to display the Open dialog box that we have just been examining.

Specifying a Drive

4. Click the **Drives** box's down arrow to display a drop-down list of the drives on your system.

5. Click *a:* to select it and list it in the **Drives** box (you may have to click the up scroll arrow to see it before you can click it).

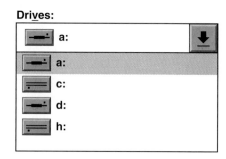

Specifying a Directory

6. Double-click the *notepad* directory in the **Directories** list box. This does two things:

   ▶ The directory changes to *notepad* and the path *a:\notepad* is shown above the list box.

   ▶ The documents in the directory with the extension *.txt* are displayed in the list of files.

The path to the selected directory is listed.

The files in the directory are listed.

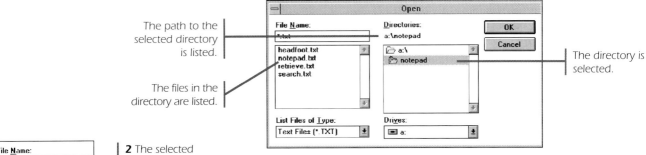

The directory is selected.

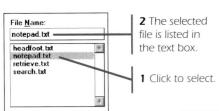

2 The selected file is listed in the text box.

1 Click to select.

Opening a Document

7. Click the *notepad.txt* filename in the list of files to select it and display its name in the **File Name** text box.

LOOKING BACK: WILDCARDS

The reason only files with the extension *.txt* are displayed is that the **File Name** text box contains the characters **.txt*. The asterisk is a wildcard standing for any filename, and *.txt* specifies the file's extension. To Windows the line reads "display files with any name but they must have the extension *.txt*."

---

8. Click the **OK** command button to open the document.

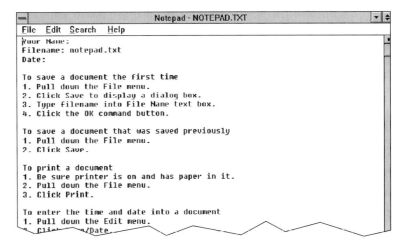

Moving Around the Document

9. Press PgDn a few times to page down through the document.

10. Press PgUp a few times to page up through the document.

11. Use the scroll bar to explore the document.

> **LOOKING BACK: USING SCROLL BARS**
>
> ▶ Click the up or down scroll arrows to scroll a line at a time.
>
> ▶ Click above or below the scroll box to scroll a screen at a time.
>
> ▶ Point to the up or down scroll arrows and hold down the left mouse button to scroll continuously.
>
> ▶ Drag the scroll box up or down the scroll bar to scroll to a specific place in the document.

Finishing Up

12. Pull down the **File** menu and click the **New** command to clear the screen.

> **PAUSING FOR PRACTICE**
>
> Opening documents and clearing the screen are basic skills. Pause here to practice opening the *notepad.txt* file in the *notepad* directory and the *readme.txt* file in the root directory until you have the procedure memorized.

ENTERING AND EDITING TEXT

Notepad is a very simple application with a limited number of commands. To use it with your own documents, all you have to know is how to move the insertion point and enter or delete text.

As you enter text with Notepad, lines normally continue past the right edge of the window until you press Enter↵. In this way, it is much like typing on a typewriter. However, to make lines automatically end when they reach the right edge of the window, you can turn on *word wrap*. With word wrap on, when a word cannot fit at the end of a line without continuing past the right edge of the window, it automatically moves, or "wraps," to the beginning of the next line. The length of the lines in the window does not reflect their length when printed. But lines longer than the page width may have words split in the middle at the right margin, or lines on the printout may be of uneven length. As you will see later, the margins and line length on the printout are controlled by the **Print Setup** command on the **File** menu.

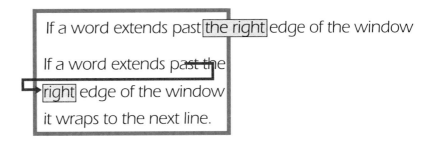

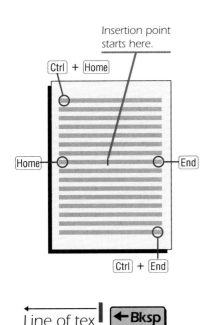

Insertion point starts here.

Ctrl + Home

Home — End

Ctrl + End

Line of tex ← Bksp

Del ine of text

The insertion point moves automatically as you enter text and always indicates where the next character you type will appear. However, to insert or delete text, you can move the insertion point to any place in the document. To move the insertion point with the mouse, point to where you want to move it and click. This moves the insertion point to where the mouse pointer is. You can also move the insertion point a character or line at a time with the arrow keys. To move in big jumps, you can press Home or End to move it to the beginning or end of a line. If you hold down Ctrl when you press either of these keys, the insertion point moves to the beginning or end of the document.

To delete text, you press ← Bksp or Del. Pressing ← Bksp moves the insertion point to the left, deleting characters as it moves. Pressing Del leaves the insertion point where it is, but draws the line of text to its right toward it, deleting characters as the line moves. If you hold either of these keys down, they rapidly delete one character after another.

To delete words, phrases, or even larger sections, it is faster to select them first. To select a word, double-click it.

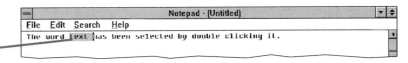

A word is selected by double-clicking it.

To select larger sections, point to the first character to be selected. Then do either of the following:

▶ Hold down the left button, and drag the mouse to the right or down the screen to expand the highlight over adjacent text. When the text that you want to select is highlighted, release the left button and it remains highlighted.

▶ Hold down ⇧ Shift and press → to extend the highlight. When the text that you want to select is highlighted, release ⇧ Shift and it remains highlighted.

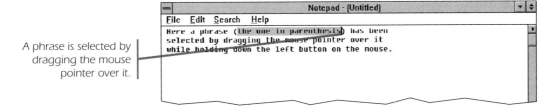

A phrase is selected by dragging the mouse pointer over it.

To select the entire document, pull down the **Edit** menu and click the **Select All** command. To remove the highlight from selected text, click anywhere in the window.

1. Pull down Notepad's **Edit** menu and if the **Word Wrap** command does not have a check (✔) in front of it to indicate that it is on, click it to turn it on. If the command does have a check mark, click anywhere outside of the menu to close the menu.

Entering a Document

2. Type the document shown here. Press ⌜Enter↵⌝ at the end of each line where the symbol ⌜Enter↵⌝ is shown. If you make mistakes, delete them with ⌜←Bksp⌝ or leave them until later.

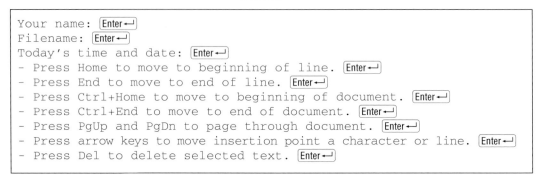

```
Your name:  Enter↵
Filename:  Enter↵
Today's time and date:  Enter↵
- Press Home to move to beginning of line.  Enter↵
- Press End to move to end of line.  Enter↵
- Press Ctrl+Home to move to beginning of document.  Enter↵
- Press Ctrl+End to move to end of document.  Enter↵
- Press PgUp and PgDn to page through document.  Enter↵
- Press arrow keys to move insertion point a character or line.  Enter↵
- Press Del to delete selected text.  Enter↵
```

Moving Through the Document

3. Use the arrow keys to move the insertion point through the text. To edit a document, you must be able to position this insertion point accurately.

▶ Press ⌜Home⌝ and ⌜End⌝ a number of times to see how the insertion point moves to the beginning or end of a line.

▶ Press ⌜Ctrl⌝+⌜Home⌝ and ⌜Ctrl⌝+⌜End⌝ a number of times to see how the insertion point moves to the beginning or end of the document.

4. Practice using the mouse to point and click to move the insertion point to specific positions.

Completing the Heading

Enter heading data

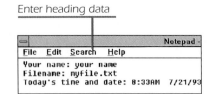

Pressing ⌜Enter↵⌝ with the insertion point at the beginning of the line inserts a blank line.

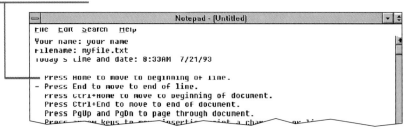

5. Fill out the heading with your name, the filename, and the time and date as shown in this illustration (although your name and the time and date will be different), following these instructions:

▶ Move the insertion point to the right end of each line and press ⌜Spacebar⌝ to insert a space, then type in your name and the filename. To enter the current time and date into the document, move the insertion point to where you want it, and then pull down the **Edit** menu and click the **Time/Date** command.

▶ If you make mistakes, press ⌜←Bksp⌝ to move the insertion point to the left and delete them.

6. Move the insertion point to the very beginning of the first item that begins "- *Press Home*" and press ⌜Enter↵⌝ to enter a blank line between the three-line heading and the rest of the text.

Inserting Text

7. Edit the body of the document by entering the words highlighted in this illustration. To do so, move the insertion point after the space where you want to insert the new words, type the words, and press ⌷Spacebar⌷.

Add these new words.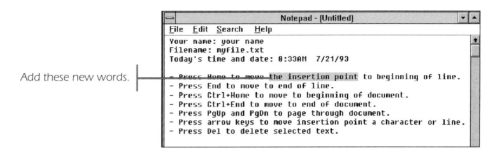

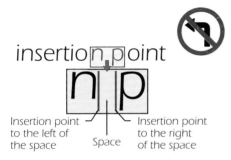

Insertion point to the left of the space   Space   Insertion point to the right of the space

COMMON WRONG TURNS: INSERTING TEXT

When you position the insertion point to insert text between two existing words, you can position it on either side of the space that separates the words. If you position it on the left side of the space, you press ⌷Spacebar⌷ before typing the new word. If you position it on the right side of the space, you press ⌷Spacebar⌷ after typing the new word.

Replacing Existing Text

8. Double-click the word *PgUp* to select it.

9. Type **PgDn** and then press ⌷Spacebar⌷ to replace it.

10. Double-click the second *PgDn* on the line to select it.

11. Type **PgUp** and then press ⌷Spacebar⌷ to replace it.

The revisions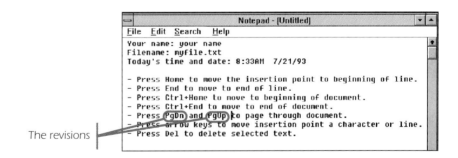

Selecting and Deleting Text

12. Point to the left of the hyphen in the last line—the line that reads *"Press Del to delete selected text."*

13. Hold down the left button and drag the cursor to extend the highlight over the entire sentence including the period at the end of the line.

14. Release the mouse button, and the sentence remains highlighted.

15. Press ⌷Del⌷ to delete the highlighted sentence. Your finished document should now look like the following illustration:

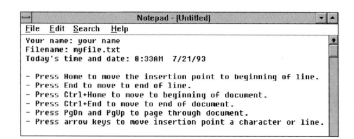

```
┌────────────────────────────────────────────────────────────┐
│ ──                    Notepad - [Untitled]            ▼  ▲  │
├────────────────────────────────────────────────────────────┤
│ File  Edit  Search  Help                                   │
├────────────────────────────────────────────────────────────┤
│ Your name: your name                                    ↑  │
│ Filename: myfile.txt                                       │
│ Today's time and date: 8:33AM  7/21/93                     │
│                                                            │
│ - Press Home to move the insertion point to beginning of line. │
│ - Press End to move to end of line.                        │
│ - Press Ctrl+Home to move to beginning of document.        │
│ - Press Ctrl+End to move to end of document.               │
│ - Press PgDn and PgUp to page through document.            │
│ - Press arrow keys to move insertion point a character or line. │
│                                                            │
└────────────────────────────────────────────────────────────┘
```

16. Leave the document on the screen as you read the following section on saving documents and clearing the screen.

PAUSING FOR PRACTICE

Moving the insertion point with the keyboard and mouse pointer and selecting text are basic skills. Continue practicing these procedures until you are comfortable with them.

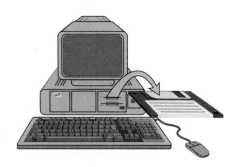

SAVING DOCUMENTS AND CLEARING THE SCREEN

When you create a new file or edit one that you have opened from a disk, it exists only in the computer's memory until you save it. Saving the document copies it from the computer's memory to the disk, where it is permanently stored.

To save a file, you pull down the **File** menu and click the **Save** command. You then fill in the necessary information in the Save As dialog box and click the **OK** command button.

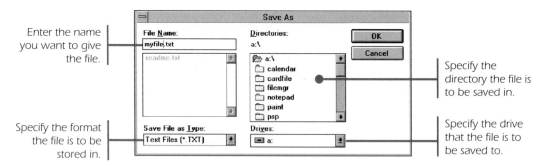

Enter the name you want to give the file.

Specify the format the file is to be stored in.

Specify the directory the file is to be saved in.

Specify the drive that the file is to be saved to.

To save the file in a specific location, it may be necessary to change the drive and directory. To change the drive, click the down arrow on the **Drives** drop-down list box to display a list of the drives on your system. Scroll the drive you want into view and click it to select it. To change the directory, double-click its name in the **Directories** list box. This takes you down into the directory and displays any of the directory's subdirectories in the **Directories** list box and any of its files in the **File Name** window.

The first time you save a document, you have to enter its filename into the **File Name** text box. When you save the file again, you needn't specify the name again unless you want to change it. In that case, you pull down the **File** menu and click the **Save As** command. Remember from PicTorial 3 that with Windows (or DOS), you can assign names to files that have up to eight characters and an extension of up to three characters separated from the name by a period. Most Windows applications assign a unique extension to the files they create so you and the applications can tell which files belong to which applications. Notepad adds the extension *.txt*.

When you are finished with a document and want to work on another, you pull down the **File** menu and click the **New** command to clear the old document from the screen.

▶▶ TUTORIAL

Saving a New File

1. Pull down Notepad's **File** menu and click the **Save** command to display the Save As dialog box. The entry *.txt in the **File Name** text box is highlighted.

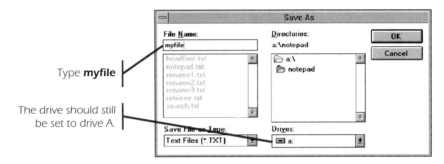

Type **myfile**

The drive should still be set to drive A.

> ▶ Check that drive A is still selected. If it isn't, select it.
> ▶ Check that the *notepad* directory is still selected. If it isn't, select it.

2. Click the **File Name** text box to move the insertion point there, and type **myfile**

3. Click the **OK** command button to save the document.

4. Pull down the **File** menu and click the **New** command to clear the screen.

Opening the Saved File

5. Pull down the **File** menu and click the **Open** command to display the Open dialog box. The path *a:\notepad* below the **Directories** heading indicates that the drive is still set to drive A and the selected directory is still *notepad*.

6. Double-click *myfile.txt* in the list of files to open the file. (The *.txt* extension was added by Notepad when you first saved the file.) The document looks just as it did when you saved it.

Saving a File a Second Time

7. Pull down the **File** menu and click the **Save** command again. This time the file is saved without displaying a dialog box.

Saving a File Under a New Name

8. Pull down the **File** menu and click the **Save As** command to dis-

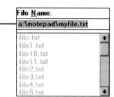

The original file-
name preceded
by its path.

play the Save As dialog box again. The original filename is high-lighted in the **File Name** text box along with its path.

9. Type **myfile2** and press ⟨Enter ←⟩ to save the file under a new name.

Opening the Saved File

10. Pull down the **File** menu and click the **New** command to clear the screen.

11. Pull down the **File** menu and click the **Open** command to display the Open dialog box.

12. Double-click the file *myfile2.txt* in the list of files to open the file. It is an exact copy of the *myfile.txt* file that you saved it from.

PRINTING DOCUMENTS

When you are ready to print a file, almost every Windows application has a **Print Setup** command on the **File** menu. You use this command to specify the printer you want to print on, change the orientation of the document on the page, or change the size and source of the paper to be used.

Click here to use
the default printer.

Click here to
change printers.

Click here to
change the orienta-
tion of the docu-
ment on the page.

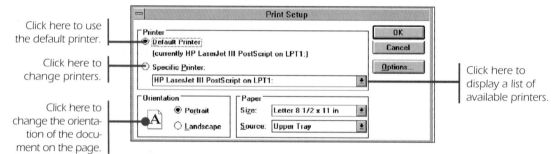

Click here to
display a list of
available printers.

Portrait

Landscape

Orientation refers to portrait or landscape mode. *Portrait mode* prints across the narrow width of the page. *Landscape mode* prints across the length of the page. The terms are taken from the fine arts, where portraits are usually painted in one orientation and landscapes in the other.

Notepad's **Page Setup** command on the **File** menu gives you some control over your printout. For example, you can change headers, footers, and margins. When you execute this command, the Page Setup dialog box is displayed. The *&f* in the **Header** text box is a code that prints the filename as a header at the top of every page. The *Page &p* in the **Footer** text box prints the word *Page* followed by the page number as a footer at the bottom of every page. The numbers in the Margin boxes specify the four margins on the printed page.

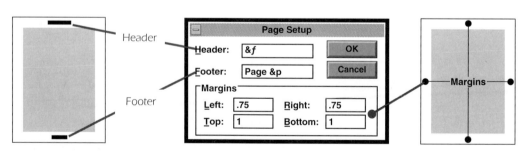

Header

Footer

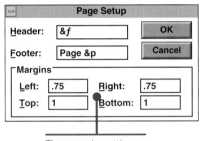

▶▶ **TUTORIAL**

Getting Started

1. Pull down Notepad's **File** menu and click the **Open** command to display the Open dialog box. The **Drives** box should indicate that the drive is still drive A and the directory is still *notepad*.

2. Click the file *notepad.txt* in the list of files to select it, and then click the **OK** command button to open the document. When the document is opened, the document that was on the screen is automatically cleared.

Changing Margins

3. Pull down the **File** menu and click the **Page Setup** command to display the Page Setup dialog box. The *&f* code in the **Header** text box is highlighted.

4. Double-click the *.75* in the **Left** Margins box to highlight it, then type **1** to replace it.

5. Press [Tab↹] to highlight the *.75* in the **Right** Margins box to highlight it, then type **1** to replace it.

6. Click the **OK** command button to complete your changes and return to the document.

The margin settings

Printing the Document

7. Pull down the **File** menu and click the **Print** command to print the document. In a moment a dialog box tells you it is being printed.

Identifying Available Printers

8. Pull down the **File** menu and click the **Print Setup** command to display the Print Setup dialog box.

9. Click the arrow for the drop-down list under the heading **Specific Printer** to list the printers that are available on your system. The name of the current printer is selected. If you have more than one printer listed, write down their names and ask what they are used for.

Click here to display a drop-down list of the printers on your system.

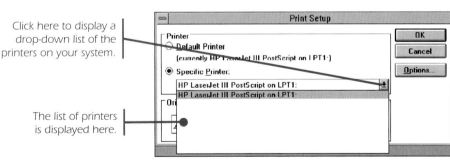

The list of printers is displayed here.

Printer's name	Use
_____	_____
_____	_____
_____	_____
_____	_____

10. Click the **Cancel** command button to close the dialog box without making any changes.

USING PRINT MANAGER

Most documents are eventually printed so a record can be filed or distributed to others. When you print a file from any Windows application, it is first printed to the disk. The file on the disk is then sent to the printer. This is done because a computer can send a file to the disk much faster than it can print it out on most printers. By printing to the disk first, Windows allows you to resume editing while it sends the file on the disk to the printer. This can save you quite a bit of time.

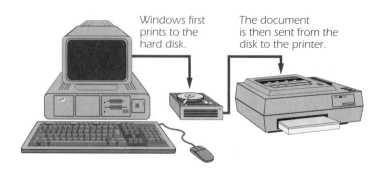

Windows first prints to the hard disk.

The document is then sent from the disk to the printer.

Printing to the disk also allows you to print one document after another without waiting for each to be finished before starting the next one. The lineup of print jobs waiting to be printed is called a *print queue*. When you have such a queue, even if it contains only one print job, Print Manager is opened and its icon appears on the desktop. To cancel or manage jobs in the queue, you double-click the icon to display the Print Manager window.

Print jobs in queue   Printer

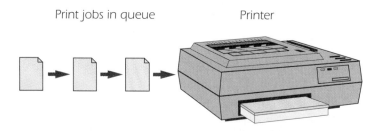

COMMON WRONG TURN: PRINT MANAGER DOESN'T APPEAR

If Print Manager does not appear when you print a document, or if you cannot resume editing until the entire document has finished printing, then Print Manager has been turned off on your system. To turn it back on, open the Main group window and double-click the Control Panel icon to open another window. Double-click the Printers icon to display a dialog box. Click the **Use Print Manager** check box to turn it on, then click the **Close** command button to return to the Control Panel. Finally, minimize or close the Control Panel window.

The Print Manager window contains a menu, command buttons, and a list of printers below each of which are listed the print jobs being processed.

Menu

Command buttons

Printers on the system, with the status of each

Print jobs being processed for the printer

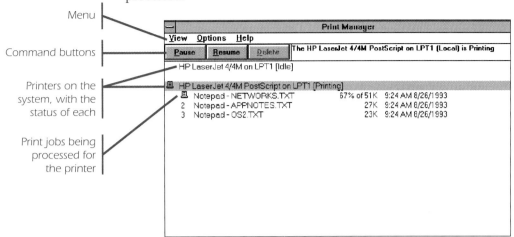

When a job is being printed to the disk, a dialog box keeps you informed of its progress.

If any problem arises, an error message is displayed.

Status of the print job

Click to cancel printing.

Fix printer and click.

Click to cancel printing.

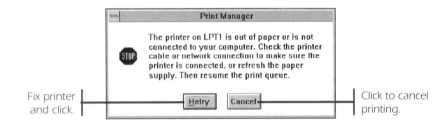

To manage printers and print jobs, you highlight either the printer or one of the jobs and then choose one of the command buttons.

Pauses the selected printer

Deletes selected print job

Resumes printing after you have paused it

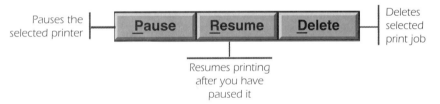

The **View** menu lists commands that specify what information is displayed by Print Manager.

Displays information about print jobs

Immediately updates the list of jobs waiting to be printed

Displays print queues for network printers

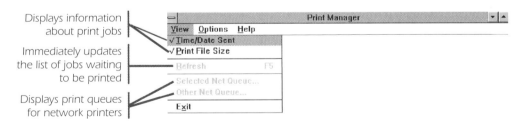

If you close Print Manager before all jobs are printed, a dialog box warns you that print jobs will be canceled.

Click to finish print-
ing before exiting.

Click to cancel
print jobs.

The commands on the **Options** menu are used to divide your processor's time between printing and other tasks, specify how error messages
are handled, and control network printing.

Higher priorities
devote more
computer resources
to printing rather
than computing.

Displays an alert if
any problems arise
with printing

Flashes Print
Manager's title bar
or icon when the
printer has a
message

Ignores messages
when Print
Manager is
inactive or an icon

Specifies your
connection to
network printers

Displays the
Printer Setup
dialog box

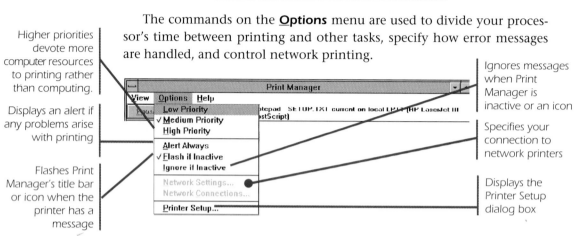

▶▶ **TUTORIAL**

Getting Ready

1. Insert your *Windows Student Resource Disk* into drive A.

Opening a Document to Print

2. Pull down Notepad's **File** menu and click the **Open** command to
display the dialog box you'll see when you open documents with
almost all Windows applications.

3 Select the
notepad.txt file.

2 Set the
directory to
notepad.

1 Set the drive
to **A.**

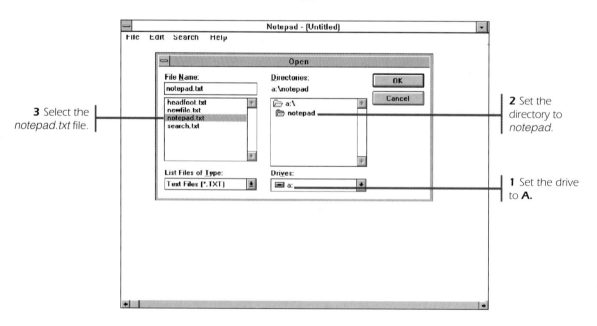

3. Open the *notepad.txt* file stored in the *notepad* directory on drive A.

Notepad - NOTEPAD.TXT

File   Edit   Search   Help

Your Name:
Filename: notepad.txt
Date:

To save a document the first time
1. Pull down the File menu.
2. Click Save to display a dialog box.

Pausing Print Manager

4. Open Program Manager's Main group window and double-click the Print Manager icon to open the application. (If you can't see the Main group window, you may want to temporarily minimize Notepad so it is displayed as an icon.)

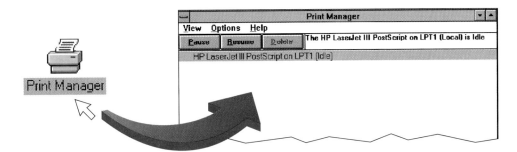

COMMON WRONG TURNS: CAN'T FIND A WINDOW OR ICON

When you are working on an application, Program Manager may be automatically minimized so it's displayed as an icon or it may be hidden behind the application window. To see Program Manager, minimize the application that is hiding it. To see Program Manager's contents, double-click its icon to open it.

5. Click the name of the printer you are using and then click the **Pause** command button. The name of your printer should be followed by the notice *[Paused]*. Now no jobs will be printed until you decide they should be. This allows you to send a number of jobs to the printer so you can experience working with a print queue.

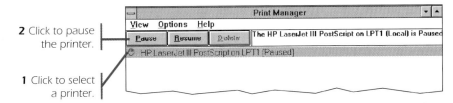

2 Click to pause the printer.

1 Click to select a printer.

Creating a Print Queue

6. Minimize Print Manager and maximize Notepad.

7. Pull down Notepad's **File** menu and click the **Print** command.

8. Repeat Step 7 five more times to send a total of six printouts to the printer.

9. Minimize Notepad and Maximize Print Manager. All six print jobs are listed under the heading for your printer.

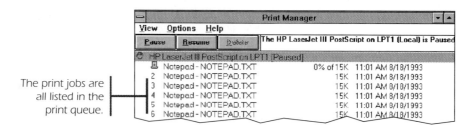

The print jobs are all listed in the print queue.

Deleting Jobs

10. Highlight the last job in the print queue and click the **Delete** command button to display a dialog box asking you to confirm the deletion.

2 Click this command button to delete the selected file.

1 Click the last file to select it.

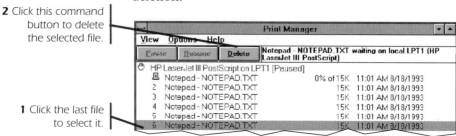

11. Click the **OK** command button to delete the job from the print queue

12. Repeat Steps 10 and 11 until all but one of the print jobs have been canceled.

Resuming the Printer

13. Click the name of the printer you are using to select it, then click the **Resume** command button. The *[Paused]* message disappears, and the last document prints.

14. Click the Print Manager's Minimize button to run it as an icon on the desktop.

USING THE CLIPBOARD TO COPY AND MOVE TEXT

Notepad, like most other applications, makes it easy for you to copy or move data in a document. To do so, you first select the data you want to copy or move, then copy or cut the selected data, and then paste it back in elsewhere in the document.

When you copy or move data, you are using Windows' Clipboard. The data that you copy or cut is first copied or moved to the Clipboard, where it remains until you copy or cut other data or exit Windows. While the data is stored on the Clipboard, you can paste it anywhere in the document you copied or cut it from. You can also paste it into another document, or even into another application's document.

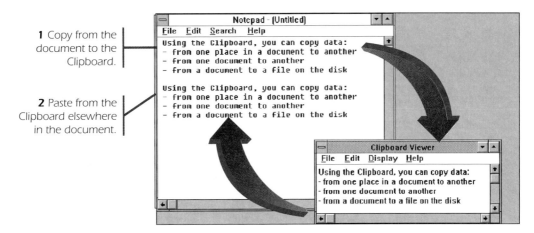

1 Copy from the document to the Clipboard.

2 Paste from the Clipboard elsewhere in the document.

COPYING OR CUTTING TO THE CLIPBOARD

You can copy or cut two types of information to the Clipboard: data or graphics. Data consists of letters and numbers like those you enter to write a letter or calculate a loan. The data can be edited and revised once you paste it into another application.

To copy or cut data onto the Clipboard, use one of these procedures:

▶ To copy or cut data from an application, select the data, then pull down the application's **Edit** menu and click the **Copy** or **Cut** command. **Copy** leaves the original data intact and makes a copy of it on the Clipboard. **Cut** removes the original data from the application's file and transfers it to the Clipboard.

▶ To copy a snapshot (bitmap) of the entire screen to the Clipboard, press PrtScr. (This only works in *386 enhanced mode.*) If this doesn't work on your system, try holding down Alt or ⬆ Shift while you press PrtScr since pressing PrtScr by itself does not work on some systems. (The graphics that you capture this way are called bitmaps because they are made up of light or dark bits arranged in a grid. These graphics are assigned the extension *.bmp* when you save them and can be pasted only into some types of applications.)

▶ To copy a snapshot (bitmap) of just the active window to the Clipboard, press Alt +PrtScr. If this doesn't work on your system, try holding down ⬆ Shift while you press PrtScr.

Viewing Data on the Clipboard

To see what is on the Clipboard, double-click the Clipboard icon to open the Viewer. The Clipboard Viewer's menu lists a number of menu names.

▶ Pull down the **File** menu to open and save the Clipboard file or to exit the Viewer. (You save the contents of the Clipboard when you want to have access to it again. The saved file has the extension *.clp*.)

▶ Pull down the **Edit** menu and click the **Delete** command to delete the contents of the Clipboard.

▶ Pull down the **Display** menu when you want to change the way data are displayed.

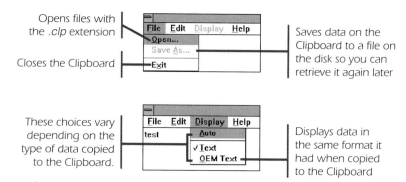

Opens files with the .clp extension

Closes the Clipboard

Saves data on the Clipboard to a file on the disk so you can retrieve it again later

These choices vary depending on the type of data copied to the Clipboard.

Displays data in the same format it had when copied to the Clipboard

Pasting Data from the Clipboard

To paste data from the Clipboard, move the insertion point to where you want it pasted, pull down the **Edit** menu, and click the **Paste** command.

▶▶ TUTORIAL

Getting Ready

1. Use Notepad to open the *search.txt* file stored in the *notepad* directory on the *Windows Student Resource Disk* on drive A.

2. Select the entire line that reads *Examples of case* (scroll or maximize the window to see it). To do so, point to the left of the *E* in *Examples,* hold down the left mouse button, and drag the mouse down to the blank line below the paragraph, then release the mouse button.

The selected paragraph is displayed in reverse video.

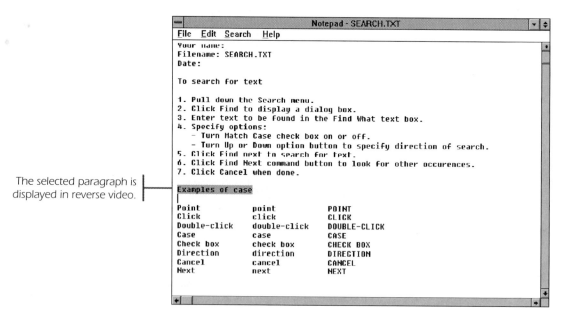

Moving Text

3. Pull down the **Edit** menu and click the **Cut** command to move the paragraph from the document to the Clipboard.

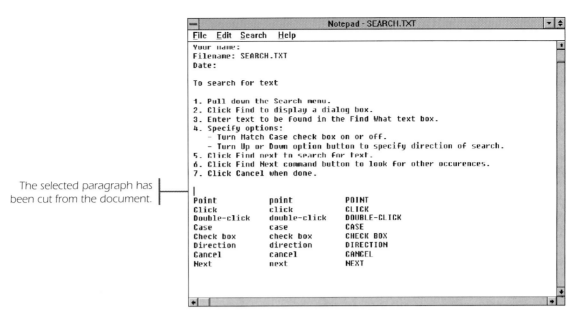

The selected paragraph has been cut from the document.

4. Press ⌈Ctrl⌉+⌈End⌉ to move the insertion point to the end of the document, and press ⌈Enter←⌉ twice to move the insertion point down two lines.

5. Pull down the **Edit** menu and click the **Paste** command to copy the paragraph from the Clipboard back into the document.

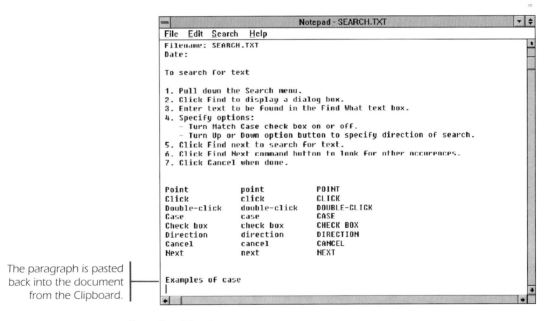

The paragraph is pasted back into the document from the Clipboard.

Copying Text

6. Select the same line of text again (in its new position) just as you did in Step 2.

7. Pull down the **Edit** menu and click the **Copy** command to copy the paragraph from the document to the Clipboard.

8. Move the insertion point to the first blank line above the three columns of terms.

9. Pull down the **Edit** menu and click the **Paste** command to copy the paragraph from the Clipboard back into the document. You now have two copies of the same paragraph.

10. Print the document.

Viewing Data on the Clipboard

11. Open the Main group and double-click the Clipboard Viewer icon to open it. Click the window's Maximize button to enlarge it. The line of text that you just copied is on the Clipboard.

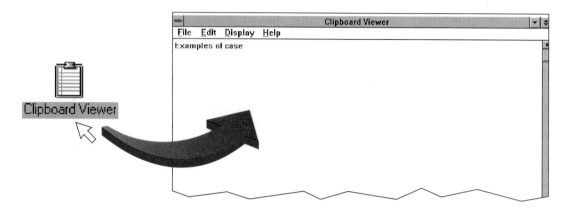

Clipboard Viewer

12. Press PrtScr, and the image of the screen is copied to the Clipboard.

PAUSING FOR PRACTICE

Cutting, copying, and pasting text are basic skills in almost all Windows applications. Pause here to practice these procedures until you have mastered them. You will not be saving the file when you are finished, so feel free to copy, move, and delete any text.

Finishing Up

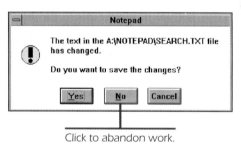

Click to abandon work.

13. Double-click the Clipboard Viewer's Control-menu box (the top-most one) to close the application.

14. Double-click the Notepad's Control-menu box to close the applica-tion. Since you have not saved your changes, a dialog box appears warning you.

15. Click the **No** command button because you don't want to save the changes.

▶▶ SKILL-BUILDING EXERCISES

1. Retrieving Documents with Notepad

Windows supplies a number of files with the extension *.txt* that you can open with Notepad. These files are normally stored in the Windows directory (usually on drive C). Open some of these files with Notepad and make a printout of at least one of them.

2. Creating a Time-Log Document

1. Clear the Notepad window and type **.LOG** in the upper-left cor-ner (it must be all uppercase).

2. Save the document in the *notepad* directory on your *Windows Student Resource Disk* in drive A as *timelog.txt*.

3. Clear the screen and then open *timelog.txt*. You'll see that the time and date have automatically been entered.

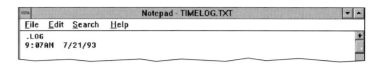

4. Type the sentence **This is my first log entry**, then save the file again and clear the screen.

5. Open the file again, and you'll see that a new time and date have been entered. You can use this document to keep track of activities, since the time and date are updated each time you open the file.

6. Print the document.

3. Exploring Notepad's Help

Explore Notepad's on-line help. You'll find definitions of such terms as *text files*, *headers*, and *footers*. You'll also find summaries of many of the procedures you have just completed.

4. Revising Headers and Footers

1. Use Notepad to open the *headfoot.txt* document supplied in the *notepad* directory on the *Windows Student Resource Disk*.

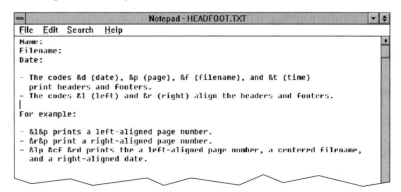

2. Before printing the document, use the Page Setup command to change the header and footer using one or more of the codes listed shown here. Experiment with these codes to change the alignment of your headers and footers. Keep in mind that you can use these codes in combinations.

5. Copying Text

1. Open the *search.txt* document supplied in the *notepad* directory on the *Windows Student Resource Disk* and make a duplicate copy of each line in the 3-line heading.

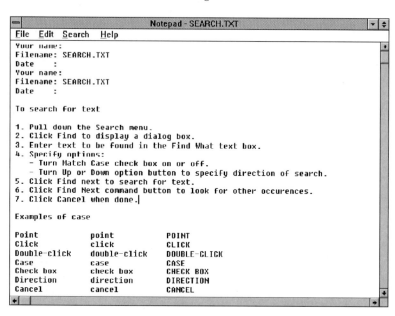

2. Reorganize the examples at the bottom of the document into ascending alphabetical order.

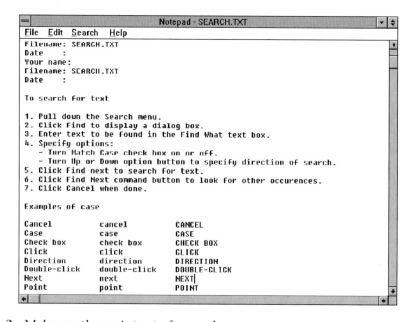

3. Make another printout of your changes.

4. Clear the screen without saving your changes.

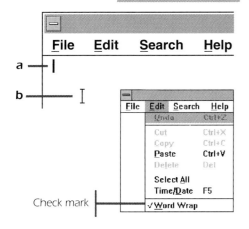

Check mark

1. This illustration shows two elements that appear on the Notepad screen. What is the name of each?

a. _____

b. _____

2. Describe what happens as you enter text when the check mark is in front of the **Word Wrap** command and when it isn't.

When it is: _____

When it isn't: _____

3. This illustration shows the dialog box that appears when you pull down the **File** menu and choose the **Open** command on almost all Windows applications. Describe what each element shows.

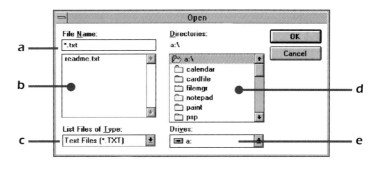

a. _____

b. _____

c. _____

d. _____

e. _____

4. This illustration shows the dialog box that appears when you pull down the **File** menu and choose the **Save** command on almost all Windows applications. Describe what each element shows.

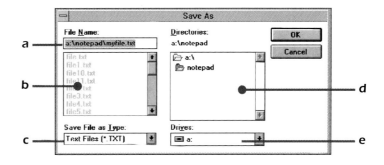

a. _____

b. _____

c. _____

d. _____

e. _____

5. This illustration shows the dialog box that appears when you pull down the **File** menu and choose the **Print Setup** command on almost all Windows applications. Describe what each element shows.

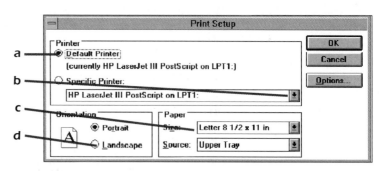

a. _____

b. _____

c. _____

d. _____

6. Describe how you would select the sections of text shown here.

a. _____

b. _____

7. Assuming the insertion point is located where shown in this illustration, list the key or keys you would press to move it to each of the indicated positions.

a. _____

b. _____

c. _____

d. _____

8. Assuming the insertion point is located where shown in this illustration, list the key you would press to delete:

the word *can* _____

the word *text* _____

Insertion point starts here

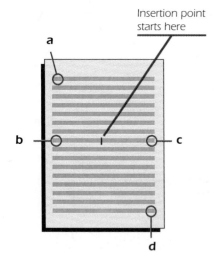

PicTorial 6

WORKING WITH WRITE

After completing this PicTorial, you will be able to:

▶ Enter and edit documents with Write

▶ Save and open documents

▶ Paginate and print documents

▶ Find and replace text in a document

▶ Format characters, paragraphs, and pages

Unlike Notepad, Write is a true word processing application. It is limited compared to many word processors used in business, but its features are sufficient for many uses. For example, you can write memos, letters, and reports as well with this application as with many others. In fact, as you will see in the next PicTorial, you can even illustrate Write documents by inserting graphics into them.

OPENING AND MOVING THROUGH DOCUMENTS

When you first open Write, the window is empty except for the insertion point, the mouse pointer, and the *end mark* that indicates the end of the document. You can't move the insertion point until you type text or open an existing document.

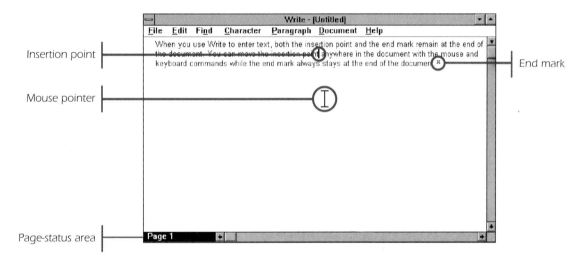

You open a Write document using the **File** menu's **Open** command just as you open documents in all Windows applications. Once a document is on the screen, you can move about it in a variety of ways. For example, you can use the scroll bars to scroll through the document just as you do in other Windows applications.

You can go directly to a page with the **Find** menu's **Go To Page** command. This command displays a dialog box into which you can type the number of a page you want to jump to. Since you are typing much of the time, using keyboard commands is frequently much faster than scrolling to move the insertion point to where you want it. Write's keyboard movement keys are shown in the following tutorial.

▶▶ TUTORIAL

1. Open the Accessories group and double-click the Write icon to open the application. Then click the Write window's Maximize button to enlarge it to full screen.

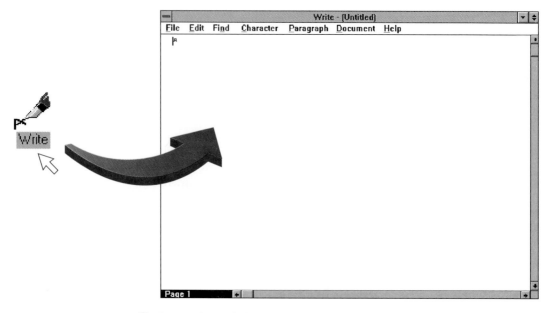

2. Insert the *Windows Student Resource Disk* into drive A.

3. Pull down Write's **File** menu and click the **Open** command to display the Open dialog box. Make the following settings:

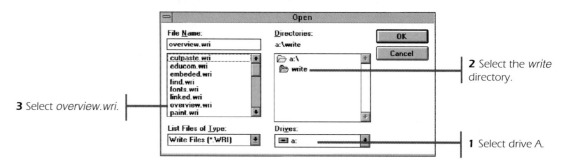

3 Select *overview.wri.*

2 Select the *write* directory.

1 Select drive A.

▶ Select drive A.

▶ Select the write directory.

▶ Select the *overview.wri* file.

4. Click the **OK** command button to open the *overview.wri* file.

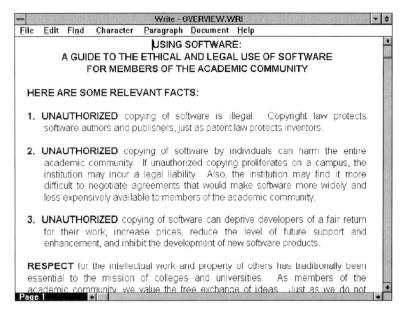

Write - OVERVIEW.WRI

File   Edit   Find   Character   Paragraph   Document   Help

USING SOFTWARE:
A GUIDE TO THE ETHICAL AND LEGAL USE OF SOFTWARE
FOR MEMBERS OF THE ACADEMIC COMMUNITY

HERE ARE SOME RELEVANT FACTS:

1. **UNAUTHORIZED** copying of software is illegal.   Copyright law protects software authors and publishers, just as patent law protects inventors.

2. **UNAUTHORIZED** copying of software by individuals can harm the entire academic community. If unauthorized copying proliferates on a campus, the institution may incur a legal liability.   Also, the institution may find it more difficult to negotiate agreements that would make software more widely and less expensively available to members of the academic community.

3. **UNAUTHORIZED** copying of software can deprive developers of a fair return for their work, increase prices, reduce the level of future support and enhancement, and inhibit the development of new software products.

RESPECT for the intellectual work and property of others has traditionally been essential to the mission of colleges and universities.   As members of the academic community we value the free exchange of ideas. Just as we do not

Page 1

5. Explore the document using the scroll bar to move around.

LOOKING BACK: USING SCROLL BARS

▶ Click the up or down scroll arrows to scroll a line at a time.

▶ Click above or below the scroll box to scroll a screen at a time.

▶ Point to the up or down scroll arrows and hold down the left mouse button to scroll continuously.

▶ Drag the scroll box up or down the scroll bar to scroll to a specific place in the document.

6. Practice using the following keys and combinations to move the insertion point around the document.

COMMON WRONG TURNS: PRESSING ↓ AND ↑ ENTERS NUMBERS

If pressing the keys on the numeric keypad enters numbers instead of moving the insertion point, press NumLock to turn off the numeric keypad.

To Move To		Press	
Previous or next screen	PgUp	or	PgDn
Beginning or end of the line	Home	or	End
Previous or next word	Ctrl+←	or	Ctrl+→
Previous or next sentence*	5+←	or	5+→
Previous or next paragraph*	5+↑	or	5+↓
Top or bottom of the screen	Ctrl+PgUp	or	Ctrl+PgDn
Beginning or end of the document	Ctrl+Home	or	Ctrl+End
* The 5 is the one on the numeric keypad; for it to work, NumLock must be disengaged.			

PAUSING FOR PRACTICE

Moving the insertion point through a document is a basic skill. Pause here to practice moving the insertion point with the commands listed in Step 6 until you can move it wherever you want with maximum speed and efficiency.

7. If you have to quit here, exit Write without saving the document. To do so, pull down the **File** menu and click the **Exit** command.

PAGINATING AND PRINTING DOCUMENTS

As you add text to a document, Write treats it as one long strip on the screen. As a result, the page-status area always indicates that the insertion point is on page 1 and commands such as **Go To Page** won't work. The **Repaginate** command on the **File** menu breaks the document into pages by calculating which lines will fit on which pages when you print the document. This command displays the symbol » in the left margin next to the first line on each page.

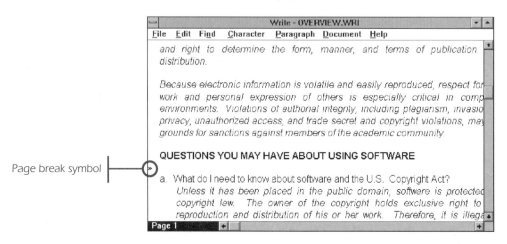

Page break symbol —

The process of breaking a document into pages is called *repagination*, and the symbols mark the location of *page breaks*. Documents are automatically repaginated when you print them. But, to determine where page breaks will fall before you print a document, you must use the **Repaginate** command.

TIP: MOVING BETWEEN PAGES

After repaginating a document, you can press ⑤+[PgUp] or ⑤+[PgDn] to move to the previous or next page in the document. When you use these keys, note that the ⑤ key is the one on the numeric keypad, not the one above the alpha keys. And the commands only work when [NumLock] is not engaged and after a document has been repaginated.

Widow

Orphan

WIDOWS AND ORPHANS

Write automatically prevents *orphans* and *widows* by not allowing the first or last line of a paragraph to print at the bottom or top of a page by itself.

CONFIRMING PAGE BREAKS

When you use the **Repaginate** command, you can turn on or off the **Confirm Page Breaks** check box. When it is on, Write pauses at each place where it proposes a page break and displays a dialog box you can use to move the break up in the document. (The **Down** command button works only after you have first used to **Up** button). Confirming page breaks is a useful feature when you want some material kept together on the same page.

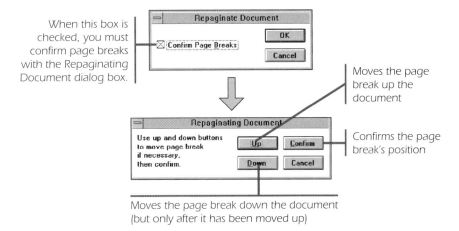

When this box is checked, you must confirm page breaks with the Repaginating Document dialog box.

Moves the page break up the document

Confirms the page break's position

Moves the page break down the document (but only after it has been moved up)

MANUALLY FORCING PAGE BREAKS

Page breaks may fall at undesirable locations—for example, in the middle of a table. To prevent unwanted page breaks, you can enter *manual page breaks*. To do so, you move the insertion point to the spot where you want to start the new page and press Ctrl+Enter←. This inserts a dotted line across the screen showing where one page will end and another begin when you print the document.

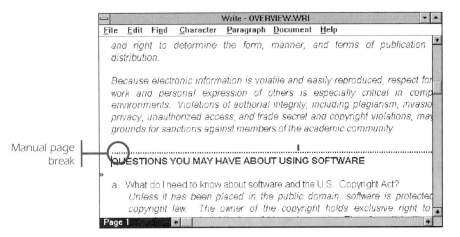

Manual page break

A manual page break doesn't move when you add or delete text above it. As a result, pages may be too short. To remove a manual page break, double-click it to select it, then press Del.

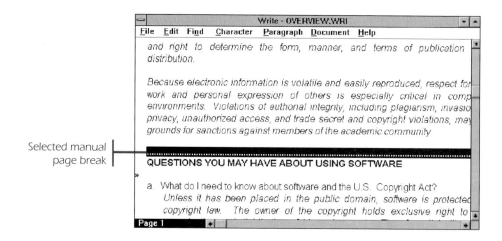

Selected manual page break

PRINTING DOCUMENTS

To print a Write document, you pull down the **File** menu and click the **Print** command to display the Print dialog box.

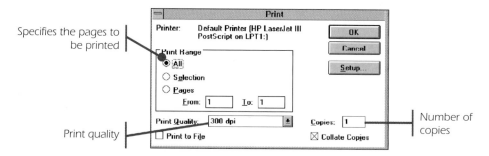

Specifies the pages to be printed

Print quality

Number of copies

This box indicates the name of the printer you are using and allows you to specify the pages to be printed, the quality of the printout, and the number of copies.

By default, the entire document is printed. However, you can print a section of the document by selecting it and then checking the **Selection** option button. You can print selected pages by clicking the **Pages** option button and entering the first and last pages in the **From** and **To** text boxes. And you can have the printer collate multiple copies of a multi-page document by checking the **Collate Copies** check box.

Some printers allow you to print a document with higher or lower print qualities. Normally, these are referred to as draft or letter-quality modes or by the number of dots printed per inch (*dpi*). Choosing a lower DPI gives you lower quality but more speed and is ideal for rough drafts. Available printing modes vary from printer to printer. To see what modes your printer offers, click the **Print Quality** drop-down list's arrow to see the options.

If the printer listed at the top of the dialog box is not the one you want to use, click the **Setup** command button to display the Print Setup Dialog box.

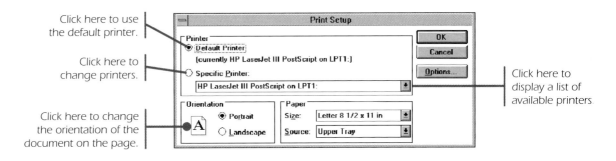

Click here to use the default printer.

Click here to change printers.

Click here to change the orientation of the document on the page.

Click here to display a list of available printers.

▶▶ **TUTORIAL**

Getting Started

1. Open the *overview.wri* file supplied on the *Windows Student Resource Disk* in the *write* directory.

Repaginating a Document

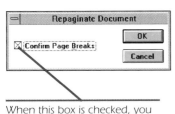

When this box is checked, you are prompted to confirm each page-break position.

2. Pull down the **File** menu and click the **Repaginate** command to display a dialog box. Click the **Confirm Page Breaks** check box to turn it on.

3. Click the **OK** command button to begin repagination. Write pauses at the first place where it proposes a page break and displays the Repaginating Document dialog box.

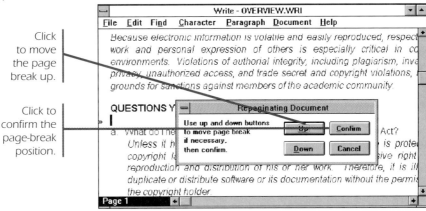

Click to move the page break up.

Click to confirm the page-break position.

4. Point to the dialog box's title bar, hold down the left mouse button, and drag the box upward and out of the way so you can see the suggested page break better. Then release the mouse button.

5. Click the **Up** command button to highlight the heading above the suggested page break, and click the **Confirm** command button. This moves the page break above the heading so that it prints on the next page along with the text that follows it.

6. Click the **Up** command button twice to highlight the heading *Alternatives to Explore* above the next suggested page break, and click the **Confirm** command button.

7. Confirm the next page break without moving it.

Moving Between Pages

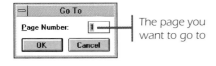

The page you want to go to

8. Pull down the **Find** menu and click the **Go To Page** command to display a dialog box. Page 1 is listed in the **Page Number** text box.

**COMMON
WRONG TURNS:**
5 + PgDn **ENTERS
NUMBERS**

If pressing 5 + PgDn
enters numbers, press
NumLock to disengage it.

9. Click the **OK** command button to move the insertion point to the beginning of page 1. Notice that the page-status area at the bottom of the screen indicates that you are on page 1.

10. Press 5 + PgDn to move to the next page, and the page-status area indicates that you are on page 2.

11. Press 5 + PgUp to move back to the previous page, and the page-status area indicates that you are back on page 1.

12. Press Ctrl + End to move to the bottom of the document, and the page-status area indicates that you are on page 4.

13. Press Ctrl + Home to move to the top of the document, and the page-status area indicates that you are on page 1.

Printing the Document

14. Pull down the **File** menu and click the **Print** command to display a dialog box.

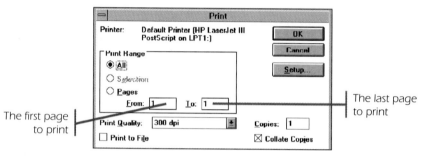

The first page to print

The last page to print

15. Double-click in the Print Range **From** text box to highlight the number *1*, then type **2** to change the first page to be printed.

16. Double-click in the Print Range **To** text box to highlight the number *1*, then type **2** to change the last page to be printed.

17. Click the **OK** command button to begin printing, and a dialog box is displayed as page 2 of the document is printed to the disk. When the dialog box disappears, you can resume editing while the document is sent from the disk to the printer.

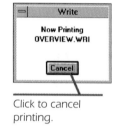

Click to cancel printing.

PAUSING FOR PRACTICE

Pause here to practice moving the insertion point to the previous or next page (5 + PgUp and 5 + PgDn) and to the beginning or end of the document (Ctrl + Home and Ctrl + End).

Finishing Up

18. If you have to quit at this point, you can do so without saving the document. If a dialog box warns you that the document has been changed and asks whether you want to save those changes, click the **No** command button.

ENTERING AND EDITING TEXT

To enter text, you just type it in. As you do so, the insertion point indicates where the next letter will appear. When you reach the end of a line, any word that won't fit automatically wraps to the next line. You

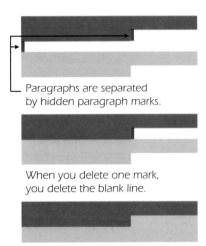

Paragraphs are separated by hidden paragraph marks.

When you delete one mark, you delete the blank line.

When you delete the second, mark, you join the paragraphs.

press ⎡Enter ⏎⎦ only when you want to end a paragraph or a line before it reaches the right margin or when you want to insert a blank line. Pressing ⎡Enter ⏎⎦ enters an invisible *paragraph mark* in the document. This hidden code can be selected and deleted just like any other character. It is the last character in a paragraph or the first on a blank line. Deleting paragraph marks is how you join separated paragraphs.

Write has tab stops set every ½-inch so you can press ⎡Tab ⇆⎦ to indent the first line of a paragraph or to align text columns.

To edit a document, you first move the insertion point to where you want to insert or delete text. To move the insertion point with the mouse, point to where you want to move it and click. To move it with the keyboard, use the keyboard movement keys listed in the table at the beginning of this PicTorial.

To delete characters to the left of the insertion point, press ⎡← Bksp⎦. To delete characters to the right of the insertion point, press ⎡Del⎦. If you hold either of these keys down, they rapidly delete one character after another.

 ▶▶ **TUTORIAL**

1. Pull down the **File** menu and click the **New** command to clear the Write document screen. If a dialog box warns you that the document has been changed and asks whether you want to save those changes, click the **No** command button.

Entering a Document

2. Type the document shown here (the type on your screen may be smaller). As you do so:

▶ Press ⎡Enter ⏎⎦ at the end of each line where the ⎡Enter ⏎⎦ symbols are shown.

▶ Press ⎡Tab ⇆⎦ at the beginning of each of the two body paragraphs where the ⎡Tab ⇆⎦ symbols are shown.

▶ To correct mistakes, delete them with ⎡← Bksp⎦ or leave them until later.

Your name: your name ⎡Enter ⏎⎦
Filename: enterdoc.wri ⎡Enter ⏎⎦
Date: today's date ⎡Enter ⏎⎦
⎡Enter ⏎⎦
⎡Tab ⇆⎦ Unlike Notepad, Write is a program. It is limited compared to many word processors, but its features are sufficient for many uses. For example, you can write memos and reports as well with this application as with many others. In fact, you can even illustrate Write documents by inserting graphics into them. ⎡Enter ⏎⎦
⎡Enter ⏎⎦
⎡Tab ⇆⎦ When you first open Write, the window is empty except for the movable insertion point, the movable mouse pointer, and the fixed end mark that indicates the end of the document. You can't move the insertion point until you type some text or open an existing document. ⎡Enter ⏎⎦

---

3. Move the insertion point to the appropriate place in the document and type the text shown underlined in this illustration. Notice how the existing text moves aside to make room for the inserted text.

Unlike Notepad, Write is a <u>true word processing</u> program. It is limited compared to many word processors <u>used in business,</u> but its features are sufficient for many uses. For example, you can write memos<u>, letters,</u> and reports as well with this application as with many others. In fact, you can even illustrate Write documents by inserting graphics into them.

---

4. Double-click each of the words shown underlined in this illustration to select them. Then pull down the **Edit** menu and click the **Cut** command to delete them.

When you first open Write, the window is empty except for the <u>movable</u> insertion point, the <u>movable</u> mouse pointer, and the <u>fixed</u> end mark that indicates the end of the document. You can't move the insertion point until you type some text or open an existing document.

---

5. Move the insertion point to the end of the word *some* in the phrase *until you type some text or open an existing document* at the end of the document, then press ⌫ Bksp to delete the word and the space that precedes it.

When you first open Write, the window is empty except for the insertion point, the mouse pointer, and the end mark that indicates the end of the document. You can't move the insertion point until you type some|text or open an existing document.

Position the insertion point here.

Joining and Separating Paragraphs

6. Move the insertion point to the end of the first body paragraph following the period at the end of the phrase *inserting graphics into them.*

Unlike Notepad, Write is a true word processing program. It is limited compared to many word processors used in business, but its features are sufficient for many uses. For example, you can write memos, letters, and reports as well with this application as with many others. In fact, you can even illustrate Write documents by inserting graphics into them.|

When you first open Write, the window is empty except for the insertion point, the mouse pointer, and the end mark that indicates the end of the document. You can't move the insertion point until you type some text or open an existing document.

Position the insertion point here.

---

7. Press Del three times to delete the invisible paragraph marks and the tab code so the two paragraphs are joined into one. Press Spacebar to separate the joined sentences with a space.

Unlike Notepad, Write is a true word processing program. It is limited compared to many word processors used in business, but its features are sufficient for many uses. For example, you can write memos, letters, and reports as well with this application as with many others. In fact, you can even illustrate Write documents by inserting graphics into them. When you first open Write, the window is empty except for the insertion point, the mouse pointer, and the end mark that indicates the end of the document. You can't move the insertion point until you type some text or open an existing document.

8. Place the insertion point just to the left of the *W* in the original second body paragraph.

Unlike Notepad, Write is a true word processing program. It is limited compared to many word processors used in business, but its features are sufficient for many uses. For example, you can write memos, letters, and reports as well with this application as with many others. In fact, you can even illustrate Write documents by inserting graphics into them. When you first open Write, the window is empty except for the insertion point, the mouse pointer, and the end mark that indicates the end of the document. You can't move the insertion point until you type some text or open an existing document.

Position the
insertion point here.

9. Press ⟨Enter ←⟩ twice to break the paragraph back into two paragraphs with a blank line between them. Then press ⟨Tab⇆⟩ to indent the second paragraph. The document should now look as it did before you joined the paragraphs.

Your name: your name
Filename: enterdoc.wri
Date: today's date

Unlike Notepad, Write is a true word processing program. It is limited compared to many word processors used in business, but its features are sufficient for many uses. For example, you can write memos, letters, and reports as well with this application as with many others. In fact, you can even illustrate Write documents by inserting graphics into them.

When you first open Write, the window is empty except for the insertion point, the mouse pointer, and the end mark that indicates the end of the document. You can't move the insertion point until you type some text or open an existing document.

Finishing Up

10. Print the document. If you proceeded here directly from the previous tutorial, reset the print range by clicking the **All** command button before you click the **OK** command button to begin printing.

11. Continue to the next section without clearing the document from the screen or quitting Windows.

SAVING DOCUMENTS

You save a Write file the same way you save a file in Notepad, by pulling down the **File** menu and clicking the **Save** command. The first time you save a document, you have to assign it a filename. When you save the file again, you needn't specify the name again unless you want to change it. In that case, you pull down the **File** menu, click the **Save As** command, enter a new filename in place of the old, and then click the **OK** command button.

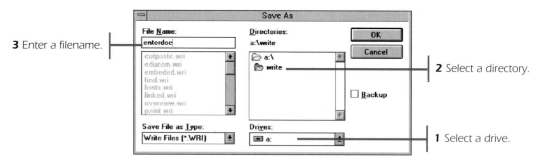

3 Enter a filename.

2 Select a directory.

1 Select a drive.

To save the file in a specific location, it may be necessary to change the drive and directory. You do this the same way in Write as in Notepad. If you don't remember how, review PicTorial 5 now.

If you enter a filename in the Save As dialog box that is the same as a filename already on the disk in the same directory, a warning dialog box is displayed giving you the option of canceling the command or overwriting the disk file with the document on the screen.

Write saves files with the extension *.wri*. With the default settings, resaving a file overwrites the old version. But you can save the old version with the extension *.bkp* by checking the **Backup** check box in the **Save As** command on the **File** menu. If you later need to open the backup copy, pull down the **File** menu and click the **Open** command to display the Open dialog box. Type the filename specification ***.bkp** into the **File Name** text box and press Enter ←. All files with the extension *.bkp* are shown in the list of files so you can select the one you want and click the **OK** command button to open it.

To clear a document from the screen so you can enter a new one, pull down the **File** menu and click the **New** command. If you do this without first saving changes to your existing document, a dialog box is displayed.

When you work on a document, Windows creates temporary files on the disk. When saving and retrieving files to a floppy disk, do not remove the disk from the drive until you have quit Write. If you do, you may see an error message telling you that there is a system error or that Write cannot find the file. If a message like this appears, reinsert the disk and click the **OK** command button. Then issue the **Save** command again.

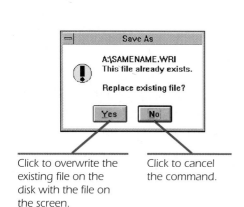

Click to overwrite the existing file on the disk with the file on the screen.

Click to cancel the command.

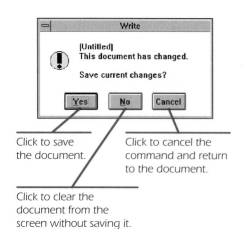

Click to save the document.

Click to cancel the command and return to the document.

Click to clear the document from the screen without saving it.

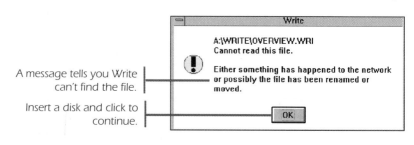

A message tells you Write can't find the file.

Insert a disk and click to continue.

►► TUTORIAL

1. With the document you typed in the previous tutorial still on your screen, insert your *Windows Student Resource Disk* into drive A.

2. Pull down the **File** menu and click the **Save** command to display the Save As dialog box. Make the following settings:

3 Enter the filename *enterdoc*

2 Set the directory to *write*.

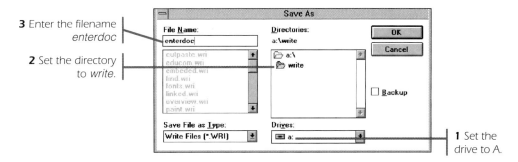

1 Set the drive to A.

   ► Select drive A.

   ► Select the write directory.

   ► Type the name **enterdoc** into the File Name text box.

3. Click the **OK** command button to save the document on your screen.

4. Pull down the **File** menu and click the **Save As** command to display the Save As dialog box again. The original drive and directory are still selected and the original filename is highlighted.

Previously entered name

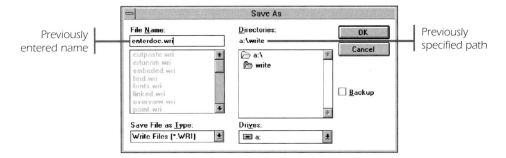

Previously specified path

5. Type **enter2** and press [Enter ←] to save the file under a new name. The new name is now displayed on the window's title bar.

6. Pull down the **File** menu and click the **New** command to clear the document from the Write document screen.

SELECTING TEXT AND CUTTING AND PASTING

When you want to rearrange text, you cut or copy it to the Clipboard and then paste it elsewhere in the document. When you *cut* a selected section of text, it is deleted from the document and moved to the Clipboard. When you *copy* it, the selected block remains in the document but a copy is stored on the Clipboard.

SELECTING TEXT

There are a number of ways to select text.

▶ To select a word, double-click it.

▶ To extend a selection to more whole words, drag the mouse in any direction after the second click without releasing the button.

▶ To select parts of words, point to the first character to be selected, hold down the left button, and drag the mouse to expand the highlight over adjacent text. When the text that you want to select is highlighted, release the left button and it remains highlighted.

▶ To select text with the keyboard, hold down ⇧Shift while you press the arrow keys.

The fastest way to select lines or paragraphs is to use the narrow, invisible strip just inside the left edge of the window called the *selection area*. When you point to this area, the mouse pointer turns into an inward pointing arrow.

With the mouse pointer in the selection area:

▶ To select a line, click once.

▶ To select a paragraph, double-click.

▶ To select the entire document, hold down Ctrl and click once.

After selecting text, you can continue to hold down the left button and drag the highlight over adjoining text.

To remove the highlight from selected text, click anywhere in the window.

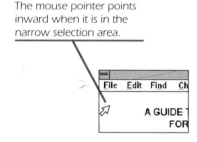

The mouse pointer points inward when it is in the narrow selection area.

TIP: SELECTING TEXT BETWEEN TWO POINTS

To select all text between two points, click at the beginning of the block, then hold down ⇧Shift when you click at the end. You can also first select a word, line, or paragraph. Then hold down ⇧Shift while you select a second word, line, or paragraph. Everything between the two points will be selected

COMMON WRONG TURNS: SELECTING PARAGRAPHS WITHOUT THEIR PARAGRAPH MARKS

If you fail to select the invisible paragraph mark at the end of a paragraph and then paste the data elsewhere in the document, it merges with an existing paragraph instead of being a new one. To be sure you select the invisible mark, double-click with the mouse pointer in the selection area. Or, when dragging the highlight to select text, drag it down to the beginning of the next line.

CUTTING AND PASTING

To cut and paste a section of text, you first select it and then pull down the **Edit** menu and click the **Cut** or **Copy** command. To paste the section in elsewhere, you move the insertion point there, pull down the **Edit** menu again, and click the **Paste** command.

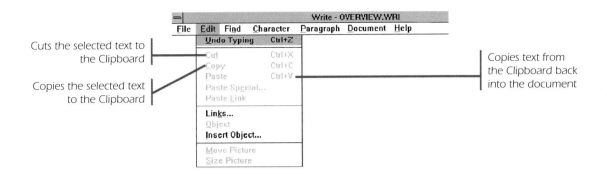

Cuts the selected text to the Clipboard

Copies the selected text to the Clipboard

Copies text from the Clipboard back into the document

COMMON WRONG TURNS: LOSING THE CLIPBOARD'S CONTENTS

The Clipboard retains data only until you cut or copy something else to it. Therefore, if you plan to paste data elsewhere in the document, do so before you use the **Cut** or **Copy** commands again.

▶▶ TUTORIAL

1. Open the *cutpaste.wri* document supplied on the *Windows Student Resource Disk* in the *write* directory. Then Maximize Write's window and enter your name and today's date in the document heading.

Moving a Phrase

2. Position the insertion point just to the left of the first *a* in the phrase *after selecting a block* on the first line of the body text. Hold down the left button and drag the mouse to the right to highlight up to and including the letter *k* just before the period at the end of the line. Release the mouse button, and the block remains highlighted.

The selected text

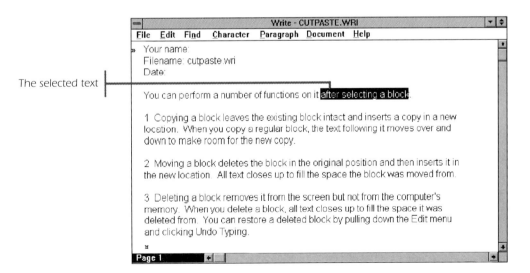

3. Pull down the **Edit** menu and click the **Cut** command to move the phrase from the document to the Clipboard.

4. Press [Home] to move the insertion point to the beginning of the line. Pull down the **Edit** menu and click the **Paste** command to copy the phrase back into the document from the Clipboard.

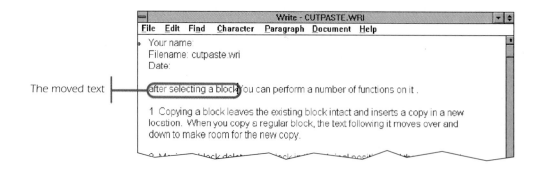

The moved text

5. Edit the sentence so that it reads *After selecting a block, you can perform a number of functions on it.*

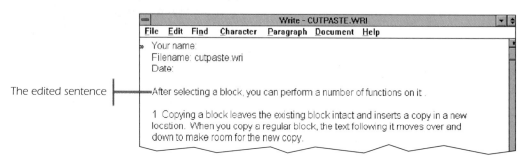

The edited sentence

Moving a Paragraph

6. Point to the selection area to the left of the number *1* in the first numbered paragraph. The insertion point turns into an inward pointing arrow.

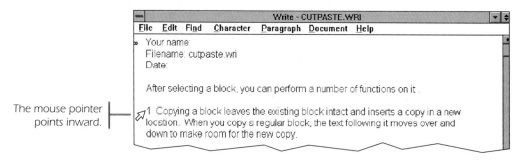

The mouse pointer points inward.

7. Double-click to select the entire paragraph.

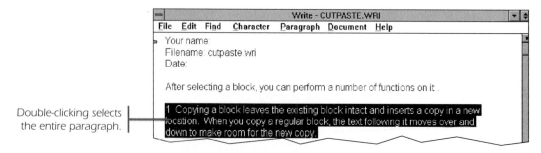

Double-clicking selects the entire paragraph.

8. Pull down the **Edit** menu and click the **Cut** command to move the paragraph from the document to the Clipboard.

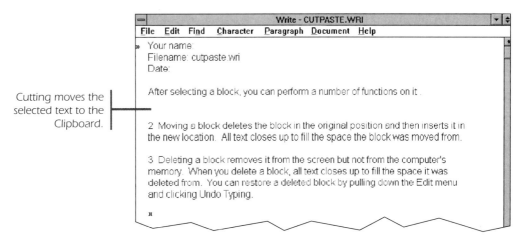

Cutting moves the selected text to the Clipboard.

9. Press ⌃Ctrl+End to move the insertion point to the end of the document.

10. Pull down the **Edit** menu and click the **Paste** command to copy the paragraph back into the document from the Clipboard.

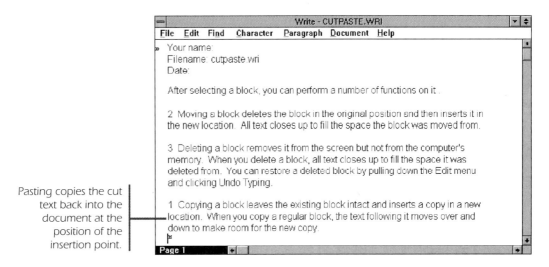

Pasting copies the cut text back into the document at the position of the insertion point.

Copying a Paragraph

11. Point to the selection area to the left of the number *2* in the paragraph with that number so the insertion point turns into an inward pointing arrow.

12. Double-click to select the entire paragraph.

13. Pull down the **Edit** menu and click the **Copy** command to copy the paragraph to the Clipboard.

14. Press ⌃Ctrl+End to move the insertion point to the end of the document and press Enter⏎ to insert a blank line.

15. Pull down the **Edit** menu and click the **Paste** command to paste a second copy of the paragraph into the document from the Clipboard.

Deleting and Undeleting a Paragraph

16. Point to the selection area to the left of the number *2* in the first paragraph with that number (you may have to press PgUp to see it) so the insertion point turns into an inward pointing arrow.

17. Double-click to select the entire paragraph.

18. Press Del to delete the paragraph.

19. Pull down the **Edit** menu and click the **Undo Editing** command to return the deleted paragraph to the document.

Finishing Up

20. Print the document.

21. Clear the document from the Write document screen without saving it.

> **PAUSING FOR PRACTICE**
>
> Open the *cutpaste.wri* document stored in the *write* directory and practice selecting text by clicking and double-clicking in the selection area and by dragging the highlight with the mouse. Practice copying and moving the three paragraphs and words or phrases within them. When you have finished, clear the document from the screen without saving it.

FINDING AND REPLACING TEXT

When you want to find text in a document or replace text with other text, you can do it automatically. When you use either of these procedures, Write begins at the insertion point and looks for matches toward the end of the document. When it reaches the end of the document, it returns to the beginning of the document and works its way back to the insertion point.

USING FIND

To find text, pull down the **Find** menu and click the **Find** command to display a dialog box. Enter the text you want to find in the **Find What** text box, and then click the **Find Next** command button to begin the search. If a match is found in the document, it is highlighted, but you may have to drag the Find dialog box out of the way so you can see it. When the text is highlighted, you have several options. You can click in the text area to edit the document without closing the dialog box, then continue to click the **Find Next** command button to find more occurrences. You can click the **Cancel** command button to close the dialog box and then press [F3] to repeat the last find command. Or you can pull down the **Find** menu again and click the **Repeat Last Find** command.

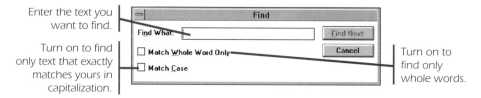

Enter the text you want to find.

Turn on to find only text that exactly matches yours in capitalization.

Turn on to find only whole words.

USING REPLACE

To replace text, you enter your find and replace text, and turn on or off the **Match Whole Word Only** and **Match Case** check boxes. You can then click any of the command buttons to begin the search. You can also click in the text area to edit the document without closing the dialog box.

When replacing text, Write will automatically preserve the case of replaced words. For example, if you search for the word *old* and replace it with the word *new*, the word *old* will be changed to *new*, *Old* to *New*, and *OLD* to *NEW*.

You can limit replace operations by selecting a part of the document before beginning the procedure. When you do so, clicking the **Replace Selection** command button (which appears in place of **Replace All** command button when you have selected text in the document) automatically replaces all text in a selected section of the document without prompting.

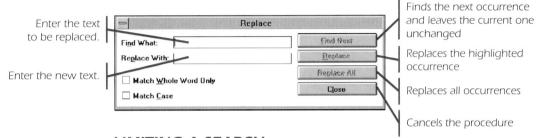

Enter the text to be replaced.

Enter the new text.

Finds the next occurrence and leaves the current one unchanged

Replaces the highlighted occurrence

Replaces all occurrences

Cancels the procedure

LIMITING A SEARCH

When searching for text, you can narrow the number of occurrences where a match is found.

▶ When you turn on the **Match Whole Word Only** check box, only words or phrases that are whole words will be found. For example, when it is on, searching for *Wind* or *Window* will not find *Windows*.

▶ When you turn on the **Match Case** check box, only words that exactly match your text in capitalization will be found. For example, when it is on, searching for *Mouse* will not find *mouse*.

TIP: STRINGS

The characters that you search for or replace are not always words or phrases. For example, you may search for initials. For this reason, many sources refer to these characters as *strings*. A string is simply a sequence of individual characters. Both *howdy* and *?*0-+* are strings.

▶▶ TUTORIAL

1. Open the *overview.wri* document supplied on the *Windows Student Resource Disk* in the *write* directory and maximize Write's window.

Finding All Occurrences

2. Pull down the **Find** menu and click the **Find** command to display the Find dialog box.

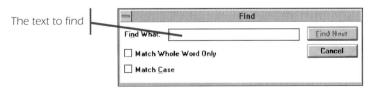

The text to find

3. Type **copy** into the **Find What** text box and click the **Find Next** command button. The first word containing *copy* is highlighted. (Drag the dialog box out of the way if you can't see the highlighted word.)

4. Continue clicking the **Find Next** command button to find additional words containing *copy*. Notice how words such as *copying* and *copyright* are highlighted because they also contain the characters *copy*. (If a dialog box appears telling you *Search operation complete*, click the **OK** command button.)

5. Click the **Cancel** command button to cancel the search operation.

Matching Whole Words Only

6. Press Ctrl+Home to move the insertion point to the top of the document.

7. Pull down the **Find** menu and click the **Find** command to display the Find dialog box. The previous entry is still in the **Find What** text box.

8. Click the **Match Whole Word Only** check box to turn it on.

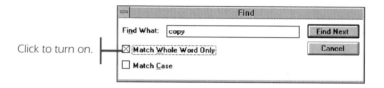

Click to turn on.

9. Click the **Find Next** command button, and the first occurrence of the word *copy* is highlighted.

10. Continue clicking the **Find Next** command button to find additional occurrences of *copy*. You are no longer finding the words *copying* and *copyright*, but you are still finding the word whether it's spelled *copy* or *Copy*. (If a dialog box appears telling you *Search operation complete*, click the **OK** command button.)

11. Click the **Cancel** command button to cancel the search operation.

Finding Just Occurrences with Matching Case

12. Press Ctrl+Home to move the insertion point to the top of the document.

13. Pull down the **Find** menu and click the **Find** command to display the Find dialog box.

14. Click the **Match Case** check box to turn it on.

Click to turn on.

15. Click the **Find Next** command button, and the first occurrence of the word *copy* is highlighted.

16. Continue clicking the **Find Next** command button to find more occurrences of the word *copy*. Notice how only words that exactly match yours are now found. The word *Copy* is no longer highlighted. (If a dialog box appears telling you *Search operation complete*, click the **OK** command button.)

17. Click the **Cancel** command button to cancel the search operation.

18. Press ⌈Ctrl⌉+⌈Home⌉ to move the insertion point to the top of the document.

19. Pull down the **Fi_n_d** menu and click the **R_e_place** command to display the Replace dialog box.

20. Type **developed** into the **Fi_n_d What** text box and **written** into the **Replace With** text box.

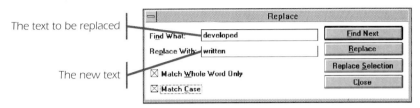

The text to be replaced

The new text

21. Click the **Find Next** command button, and the first occurrence of the word is highlighted.

22. Click the **R_e_place** command button to replace the word *developed* with the word *written*, and a dialog box informs you the search operation is complete.

23. Click the **OK** command button to return to the Replace dialog box, then click its **C_l_ose** command button.

Finishing Up

24. Clear the document from the Write document screen without saving it.

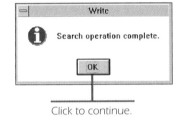

Click to continue.

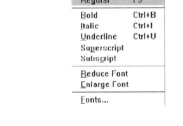

FORMATTING CHARACTERS

One of the reasons that Windows is so popular is that it has a WYSIWYG (pronounced "wizzy-wig") display. This acronym stands for "What you see is what you get," meaning that the screen display closely matches the final printout. This feature is especially obvious when you begin to change the look and size of type used in a document.

You format characters, words, phrases, or other selections with *character formats*. These formats affect only those characters selected at the time you execute the command or those that you enter at the point where you make a change. The character formats from which you can choose are listed on the **_C_haracter** menu.

The characters that appear on your screen and on your printouts are referred to as fonts. Write, like most other Windows applications, allows you to specify the fonts used in your documents. When you specify a font, you also specify a style and a size.

FONTS AND FONT STYLES

There are a wide variety of *fonts* available for use with Windows. Each has its own unique design. Some fonts, called TrueType fonts, are supplied with Windows, including Arial, Courier New, and Times New Roman; and many others may be added to a system. The fonts available to you depend on what printer has been selected. If you change the printer selection, you may see a different list of fonts when you format characters.

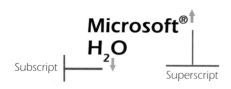

Arial 8 point
Arial 10 point
Arial 12 point
Arial 14 point
Arial 18 point
Arial 24 point

Microsoft®
H₂O

Subscript | Superscript

Some of these fonts are called *serif* and other *sans serif*. Serif fonts, such as Times New Roman, have small crossbars on their bases. Sans serif fonts, such as Arial, do not. In fact, *sans* is French for "without." *Font styles* supplied by Windows include regular, bold, italic, and bold italic.

FONT SIZES

Font sizes in Write can range from 4 to 127 points. A point is about $\frac{1}{72}$ of an inch, so 72-point type is 1 inch high, 36-point type is $\frac{1}{2}$ inch high, and 18-point type is $\frac{1}{4}$ inch high. Normally, body text in books, magazines, and newspapers will be 10 to 12 points in size.

SUPERSCRIPTS AND SUBSCRIPTS

In some cases, you may want to superscript or subscript characters. *Superscripted characters* print in a smaller size type raised above the line. *Subscripted characters* print in a smaller type sunk below the line.

FORMATTING AND UNFORMATTING CHARACTERS

To format any characters in the document, select them; then pull down the **Character** menu and click the **Fonts** command to display the Fonts Dialog box. There are three list boxes from which you can select a font, font style, and size. After selecting your choices, click the **OK** command button.

Select a font style. / Select a font.

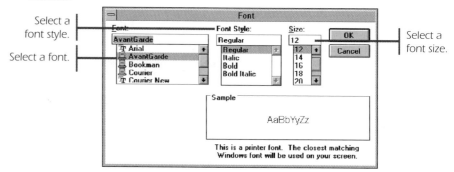

Select a font size.

To cancel a character style, select the formatted characters and pull down the **Character** menu again. Click the **Regular** command to cancel all character styles or click just one of the formats marked with a check mark to cancel that specific format.

▶▶ **TUTORIAL**

1. Open the *fonts.wri* document supplied on the *Windows Student Resource Disk* in the *write* directory.

Formatting with Font Styles

2. Select each of the lines under the *STYLES* heading one at a time, pull down the **Character** menu, and choose the matching style from the menu.

Formatting with Font Sizes

3. Selecting first the line *Reduce Font* and then the line *Enlarge Font*, pull down the **Character** menu and choose the matching style from the menu.

4. Select each of the lines listing a specific point size from 9 to 72

STYLES

Regular
Bold
Italic
<u>Underline</u>

points. Then pull down the **Character** menu and click the **Fonts** command to display the Fonts dialog box. Notice how there are three list boxes, one for the font, one for its style, and one for its size. A sample of text formatted with the current combination of these three settings is shown in the Sample box.

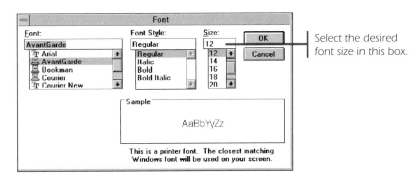

Select the desired font size in this box.

5. Select the size from the menu that matches the selected line (you can drag the dialog box out of the way if you can't see it), and click the **OK** command button to return to the document.

TIP: SLOW SYSTEM?

As you continue to format a document, you may begin to notice that your system slows down, especially when you scroll the screen. This is normal for all systems, although on more powerful systems the effect is less noticeable and less bothersome.

Arial
Arial Bold
Arial Bold Italic
Arial Italic
Courier New
Courier New Bold
Courier New Bold Italic
Courier New Italic
Times New Roman
Times New Roman Bold
Times New Roman Bold Italic
Times New Roman Italic

Formatting with Fonts

6. Point to the selection area to the left of the word *Arial* under the heading *Fonts*, and click to select the line.

7. Pull down the **Character** menu and click the **Fonts** command to display the Fonts dialog box.

8. Select the font and font style from the list boxes that match the selected line and click the **OK** command button to return to the document. (If the line doesn't specify a style, it's Regular.)

Finishing Up

9. Save the formatted document.

10. Print the document.

PAUSING FOR PRACTICE

Selecting and formatting are two basic skills. Point anywhere in the selection area so the insertion point turns into a inward facing arrow. Hold down [Ctrl] and click the mouse to select the entire document. Pull down the **Character** menu, select *Arial*, *Regular*, and *12*, then click the OK command button to reset all fonts back to regular. Now practice selecting and formatting them again. There is no need to save your work, so you can quit at any time.

FORMATTING PARAGRAPHS

Many formats, such as alignment and spacing, apply only to selected paragraphs. The commands you use to format paragraphs can be found on the **Paragraph** menu. However, the same commands can be executed by clicking icons on the Ruler if you display it.

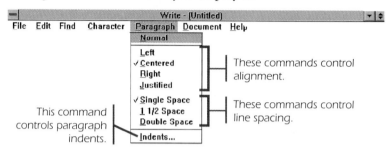

To change the alignment of a paragraph, position the insertion point in it before using these commands. To change more than one paragraph, select them. When you press [Enter ←] at the end of a paragraph to start a new paragraph, the new paragraph has the same formats as the one it was created from.

DISPLAYING THE RULER

The **Ruler On** command on the **Document** menu displays or hides Write's Ruler at the top of the document. The Ruler allows you to set tabs, space and align paragraphs, and set indents and margin settings by clicking icons and dragging markers.

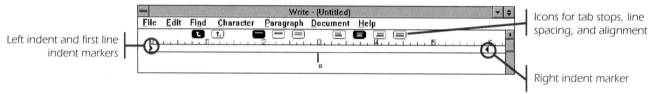

ALIGNING TEXT WITH MARGINS

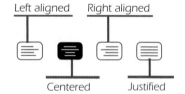

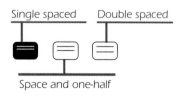

Paragraphs in a document can be aligned in any of four ways.

▶ Paragraphs can be aligned with the left margin or the right margin. When aligned in either of these ways, the other margin is uneven, or *ragged*.

▶ Paragraphs can be centered between the margins.

▶ Paragraphs can be justified. *Justified text* is aligned with both left and right margins. This alignment gives a very finished appearance to a document and is therefore often used in publications.

The commands you use to align paragraphs are located on the **Paragraph** menu. You can also display the Ruler and click icons to align selected text.

SPACING LINES OF TEXT

Text can be single-spaced, 1½-spaced, or double-spaced.

INDENTING PARAGRAPHS

To indent the first line of a paragraph, you just press [Tab ⇆]. However, there are other indents you can use.

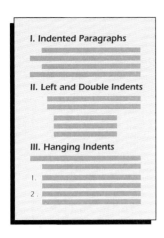

To indent a paragraph, you first move the cursor into it (or select a group of paragraphs), and then either use the **Indents** command on the **Paragraph** menu or drag markers on the Ruler.

Clicking the **Indents** command on the **Paragraph** menu displays an Indents dialog box into which you type indent settings.

▶ A paragraph with a *left indent* has all lines indented from the left margin by a specified amount.

▶ A paragraph with a *right indent* has all lines indented from the right margin by a specified amount.

▶ A paragraph with both a right and left indent has all lines indented from both margins by a specified amount.

▶ A paragraph with a *hanging indent* has the first line indented less than the other lines in the paragraph or not indented at all. To format a hanging indent, first specify the left indent distance and then enter a negative indent for the first line. For example, a left indent of 1 and a first line indent of –1 means the entire paragraph is indented 1 inch and then the first line is brought back 1 inch in the other direction. As a result, the first line isn't indented at all and is left hanging.

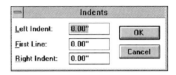

To use the Ruler to change indents, point to one of the indent markers, hold down the left mouse button, and drag the marker to a new position. At the left margin there are two indent markers—initially in the same position. The triangle controls the left paragraph indent, and the dot controls the first line indent.

To indent the entire paragraph (a left indent), drag both left indent markers to where you want the paragraph indented.

For a paragraph indent, position the triangle to the left of the dot.

For a hanging indent, position the dot to the left of the triangle.

For an enumerated list, arrange the indent markers as you would for a hanging indent but set a tab stop on the same position as the left indent marker to align the first line of text with the rest of the paragraph. (We will see how to set tabs later in this PicTorial.) Then when you type the list, press Tab⮐ after entering the period following each number.

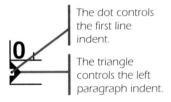

The dot controls the first line indent.

The triangle controls the left paragraph indent.

Left Indent

Left and first line indent markers indent the left side of the paragraph.

Paragraph Indent

Left paragraph indent marker

First line indent marker

The first line is indented.

Hanging Indent

Left paragraph indent marker

First line indent marker

The first line hangs to the left.

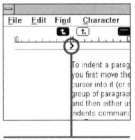

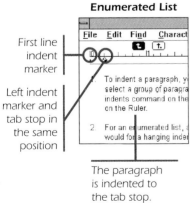

Enumerated List

First line indent marker

Left indent marker and tab stop in the same position

The paragraph is indented to the tab stop.

▶▶ TUTORIAL

1. Open the *paragrph.wri* document supplied on the *Windows Student Resource Disk* in the *write* directory.

2. Pull down the **Document** menu and click the **Ruler On** command to display the Ruler at the top of the document.

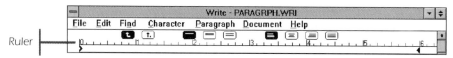

Ruler

Aligning Paragraphs with Margins

The highlighted icon indicates the paragraph's format.

3. Click anywhere in the paragraph below the heading *Left-Aligned Paragraph*. Notice how the left-align icon on the Ruler is highlighted to indicate the paragraph's alignment.

4. Click anywhere in the paragraph below the heading *Justified Paragraph*, then click the justified icon on the Ruler.

Click to justify the paragraph.

5. Click anywhere in the paragraph below the heading *Centered Paragraph*, then click the centered icon on the Ruler.

6. Click anywhere in the paragraph below the heading *Right-Aligned Paragraph*, then click the right-align icon on the Ruler.

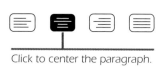

Click to center the paragraph.

Spacing Lines of Text in Paragraphs

7. Click anywhere in the paragraph below the heading *One-and-One-Half Spaced Paragraph*, then click the 1½-space icon on the Ruler.

Click to right-align the paragraph.

Click this icon for one-and-one-half spacing.

8. Click anywhere in the paragraph below the heading *Double-Spaced Paragraph*, then click the double-space icon on the Ruler.

Click this icon for double spacing.

Indenting Paragraphs

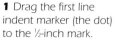

1 Drag the first line indent marker (the dot) to the ½-inch mark.

9. Move the insertion point to the beginning of the first paragraph below the heading *Indented Paragraph*, then press ⟨Tab⟩ to indent the first line.

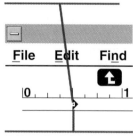

2 Drag the left indent marker to the ½-inch mark.

10. Click anywhere in the paragraph below the heading *Left-Indented Paragraph*, then drag first the first line indent marker (the dot) and then the left indent marker to the ½-inch mark on the Ruler.

11. Click anywhere in the paragraph below the heading *Double-Indented Paragraph*, then drag both left indent markers to the ½-inch mark on the Ruler. Drag the right indent marker to the 5½-inch mark on the Ruler.

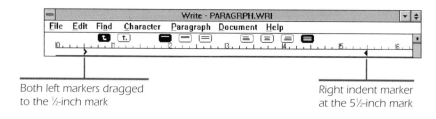

Both left markers dragged to the ½-inch mark

Right indent marker at the 5½-inch mark

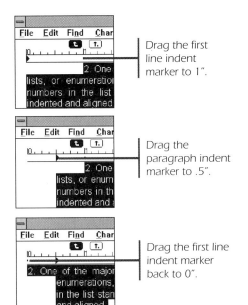

Indents paragraph .5"

Brings first line back to the left .5"

Drag the first line indent marker to 1".

Drag the paragraph indent marker to .5".

Drag the first line indent marker back to 0".

Creating Hanging Indents with the Menu

12. Click anywhere in the paragraph numbered *1* under the heading *Hanging-Indented Paragraph*.

13. Pull down the **Paragraph** menu and click the **Indents** command to display the Indents dialog box.

14. Enter .5 in the **Left Indent** text box and –.5 as the **First Line** text box, then click the **OK** command button.

15. Delete the space following the number *1.* at the beginning of the paragraph and press `Tab⇆` to align the paragraph following the number.

Creating Hanging Indents with the Markers on the Ruler Line

16. Select the paragraphs numbered *2* and *3* under the heading *Hanging-Indented Paragraphs*.

17. Drag the first line indent marker (the dot) to the 1-inch marker on the Ruler to get it out of your way for now.

18. Drag the triangular paragraph indent marker to the ½ inch mark on the Ruler.

19. Drag the first line indent marker (the dot) back to the *0* mark on the Ruler.

20. Delete the spaces following the numbers *2.* and *3.* at the beginning of the paragraphs and press `Tab⇆` to align the paragraphs following the numbers.

Finishing Up

21. Print the document.

22. Save the formatted document and then clear it from the Write document screen.

FORMATTING PAGES

Normally a document has no headers or footers, tabs are set every ½ inch, and margins are 1 inch top and bottom and 1.25 inches left and right. Commands to change these settings are located on the **Document** menu and affect the entire document.

ADDING HEADERS AND FOOTERS

Headers are lines of text that print at the top of pages and *footers* are lines of text that print at the bottom. Normally they print ¾-inch from the edge of the page and are left-aligned, but you can change these settings when you enter them.

When you choose the **Header** or **Footer** command from the **Document** menu, a Header or Footer text window and dialog box are displayed.

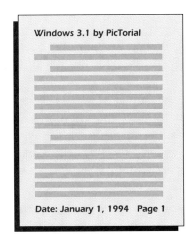

Windows 3.1 by PicTorial

Date: January 1, 1994   Page 1

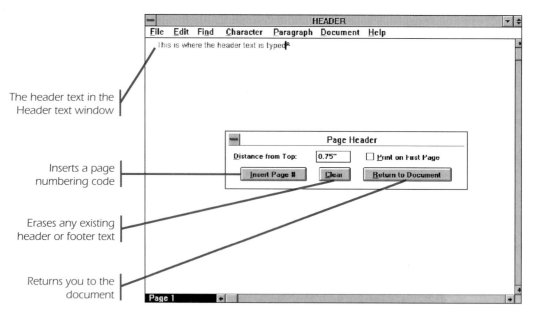

The header text in the Header text window

Inserts a page numbering code

Erases any existing header or footer text

Returns you to the document

The Header or Footer text window is where you enter, edit, or format the text that will print as the header or footer. You can use the commands listed on the **Character** and **Paragraph** menus to format and align text in this window just as you do in the normal document window.

The dialog box allows you to specify the distance between the header and footer and the top or bottom of the page. You can also click the **Print on First Page** check box if you want the header or footer to print on the first page or click it off if you don't.

The dialog box also has command buttons that you can click to insert a code to print page numbers in the header or footer, clear any text already entered in the header or footer window, or return to the document. You can click the **Insert Page** # command button at any point in the header or footer, and you can combine it with text. For example, if you type **Page** and then click it, the header or footer will print Page 1, Page 2, and so on.

SETTING TAB STOPS

Write has tab stops set every ½ inch even though they are not displayed on the Ruler. You can use these default settings, or you can change them by setting two kinds of tab stops; left-aligned and decimal.

▶ Left-aligned tab stops are normally used to align columns of text. When you press Tab↹ and type text, the text aligns flush left with the tab stop.

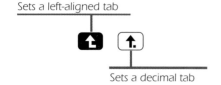

Sets a left-aligned tab

Sets a decimal tab

▶ Decimal tab stops are used to align columns of numbers containing decimal points. When you press Tab↹ to move the insertion point to one of these tab stops, characters you type align flush right with the stop until you type a decimal point. You can use this feature to right-align text with tab stops. Just enter it without typing a period, or make the period the last character.

You can set tabs by choosing the **Tabs** command on the **Document** menu or by displaying the Ruler and clicking where you want them.

▶ Clicking the **Tabs** command on the **Document** menu displays a Tabs dialog box into which you type tab settings. For decimal tabs you click the appropriate option box. To clear tabs, you click the **Clear All** command button.

▶ To use the Ruler to enter tab stops, first click one of the two tab icons and then click the Ruler where you want to insert the tab icon. You can also point to a tab symbol on the Ruler, hold down the left mouse button, and drag it to a new position. To delete a tab stop, drag it up or down off the Ruler and release the mouse button.

PAGE LAYOUT

When using Write, you can specify starting page numbers and change a document's margins. The dialog box into which you enter these changes is displayed when you choose the **Page Layout** command from the **Document** menu.

As you've seen, you enter page numbers using the **Header** or **Footer** commands on the **Document** menu. Once you have specified where they print, you can then change the number they start at. This is useful when your document is stored in more than one file. If pages 5 through 10 are in a separate file, you can change the starting page number for that document to 5. That way, the files will all be numbered sequentially when printed and assembled.

Margins are the white area on the page around the block where the text is printed. Normally, these are set to 1 inch at the top and bottom and 1.25 inches on the sides. You can change one or all of these margin settings. For example, you may want more room on the left edge so you can punch pages for a binder. Or you may want more room at the top for a header.

Specifies the beginning page number

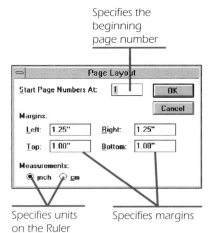

Specifies units on the Ruler

Specifies margins

▶▶ TUTORIAL

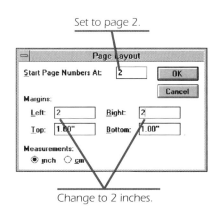

1. Open the *overview.wri* document supplied on the *Windows Student Resource Disk* in the *write* directory.

Specifying Page Numbers and Margins

2. Pull down the **Document** menu and click the **Page Layout** command to display the Page Layout dialog box. The number in the **Start Page Number At** box is highlighted. Make the following settings:

▶ Type **2** to change it from 1 to 2.

▶ Double-click the number in the Left margins box to select it, and then type **2** to change it.

▶ Double-click the number in the Right margins box to select it, and then type **2** to change it.

3. Click the **OK** command button to close the dialog box. The margins of the document change on the screen.

Adding a Footer

4. Pull down the **Document** menu and click the **Footer** command to display the Footer text window and dialog box.

Set to page 2.

Change to 2 inches.

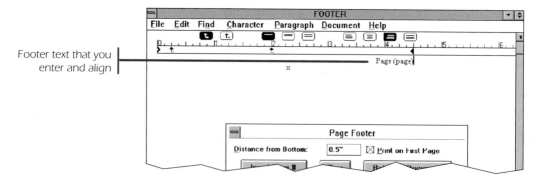

Footer text that you enter and align

5. Type **Page**, press [Spacebar], then click the **Insert Page #** command button to insert the page numbering code in the footer.

6. If the Ruler is still displayed, click the right-align icon, or pull down the **Paragraph** menu and click the **Right** command to right-align the footer.

7. Click the **Return to Document** command button to remove the dialog box.

Adding a Header

8. Pull down the **Document** menu and click the **Header** command to display the Header text window and dialog box.

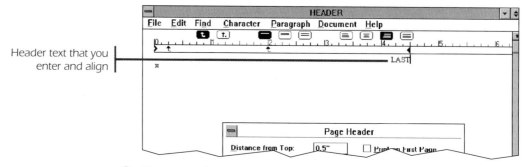

Header text that you enter and align

9. Type your last name in all uppercase letters.

10. If the Ruler is still displayed, click the right-align icon; otherwise, pull down the **Paragraph** menu and click the **Right** command to right-align the header.

11. Click the **Return to Document** command button to remove the dialog box.

Finishing Up

12. Print the document and notice the following about the printout:

▶ The left and right margins are now 2 inches instead of 1.25 inches.

▶ The headers and footers print at the top and bottom of the page.

▶ The original page numbers at the bottom center of the page are turned off, and each page is now numbered in the footer.

13. Save the revised document and clear the document from the screen.

PAUSING FOR PRACTICE

Using the Ruler to change indents and set tab stops is a common feature on many Windows word processing applications. Since it such a superior way to enter these formats, pause here to practice the procedures until they fell comfortable to you. Try different combinations of indents and different tab stop settings. You can reset margins, indents, and tabs at any point by just clearing the screen.

▶▶ SKILL-BUILDING EXERCISES

Exercise 1. Retrieving Documents with Write

Windows supplies a number of files with the extension *.wri* that you can open with Write. For example, there are *readme.wri*, *printers.wri*, *networks.wri*, *sysini.wri*, and *winini.wri*. These files are normally stored in the *Windows* directory (usually on drive C). Open some of these files with Write and make a printout of at least one of them.

Exercise 2. Sending a Letter

1. Using Write, enter and edit the letter home asking for money. Fill in the customized information in places where it is indicated. (If you have kids yourself, enter the letter anyway. It will prepare you for the devious ways of younger students.)

2. Save the document in the *write* directory as *ltrhome.wri* and print it.

3. Proofread the printout and correct the document if necessary. If you make any changes, print it again.

4. Save the edited document.

Jobs List
a. sewer cleaner
b. dog catcher's assistant
c. blast furnace operator in the steel mill
d. dynamite detonator in the local coal mine

Seminars List
a. space science
b. nuclear physics
c. computer programming
d. environmental studies

Professions List
a. lawyer
b. business executive
c. doctor
d. teacher

Date

Dear Mom and Dad,

This year is progressing extremely well and I'm working harder than ever (really!). All I do is work, but it's paying off. For example, I've written this letter on a state-of-the-art (*enter the name of your computer*) using (*enter the name of your word processing application*). I have mastered word processing in half the time it has taken the others in the class. The only glitch is that I'm out of money. To raise the lousy (*fill in the amount needed—make it big!*) I need, I am considering taking a job as a (*choose a job from the Jobs List*).

I realize that this will detract from my studies and jeopardize the thousands you have already invested in my education, but I have no other choice. I have overspent on textbooks, reference books, seminars on (*choose a seminar from the Seminars List*), computer supplies, and other things needed to ensure the quality of my education. I guess working as a (*enter the job you used above*) for a few months is a small price to pay. Although it will result in my being less well educated, it at least makes it possible to muddle through. Your dreams of my becoming a (*choose a profession from the Professions List or use your own*) will probably not now be fulfilled, but there are plenty of lower paying and less fulfilling jobs that I will be qualified for.

Sorry to share my minor problem with you, but other than this, everything is going VERY well! Don't worry about me; be happy.

Love,

Symbol Format

```
1234567890 -
~!≅#≡%⊥&*() ┐
θωεΡΤψυιοπ[].
θ⌂ΩΣΕΡΤΨΥΙΟΠ}{
αοδφγηφκλϑ
ΑΣΔΦΓΗϑΚΛ:∀
ζξϖϱνμ,./
ΖΞΧ¢ΒΝΜ<>?
```

Wingdings Format

(Wingdings symbol characters)

To enter	Hold down [Alt] and type
£	0163
¥	0165
©	0169
®	0174
±	0177
¶	0182
¼	0188
½	0189
¾	0190

1. $^{1}/_{2}$
2. Trademark^{TM}
3. Registered$^{®}$
4. $30^{O}F$
5. H_2O
6. $1 - ^{3}/_{4} = ^{1}/_{4}$

Exercise 3. Using Special Characters

1. Open the *special.wri* document supplied on the *Windows Student Resource Disk* in the *write* directory and enter your name and today's date.

2. Format all characters under the *Symbol Format* heading with the Symbol font.

3. Format all characters under the *Wingdings Format* heading with the Wingdings font.

4. Save and print the document.

5. Change the size of the characters in the Wingdings section to 14 points and print the document again.

6. Clear the document from the Write document screen without saving it again.

Exercise 4. Entering Special Characters

Occasionally, you may want to use special characters that do not appear on the keyboard. You can enter a character and format it with the Symbol and Wingding fonts supplied with Windows. The regular text fonts also have special characters available that you can use by holding down [Alt] and typing their codes on the numeric keypad.

1. Open a new document.

2. Press [NumLock] if necessary to engage the numeric keypad.

3. Hold down [Alt] and type the codes shown at the left on the numeric keypad to enter special characters. Some of the most commonly used special characters are listed here along with the codes that you type to enter them into a document.

4. Save the document as *special2.wri* and make a printout. Then clear the screen.

Exercise 5. Using Subscripts and Superscripts

1. Open the *scripts.wri* document supplied on the *Windows Student Resource Disk* in the *write* directory.

2. Format it using superscripts and subscripts so it looks like the illustration at the left.

3. Save the formatted document and make a printout. Then clear the screen.

Exercise 6. Exploring Find and Replace

1. Open the *find.wri* document supplied on the *Windows Student Resource Disk* in the *write* directory.

2. Explore using wildcards and special codes in either the **Find What** or **Replace What** text boxes. For example, you could enter **h?t** to find *hat, hot, hut,* and *hit.* You could enter **h??t** to find *hoot, hurt,* and *hunt.* When you want to find formatting in a document, you can use special codes. For example, to find tabs, enter **^t** (the ^ character is a caret and is on the keyboard, usually on the ⑥ key); to find paragraph marks, enter **^p**; and to find spaces, enter **^w**.

To Find or Replace With	Enter
Any single character	?
Spaces entered by pressing [Spacebar]	^w
Tab codes entered by pressing [Tab⇆]	^t
Paragraph marks entered by pressing [Enter←]	^p
Manual page breaks entered by pressing [Ctrl]+[Enter←]	^d

3. If you replaced any codes, print the document. Clear the screen without saving the document.

PicTorial 6 ▶ VISualQuiz

1. This illustration shows four of the elements you always see when working with the Write application. Label each part in the spaces provided.

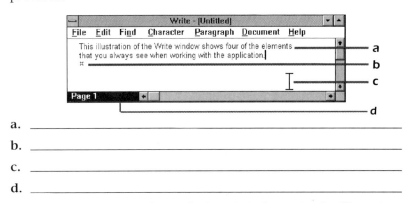

a. _____

b. _____

c. _____

d. _____

2. If the insertion point is located where it is shown in the illustraion, where does it move when each of the following keys or key combinations is pressed? Enter the proper letter in the blank.

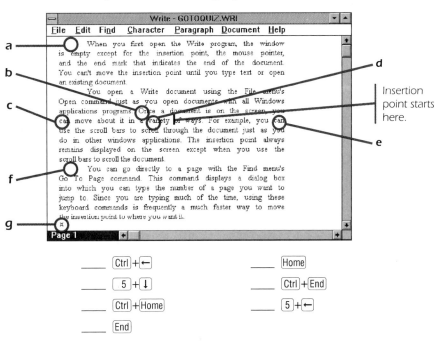

_____ [Ctrl]+[←]   _____ [Home]

_____ [5]+[↓]   _____ [Ctrl]+[End]

_____ [Ctrl]+[Home]   _____ [5]+[←]

_____ [End]

3. This figure shows two page breaks. Identify each type and briefly describe how each is entered.

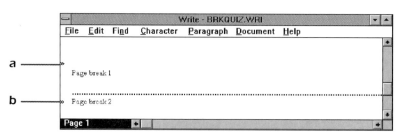

a. _____

b. _____

4. When the mouse pointer takes on the shape shown here, describe what happens when you point anywhere in the document and then:

a. Click _____

b. Double-click _____

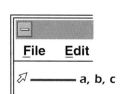

5. When the mouse pointer takes on the shape show here, describe what happens when its pointing to a paragraph and you then:

a. Click _____

b. Double-click _____

c. Hold down [Ctrl] and click _____

6. One of the items labeled in the illustration at the left is a widow and one is an orphan. Identify which is which and describe each.

a. _____

b. _____

7. List the steps you would follow to join these two paragraphs into one.

> Unlike Notepad, Write is a true word processing program. It is limited compared to many word processors used in business, but its features are sufficient for many uses. For example, you can write memos, letters, and reports as well with this application as with many others. In fact, you can even illustrate Write documents by inserting graphics into them.
>
> When you first open Write, the window is empty except for the insertion point, the mouse pointer, and the end mark that indicates the end of the document. You can't move the insertion point until you type some text or open an existing document.

a. Move the insertion point to _____

b. Press _____ _____ times to _____

c. Press _____ if necessary to _____

8. When trying to find the word shown here, indicate which words will be found when each of the check boxes is on by itself and then when both are on:

(1) case (2) Case (3) CASE (4) cased (5) Cased (6) CASED

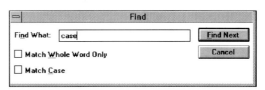

a. **Match Whole Word Only** on _____

b. **Match Case** on _____

c. Both on _____

9. What is the name of this screen element?

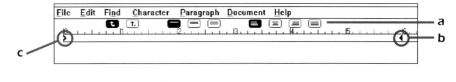

Describe how you display it. _____

_____

Identify each of the labeled items.

a. _____

b. _____

c. _____

10. Describe what happens to the paragraph containing the insertion point when you click each of these icons.

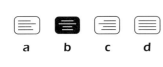

a. _____

b. _____

c. _____

d. _____

11. Describe what happens to the paragraph containing the insertion point when you click each of these icons.

a. _____

b. _____

c. _____

12. This illustration shows three paragraphs each indented in a different way.

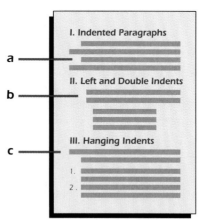

These illustrations show how the left paragraph indent marker and the first line indent marker appear for each of the three paragraphs. Write in, in the space provided, the letter of the paragraph that you think is formatted with each of the settings.

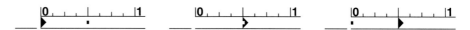

13. This figure shows two tab stop icons. Identify each type and briefly describe how text or numbers align with each.

a. _____

b. _____

PicTorial 7

WORKING WITH PAINTBRUSH AND MULTIPLE APPLICATIONS

After completing this topic, you will be able to:

▶ Load Paintbrush and describe its window and tools

▶ Open, view, and print Paintbrush documents

▶ Save Paintbrush documents and clear the screen

▶ Create your own Paintbrush drawings

▶ Switch between open applications

▶ Copy or move data between applications

▶ Link or embed data from one application into another

▶ Open files stored on the disk in other formats

Windows lets you keep two or more applications open at the same time and move data from one to the other through the Clipboard. It also lets you link or embed an object created in one application into a document created in another. Paintbrush, the Windows application used for creating graphics, can also serve as an introduction to linking and embedding.

UNDERSTANDING THE PAINTBRUSH WINDOW

When you load Paintbrush, the window displays a drawing area, a Toolbox, a Linesize box, and a Palette.

▶ The *drawing area* is where you create or edit a drawing using the tools in the Toolbox.

▶ The *Toolbox* contains a number of tools you can use to create or edit drawings. To select a tool, you click its icon. The mouse pointer (called a *cursor* in Paintbrush) changes in the drawing area when you change the tool. In the drawing area it always indicates where an action will begin.

▶ The *Linesize box* controls the width of lines drawn with some of the tools.

▶ The *Palette* selects the color and pattern to be used when drawing with some of the tools. The currently selected foreground and background colors are displayed in the leftmost box in the Palette—called the *Selected Colors box*.

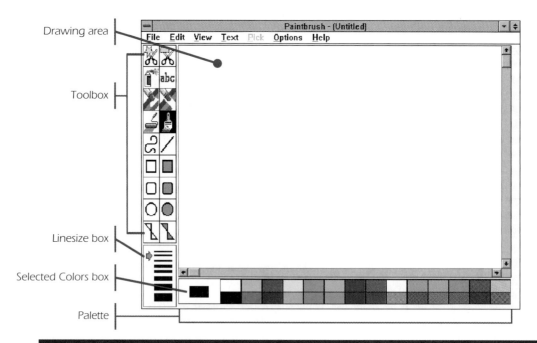

Drawing area

Toolbox

Linesize box

Selected Colors box

Palette

▶▶ TUTORIAL

1. Open the Accessories group and double-click the Paintbrush icon to open the application.

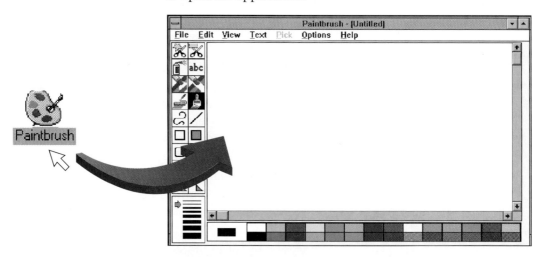

Paintbrush

2. Look carefully at the screen and locate the drawing area, the Toolbox, the Palette, and the Linesize box.

3. Move the cursor around the screen and see how it changes from an arrow outside of the drawing area into a tool inside. When first loaded, the cursor is a small square dot that represents the Brush tool.

OPENING, VIEWING, AND PRINTING DOCUMENTS

You open a Paintbrush document just like all other Windows documents. You pull down the **File** menu, click the **Open** command, and then use the Open dialog box to load the desired document.

Once a Paintbrush document is displayed on the screen, you can zoom in and out or display it using the full screen.

▶ To zoom in, pull down the **View** menu and click the **Zoom In** command. This displays a small rectangular outline on the screen that indicates the size of the area you can zoom into. Point the outline to the area you want to enlarge, and click.

▶ To zoom out, you must first have zoomed in. To zoom out, you pull down the **View** menu and click the **Zoom Out** command.

▶ To display a picture at full screen, pull down the **View** menu and click the **View Picture** command. To return to the normal view, click anywhere in the picture.

You print a Paintbrush document just like all other Windows documents. Pull down the **File** menu and click the **Print** command. This displays the Print dialog box, where you can specify the quality of the printout, the part to be printed, the number of copies, and scaling.

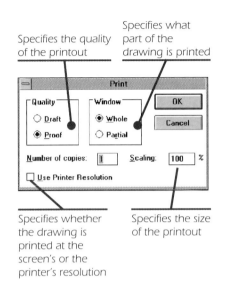

Specifies the quality of the printout

Specifies what part of the drawing is printed

Specifies whether the drawing is printed at the screen's or the printer's resolution

Specifies the size of the printout

▶ To specify the print quality, click one of the option buttons in the Quality box. On many printers, proof quality will be higher than draft quality but it will take longer to print. (On other printers, including laser printers, there is no difference.) The quality of a printout is determined by its *resolution*, the number of dots printed per inch. Normally, documents are printed at screen resolution, but your printer may have a higher resolution than the screen. If it does, you may get better results if you turn on the **Use Printer Resolution** check box. On some printers, turning on this box produces a tiny picture.

▶ To print just a part of the drawing, turn on the **Partial** option button. Click the **OK** command button, and the entire drawing is displayed on the screen. Then point to one corner of the area you want to print, hold down the left button, and drag an outline over the area to be printed. When you release the button, only the area you selected is printed.

▶ To print the drawing smaller or larger, change the number in the **Scaling** box. Enter 50 to print it at half size or 200 to print it at double size.

To add headers or footers or change the margins for your printout, pull down the **File** menu and click the **Page Setup** command to display a dialog box. To add a header or footer, type it into the appropriate text box. To change margins, enter new settings in the margin boxes.

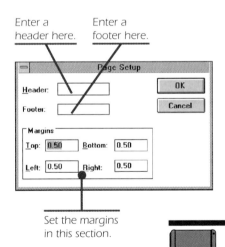

Enter a header here.

Enter a footer here.

Set the margins in this section.

▶▶ **TUTORIAL**

Getting Ready

1. Insert the *Windows Student Resource Disk* into drive A.

Opening a Document

2. Pull down Paintbrush's **File** menu and click the **Open** command to display the Open dialog box.

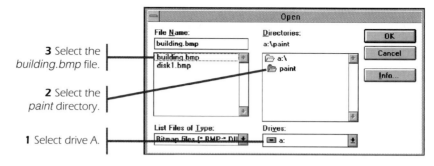

3 Select the *building.bmp* file.

2 Select the *paint* directory.

1 Select drive A.

▶ Select drive A.

▶ Select the *paint* directory.

▶ Click the file named *building.bmp* to select it.

3. Click the **OK** command button to open the document. This illustration actually started out as a photograph and was converted on the computer to the drawing you see here.

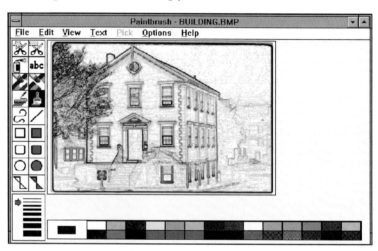

Zooming the Painting

4. Pull down the **View** menu and click the **Zoom In** command to display a rectangular outline on the screen. This outline defines the area that will be zoomed to fill the screen.

5. Practice moving the outline around the drawing area with the mouse and then position it around the cornice over the front door in the drawing.

6. Click the mouse, and the area within the outline is zoomed so that you can see the individual square pixels (picture elements) that make up the drawing. A broader view of the enlarged area is shown in the upper-left corner so you can tell where you are in the drawing.

Position the outline over the cornice.

The larger view helps you stay oriented.

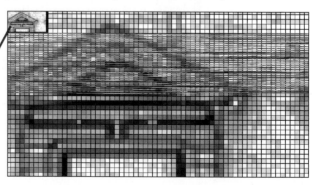

7. Pull down the **View** menu and click the **Zoom Out** command to return to the normal view.

8. Pull down the **View** menu and click the **View Picture** command to display the picture at full screen.

9. Click anywhere to return to the normal view.

Adding your Name

10. Click the Text tool (labeled *abc*) in the Toolbox to select it.

Click the Text tool to select it.

11. Click in the blank area of the upper-right corner of the screen to position the cursor in the drawing, then type your name. Leave the cursor where it is when you finish typing.

12. Pull down the **Text** menu and click the **Italic** command to italicize your name. (This works only if you haven't moved the cursor on the screen.)

Printing the Drawing

13. Pull down the **File** menu and click the **Print** command to display the Print dialog box.

14. Click the **Draft** option button in the Quality box to turn on draft printing, then click the **OK** command button to begin.

15. Some printers support only one print setting. To see whether your printer supports more than one setting, repeat Steps 13 and 14 but this time click the **Proof** option button in the Quality box before printing the document. If your printer supports two settings, the printout will be much sharper and more detailed but will take longer to print.

Finishing Up

16. Continue to the next section without clearing the document from the screen or quitting Paintbrush.

Click here and then type your name.

Your Name

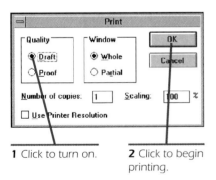

1 Click to turn on.   2 Click to begin printing.

SAVING DOCUMENTS AND CLEARING THE SCREEN

You save Paintbrush documents the same way you save all other Windows documents. Pull down the **File** menu and click the **Save** command to display the Save As dialog box. After entering a name and specifying a drive, click the **OK** command button. When you resave the same document, no dialog box is displayed. To save the file under a new name or to a new drive, use the **Save As** command on the **File** menu.

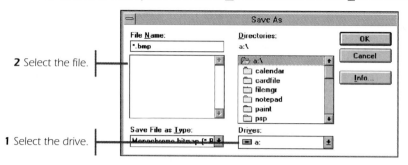

2 Select the file.

1 Select the drive.

To clear the screen to begin a new drawing, pull down the **File** menu and Click the **New** command. If you haven't saved your work, a dialog box is displayed offering you the chance to do so before clearing it from the screen.

 ▶▶ **TUTORIAL**

1. Pull down the **File** menu and click the **Save** command. Since you opened the document from the disk, it is saved without a dialog box being displayed.

2. Pull down the **File** menu and click the **New** command to clear the screen.

CREATING DRAWINGS

To create a drawing, you begin by performing three simple steps: selecting the colors to be used, selecting the width of the lines, and selecting a tool.

Three sets of drawing tools are displayed on the screen. They include the Toolbox, the Palette, and the Linesize box. These tools can be hidden (or turned back on) using the **Tools and Linesize** and **Palette** commands on the **View** menu.

UNDOING CHANGES

When working on a drawing, it is very easy to make a mistake. For this reason you should concentrate on what you are doing. If you notice a mistake immediately, pull down the **Edit** menu and click the **Undo** command. If you complete another procedure before undoing a mistake, it may be too late.

SELECTING COLORS

The Palette specifies the foreground and background colors that appear when you use the drawing tools. The currently selected colors are shown in the Selected Colors box at the left end of the Palette. When you first load Paintbrush, the foreground color is black and the background color is white. To change these colors, you use both the right and left mouse buttons.

Selected Colors box

Foreground color

Background color

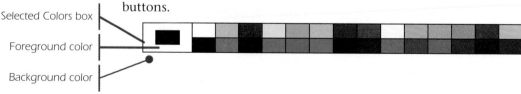

- To select a new foreground color, point to it on the Palette and click the left button.

- To select a new background color, point to it on the Palette and click the right button.

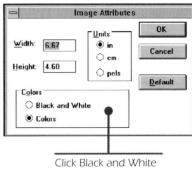

Click Black and White or Colors to turn it on.

Keep in mind that colors look great on the screen but that most printers don't print colors. To get a better approximation on the screen of what your document will look like when printed, use the black and white Palette. You can switch between color and black and white using the **Image Attributes** command on the **Options** menu.

You can adjust any color on the Palette by double-clicking it to display a dialog box with scroll bars for the red, green, and blue components.

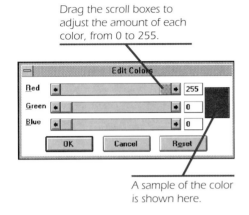

Drag the scroll boxes to adjust the amount of each color, from 0 to 255.

A sample of the color is shown here.

SELECTING LINE WIDTHS

The *Linesize box* is used to specify drawing widths when using the Curve, Line, and Box tools. The currently selected width is indicated with an arrow. To change sizes, click a new width. The thinnest line is one pel (one pixel or picture element) wide.

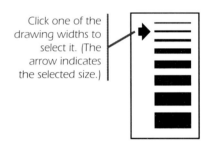

Click one of the drawing widths to select it. (The arrow indicates the selected size.)

SELECTING TOOLS

Normally, the *Toolbox* is displayed at the left side of the Paintbrush screen. Outside the drawing area, the cursor (mouse pointer) always appears as an open arrow. Inside the drawing area, it takes different shapes depending on which tool and which drawing width are selected. recall that when you first open Paintbrush, the Brush tool is selected and the cursor is a small square dot in the drawing area. To select another tool, click its icon. The currently selected tool is shown in reverse video. The color of what you draw is governed by the colors you have selected from the Palette.

Paintbrush has 18 tools. This may seem like a lot to learn, but many of the tools work the same way:

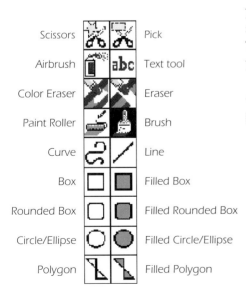

Scissors   Pick
Airbrush   Text tool
Color Eraser   Eraser
Paint Roller   Brush
Curve   Line
Box   Filled Box
Rounded Box   Filled Rounded Box
Circle/Ellipse   Filled Circle/Ellipse
Polygon   Filled Polygon

- *Scissors* draws a freehand line around any object when you hold down the left button and drag the mouse. When you release the button, the line remains. You can pull down the **Edit** menu and click the **Cut** or **Copy** command to move the data to the Clipboard so you can paste it elsewhere in the drawing. You can also click the **Copy To** command to copy it to a file of its own.

  When you pull down the **Edit** menu and click the **Paste** command, the cut section appears in the upper-left corner of the screen, and the Pick tool is automatically selected. To paste it, drag it to where you want it positioned, and then click anywhere but in the pasted section.

- *Pick* is just like Scissors, but it draws a rectangle around any object.

- *Airbrush* sprays the drawing with a circular spray of dots of the foreground color when you hold down the left button and drag the cursor. The speed at which you drag the circle determines the density of the spray. To change the diameter of the spraying circle, click a different drawing width in the Linesize box.

- *Text tool* enters text in the drawing area. After selecting this tool, click in the drawing area to place the insertion point. Then type the text. Before you type, or before you 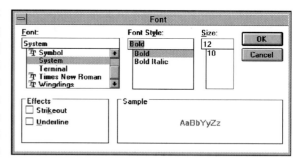 click another tool, you can pull down the **Text** menu and select a type style such as bold, italic, underline, outline, or shadow. (All don't work on every printer.) Or you can click the **Fonts** command on the same menu and specify a font the same way you do in Write. If you make a mistake, correct it with (←Bksp) while you are typing. Once you finish typing and go to another procedure, you won't be able to edit the text. You will have to cut it and start over.

- *Color Eraser* changes a color in the drawing to any other color selected from the Palette. To use this command:

  1. Select the foreground color—the color in the drawing that you want to change. To do so, point to the desired color on the Palette and click the left button.

  2. Select the background color—the color in the drawing that you want to change to. To do so, point to the desired color on the Palette and click the right button.

  3. Click the Color Eraser tool and drag it over the drawing, and the selected foreground color changes to the selected background color. To change the size of the area affected, click a new drawing width in the Linesize box. To restrain the tool to only vertical and horizontal movements, hold down (⇧Shift) while you drag it. You can change all occurrences of the color throughout the drawing by double-clicking the Color Eraser tool.

- *Eraser* changes all colors that it is dragged over to the selected background color. Otherwise it works like the Color Eraser tool.

- *Paint Roller* fills any space enclosed by a border with the selected foreground color. If the border is not closed, the color "leaks through" into the surrounding area or whole screen. You can undo the mistake with the **Undo** command on the **Edit** menu.

- *Brush* draws freehand shapes using the selected foreground color and drawing width. To restrain the Brush to only vertical and horizontal movements, hold down (⇧Shift) while you drag the tool. You can also change the shape of the Brush using the **Brush Shapes** command on the **Options** menu or by double-clicking the Brush tool.

To position a perfect circle accurately with the Circle/Ellipse tool:

Point here to begin and hold down the left mouse button.

Hold down ⇧ Shift and drag the cursor to expand the circle.

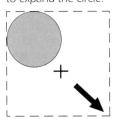

Release the button when the circle fills the imaginary square.

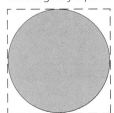

▶ *Curve* draws curves. Point to where you want a curved line to begin, hold down the left button, and drag the cursor to where you want the line to end. Release the button, and a straight line is displayed on the screen. Hold down the left button again, move the mouse to pull the line in the direction the mouse moves, then release the button. To curve the line in the other direction, hold down the mouse button again and drag the line. Release the button when finished.

▶ *Line* draws a line in the selected foreground color and width. Position the cursor where you want the line to start, hold down the left button, and drag the mouse to draw a line. You can move the free end of the line about until you release the mouse button. To restrain the line to only vertical, horizontal, and 45-degree movements, hold down ⇧ Shift while you drag the tool.

▶ *Box* draws a hollow rectangle using the selected foreground color. To draw a perfect square, hold down ⇧ Shift while you drag the tool.

▶ *Filled Box* draws a box bordered by the selected background color and filled by the selected foreground color.

▶ *Rounded Box* is like Box, but its corners are rounded.

▶ *Filled Rounded Box* is like Filled Box, but its corners are rounded.

▶ *Circle/Ellipse* is like Box, but the shape is a circle. To draw a perfect circle, hold down ⇧ Shift while you drag the tool. To position a circle accurately, point to the upper-left corner of an imaginary box that would contain it, and then drag down and to the right.

▶ *Filled Circle/Ellipse* is like Filled Box, but the shape is a circle.

▶ *Polygon* draws polygons of the selected foreground color. Point to where you want the line to begin, and hold down the left button. Drag the tool to where the first line should end, and click to anchor the point. Repeat dragging and clicking until all line segments except the last are completed, then double-click to close the polygon.

▶ *Filled Polygon* is like Polygon, but the shape is filled with the selected foreground color.

▶▶ TUTORIAL

Drawing Shapes

1. Click the Box tool to select it. Then point anywhere in the drawing area, hold down the left button, and drag the mouse to draw a box. When it's the size you want, release the mouse button.

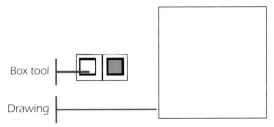

Box tool

Drawing

2. Click a thicker drawing width in the Linesize box to select it. Then point anywhere in the drawing area, hold down the left button, and drag the mouse to draw a box. When it's the size you want, release the mouse button.

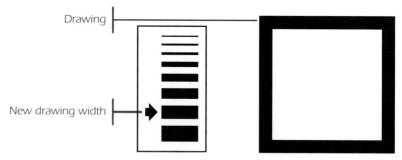

Drawing

New drawing width

3. Click the thinnest drawing width and then the Filled Box tool to select them. Then point anywhere in the drawing area and hold down ⟨⇧ Shift⟩ and the left button while you drag the mouse to draw a perfect square. When it's the size you want, release first the mouse button and then ⟨⇧ Shift⟩.

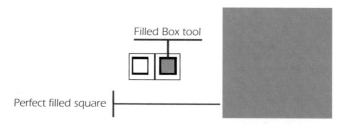

Filled Box tool

Perfect filled square

4. Double-click the Eraser tool to clear the screen. When a dialog box asks if you want to save current changes, click the **No** command button.

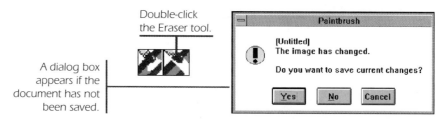

Double-click the Eraser tool.

A dialog box appears if the document has not been saved.

Paintbrush

[Untitled]
The image has changed.

Do you want to save current changes?

Yes   No   Cancel

5. Click the Rounded Box tool to select it. Then point anywhere in the drawing area, hold down the left button, and drag the mouse to draw a box with rounded corners. When it's the size you want, release the mouse button.

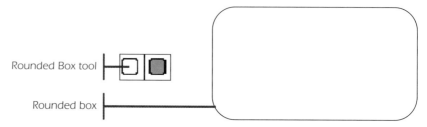

Rounded Box tool

Rounded box

6. Click the Filled Rounded Box tool to select it. Then point anywhere in the drawing area, hold down ⟨⇧ Shift⟩ and the left button, and drag the mouse to draw a perfect square. When it's the size you want, release first the mouse button and then [⇧ Shift].

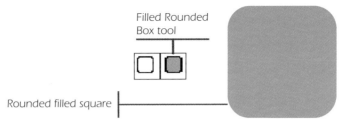

Filled Rounded Box tool

Rounded filled square

7. Double-click the Eraser tool to clear the screen. When a dialog box asks if you want to save current changes, click the **No** command button.

8. Click the Circle/Ellipse tool to select it. Then point anywhere in the drawing area, hold down the left button, and drag the mouse to draw a circle or ellipse. When it's the size you want, release the mouse button.

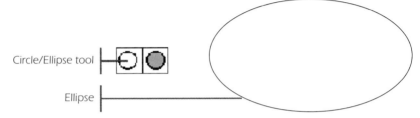

Circle/Ellipse tool

Ellipse

9. Click the Filled Circle/Ellipse tool to select it. Then point anywhere in the drawing area, hold down [⇧ Shift] and the left button, and drag the mouse to draw a a perfect circle. When it's the size you want, release first the mouse button and then [⇧ Shift].

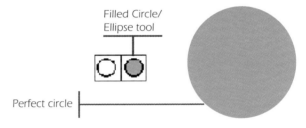

Filled Circle/ Ellipse tool

Perfect circle

Drawing Lines

10. Click the Line tool to select it. Then point anywhere in the drawing area, hold down the left button, and drag the mouse to draw a line. Until you release the mouse button, you can move the line all over the screen. Only the point where you first held down the mouse button is anchored. When the line is the length you want, release the mouse button.

11. Click a thicker drawing width in the Linesize box to select it. Then point anywhere in the drawing area, hold down the left button, and drag the mouse to draw a line. When it's the length you want, release the mouse button.

Airbrushing

12. Double-click the Eraser tool to clear the screen. When a dialog box asks if you want to save current changes, click the **No** command button.

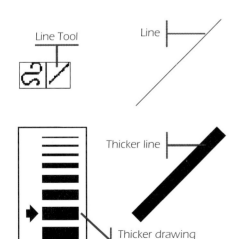

Line Tool

Line

Thicker line

Thicker drawing width

13. Click the thinnest drawing width and then the Airbrush tool to select them. Then hold down the left button and drag the mouse to spray paint. When finished spraying, release the mouse button.

14. Click a thicker drawing width in the Linesize box to select it. Then hold down the left button and drag the mouse to spray paint. Notice how the line thickness affects the area covered by the spray. When finished, release the mouse button.

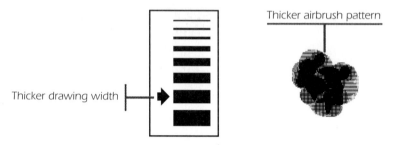

Painting

15. Click the thinnest drawing width and then the Brush tool to select them. Then hold down the left button and drag the mouse to paint. When finished, release the mouse button.

16. Click a thicker drawing width in the Linesize box to select it. Then hold down the left button and drag the mouse to paint. When finished, release the mouse button. Notice how the drawing width affects the area covered by the Brush.

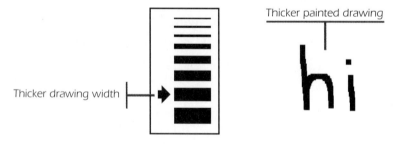

Using Colors or Shades

17. Double-click the Eraser tool to clear the screen. When a dialog box asks if you want to save current changes, click the **No** command button.

18. Point to red on the Palette and click the left button. Then point to yellow on the Palette and click the right button. The Selected Colors box at the left end of the Palette shows the color choices.

Clicking a color with the left button changes the inner color, and clicking a color with the right button changes the outer color.

Click here with the left button.

Click here with the right button.

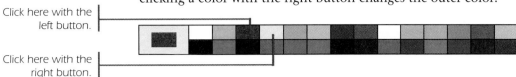

19. Click the Filled Box tool to select it. Then point anywhere in the drawing area, hold down the left button, and drag the mouse to draw a box. Release the mouse button. Notice how the inner and outer colors of the box match the inner and outer colors in the Palette's Selected Colors box.

The inner and outer colors match.

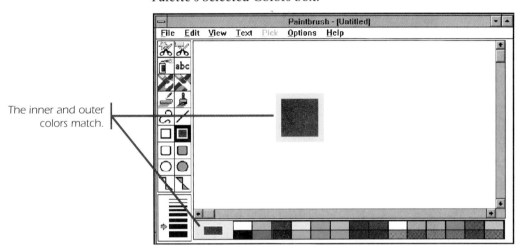

20. Click the Color Eraser tool and drag it in the inner area of the box. Notice how it replaces the red with yellow. However, when you drag it outside of the box it has no effect. You can't paint with it since it only replaces one color with another.

The outer color replaces the inner color.

Color Eraser

Finishing Up

21. Double-click the Eraser tool to clear the screen, and a dialog box asks if you want to save your changes. Click the **No** command button to clear the screen.

22. Double-click Paintbrush's Control-menu box to close the application.

SWITCHING AMONG APPLICATIONS

Although you can have a number of applications open at the same time, only one of them can be active. To make an application active, you select it, and it moves to the top of the pile if windows overlap. When there is more than one window open on the desktop, you can switch between them even if some are hidden by windows on top of them.

▶ If you can see any part of the application's or document's window, click it.

▶ If the application is running as an icon, double-click the icon.

▶ Pull down the application's **Window** menu and click the one you want to make active.

▶ To cycle through all open applications, press [Alt]+[Esc].

▶ Hold down [Alt] and press [Tab⇆] repeatedly to display the names of open applications in the middle of the screen. When the name of the application you want to switch to is displayed, release [Alt].

▶ To cycle through document windows within an application, press [Ctrl]+[F6].

You can use the Task List to move between applications. To display the Task List, double-click anywhere on the desktop (other than in an open window) or display the active window's Control menu and click the **Switch To** command. To switch to another open application, double-click the application's name, or click its name to select it and then click the **Switch To** command button.

You can also use the Task List to arrange windows and icons on the desktop.

▶ To rearrange windows, click the **Cascade** command button to arrange the windows so they overlap or the **Tile** command button to fit them all into the window.

▶ To rearrange icons, click the **Arrange Icons** command button to line up the icons along the lower portion of the window.

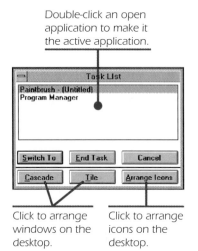

Double-click an open application to make it the active application.

Click to arrange windows on the desktop.

Click to arrange icons on the desktop.

▶▶ TUTORIAL

Getting Started

1. Pull down Program Manager's **Options** menu and click the **Minimize on Use** command to turn it on if it isn't already on. Now wherever you open another application, Program Manager will automatically run as an icon.

2. Open the Accessories group and double-click Write's icon to open it.

Switching Back to Program Manager

3. Click Write's Control-menu box to display its Control menu.

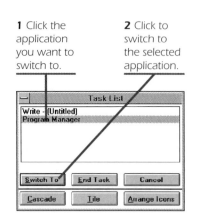

1 Click the application you want to switch to.

2 Click to switch to the selected application.

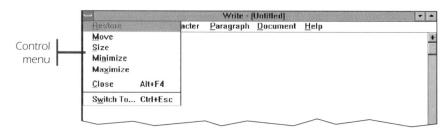

Control menu

4. Click the **Switch To** command to display the Task List. Click the Program Manager application to select it, then click the **Switch To** command button and you return to Program Manager.

Opening and Arranging a Second Application

5. Double-click Paintbrush's icon to open it.

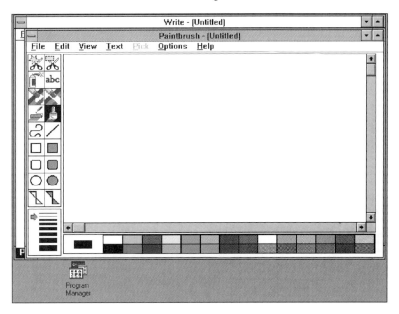

6. Click Paintbrush's Control-menu box to display its Control menu, then click the **Switch To** command to display the Task List.

7. Click the **Tile** command button to tile the application windows.

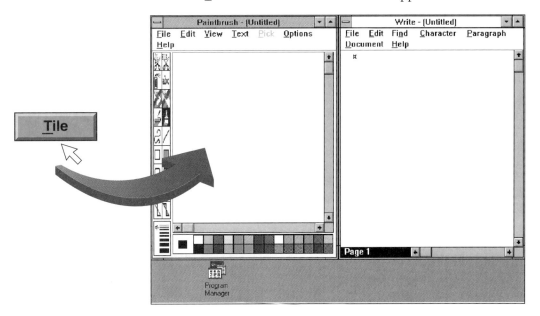

8. Click Paintbrush's Control-menu box to display its Control menu, then click the **Switch To** command to display the Task List.

9. Click the **C**ascade command button to cascade the application windows.

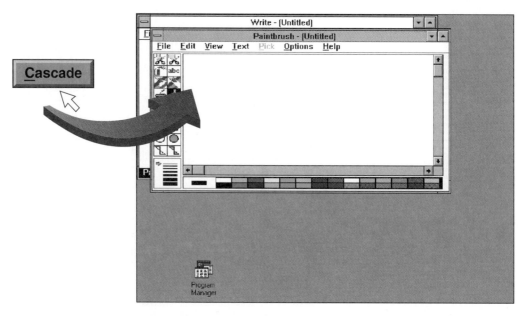

Switching Between Applications

10. Click any part of the Write window peeking out from behind the Paintbrush window, and it moves to the front as the active window.

11. Hold down [Alt] and press [Tab⇆] a few times, and you'll see the names of open applications displayed in the middle of the screen. When the name of the Paintbrush application is displayed, release [Alt], and you switch to it.

Pressing [Alt]+[Tab⇆] displays the names of open applications one at a time.

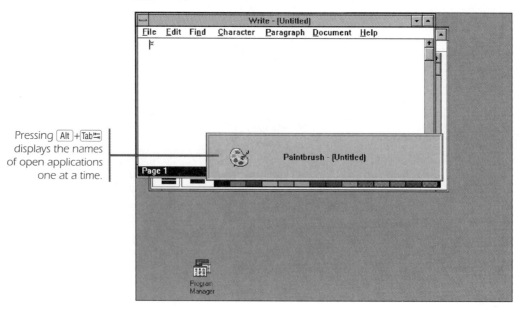

PAUSING FOR PRACTICE

Switching between open applications is a basic skill that you should master, and pressing [Alt]+[Tab⇆] is the fastest and easiest way to do it. Pause here to practice switching among the three open applications until you have mastered the procedure.

12. Click any part of the Write window peeking out from behind the Paintbrush window, and it moves to the front as the active window.

13. Click Write's Control-menu box to display the Control menu.

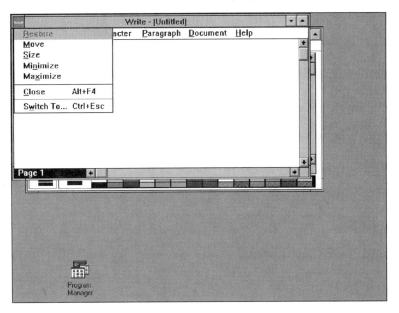

14. Click the **Switch To** command to display the Task List.

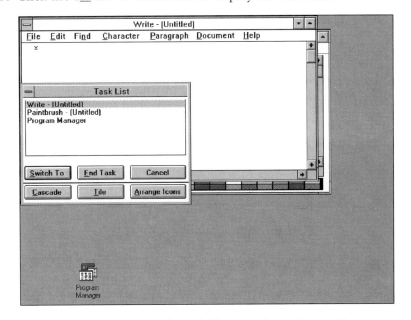

15. Double-click *Paintbrush - [Untitled]* to switch to that application.

16. Double-click anywhere on the desktop (other than an open window or icon), and the Task List appears where you double-click.

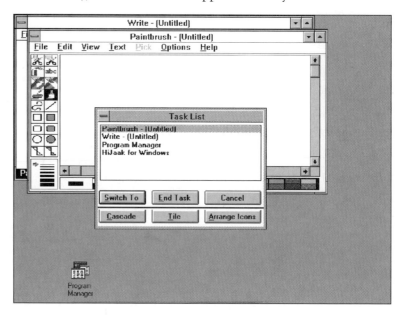

17. Click *Write - [Untitled]* to select it, then click the **Switch To** command button to make Write the current application.

Finishing Up

18. If time permits, continue to the next section without closing the two application windows.

COPYING DATA BETWEEN APPLICATIONS

To copy data from one application to another, you copy it to the Clipboard, switch to the other application, and paste it in. The data is pasted into the application in a format that the application recognizes.

▶▶ TUTORIAL

Getting Ready

1. If both Write and Paintbrush are not open on the desktop, open them and make Paintbrush the active application.

Capturing a Snapshot of the Screen on the Clipboard

2. Press [Alt]+[PrtScr] to copy a snapshot of the active window to the Clipboard.

3. Open Program Manager's Main group and double-click the Clipboard icon to open the Viewer. Click the window's Maximize button so you can see the image of the Paintbrush screen. (If it isn't on the Clipboard, repeat Step 1, and try pressing [⇧ Shift]+[PrtScr] in Step 2.)

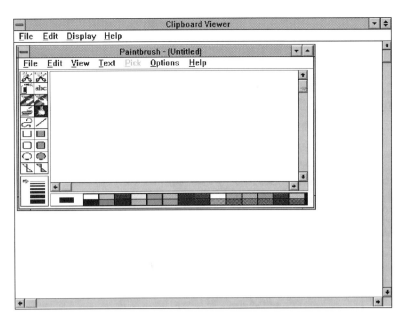

4. Click the Minimize button to minimize the Viewer to an icon.

Pasting the Snapshot into a Write Document

5. Make Write the active application, then maximize it to full screen.

6. Type your name and press Enter⤶ twice to insert a blank line.

7. Pull down the **Edit** menu and click the **Paste** command to paste the picture on the Clipboard into the document. If necessary, press PgUp to see it. If the drawing area is black, press ↑ to unselect it.

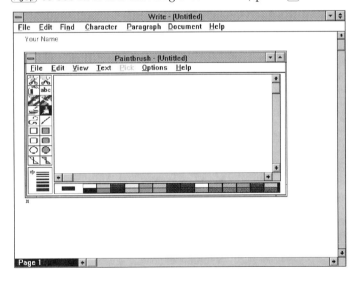

Finishing Up

8. Clear the screen without saving the document.

EMBEDDING DATA

Windows gives you more than one way to move information from one application into another. Some Windows applications support *object linking and embedding* (OLE). OLE allows you to open one application from within another, so that an object created in one application can be edited from within the second, within which it is embedded.

Applications that support OLE can be either *servers* or *clients* or both. Servers create documents or graphics (called *objects*) that can be embedded in documents created with client applications. Paintbrush is a server. Write is a client. Paintbrush objects can therefore be embedded in Write documents. The resulting Write document, containing material created in another application, is called a *compound document.*

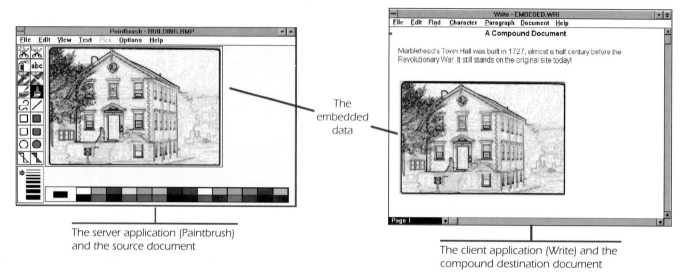

The server application (Paintbrush) and the source document

The embedded data

The client application (Write) and the compound destination document

When you use object embedding, the *object* is any piece of data created by another Windows application. The object originates in the *source document* and is embedded into the *destination document.*

Embedding data has one major advantage over copying data. When data is copied, it is no longer connected to the application that created it. When it is *embedded*, the creating application can be opened from within the client application's document so you can edit it.

When you *embed* an object, a copy of the data in the source document is copied to the destination document just as if you had copied it. The link between the object and the source document is broken. If you double-click the object in the destination document, the server application is displayed so you can edit it; but any changes you make affect only the copy in the destination document. The source document remains unchanged.

After embedding an object in a document, you can just double-click the object to automatically load it and its server application. After making any changes, pull down the server application's **File** menu and click the **Update** command to carry the changes to the destination document.

▶▶ TUTORIAL

Getting Ready

1. Insert the *Windows Student Resource Disk* into drive A.

2. Use the Write application to open the *embeded.wri* document stored in the *write* directory on the disk in drive A.

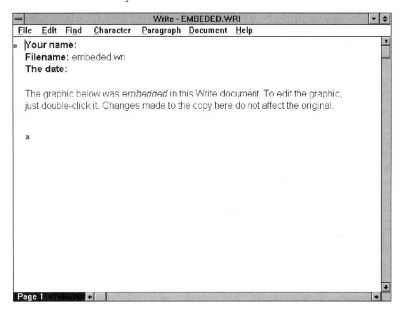

Embedding the Graphic

3. Press [Ctrl]+[End] to move the insertion point to the end of the document.

4. Pull down Write's **Edit** menu and click the **Insert Object** command to display a dialog box. (The Object Types in your dialog box may be different from those shown here.)

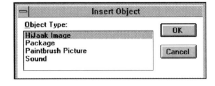

5. Double-click *Paintbrush Picture* to choose it, and the Paintbrush application appears. Notice how the title bar reads *Paintbrush Picture in EMBEDED.WRI* to indicate that you are working on an object.

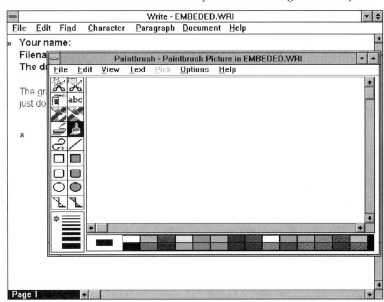

6. Pull down Paintbrush's **Edit** menu and click the **Paste From** command to display a dialog box.

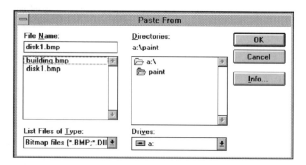

COMMON WRONG TURNS: APPLICATION WINDOW DISAPPEARS

Whenever there are two applications open, you may be able to see two windows and two menus. If you click the wrong menu, that window becomes the active application and moves to the front. When it does so, it may cover the other application. If this happens, use the ⟨Alt⟩+⟨Tab⟩ command to return to the application whose menu you meant to click.

7. Select the *paint* directory (you may have to double-click *a:* first to return to the root directory), then double-click *disk1.bmp* to open the document.

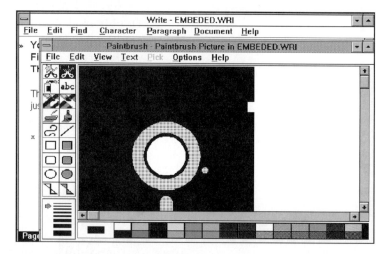

8. Pull down Paintbrush's **File** menu and click the **Update** command to embed the graphic into the Write document. (You may be able to see the graphic appear in the Write document behind the Paintbrush window.)

9. Pull down Paintbrush's **File** menu and click the **Exit & Return to EMBEDED.WRI** command to return to the Write document. The graphic appears in the document where the insertion point was positioned. If necessary, press PgUp to see it. If the drawing area is black, press ↑ to unselect it.

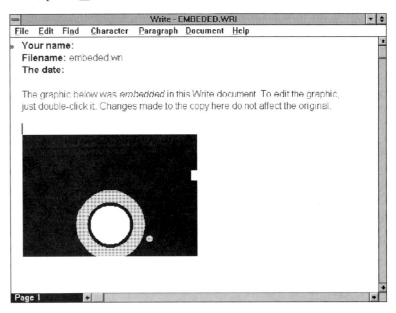

Editing the Embedded Graphic

10. Double-click the graphic in the Write document, and you return to the Paintbrush application.

11. Click the white color on the Palette with the left button to make it the foreground color.

12. Click the Text tool (*abc*) to select it, then click anywhere on the illustration of the disk and type your name.

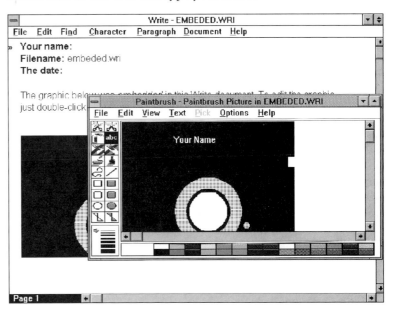

13. Pull down Paintbrush's **File** menu and click the **Update** command to update the graphic's link to the Write document.

14. Pull down Paintbrush's **File** menu and click the **Exit & Return to EMBEDED.WRI** command to return to the Write document. Your name appears on the graphic in the document.

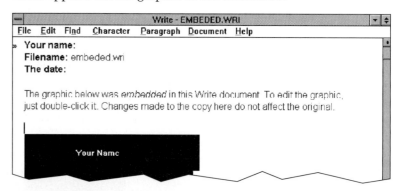

Checking the Original Graphic

15. Minimize Write and open the Paintbrush application.

16. Open the original *disk1.bmp* file stored in the *paint* directory on the disk in drive A, and you'll see that the changes you made to the embedded graphic were not carried to the original file.

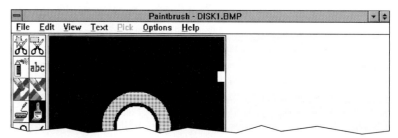

17. Close the Paintbrush application.

Finishing Up

18. Maximize the Write application and make a printout if time permits.

19. Clear the screen without saving the document. The document with the embedded art would take up 141KB on the disk. That is a very large file considering the document has a few lines of text and one simple graphic.

20. Close all open applications without saving your changes.

LINKING DATA

Linking is similar to embedding with a few key exceptions. When you *link* an object, it isn't copied into the destination document, but a link between the destination and source documents is established. Linking files keeps the destination document's size smaller because a copy of the linked file is not stored in the document. However, if you want to send the client application to someone who will edit it, you must also send the file containing the original graphic.

The biggest difference between embedded and linked documents is what happens when you edit them. When you edit an embedded document, only the embedded copy is affected. The original document on the disk remains unchanged. When you edit a linked document, you are actually editing the original copy. Changes are made to this original and then are carried to the document when the link is updated. Many destination documents can be linked to the same source document. If the source document is then revised, any changes are reflected in all the destination documents.

After linking an object in a document, you double-click the object to load it and its server application. After making any changes, pull down the server application's **File** menu and click the **Save** command to save the changes. The changes are normally automatically carried to the destination document.

You can control the way links are managed in Write by pulling down Write's **Edit** menu and clicking the **Links** command to display the Links dialog box.

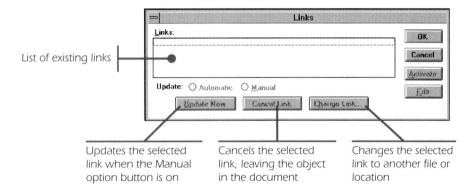

List of existing links

Updates the selected link when the Manual option button is on

Cancels the selected link, leaving the object in the document

Changes the selected link to another file or location

▶▶ TUTORIAL

1. Insert the *Windows Student Resource Disk* into drive A.

Copying the Graphic to the Clipboard

2. Open the Paintbrush application and open the *disk1.bmp* graphic stored in the *paint* directory on the disk in drive A. Maximize the Paintbrush window so you can see all of the graphic.

3. Select the Pick tool and use it to select just the graphic. To select the graphic, position the tool in the upper-left corner of the disk painting. (If you are too high or to the left, the tool turns from a cross into an arrow.) Hold down the left button and drag the dotted outline to the lower-right corner and then release the button. If you make a mistake, click the Pick tool again to remove the dotted outline and try again.

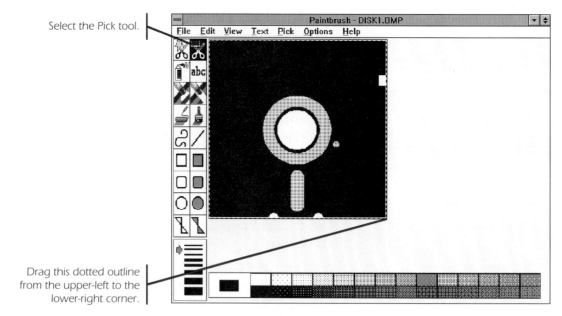

Select the Pick tool.

Drag this dotted outline from the upper-left to the lower-right corner.

4. Pull down the **Edit** menu and click the **Copy** command to copy the selected graphic to the Clipboard.

5. Double-click Paintbrush's Control-menu box to close the application.

Linking the Graphic to the Document

6. Open the Write application and open the *linked.wri* document stored in the *write* directory on the disk in drive A.

7. Press Ctrl+End to move the insertion point to the end of the document.

8. Pull down the **Edit** menu and click the **Paste Link** command to link the graphic to the document. The graphic appears in the document. Press PgUp to move back to the top of the document.

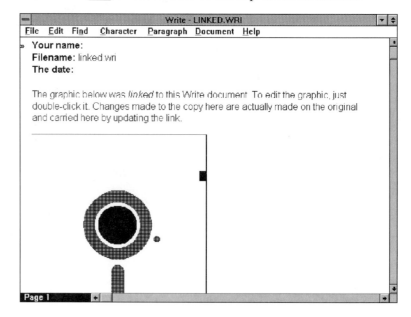

Editing the Linked Graphic

9. Double-click the graphic, and Paintbrush is again loaded and the graphic opened.

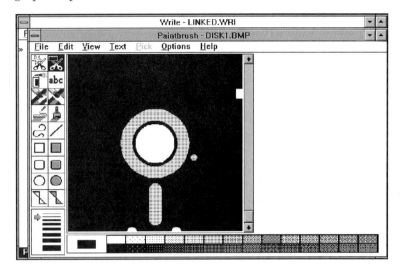

10. Click the white color on the Palette with the left mouse button to make it the foreground color.

11. Click the Text tool (*abc*) to select it, then type your name anywhere on the illustration of the disk.

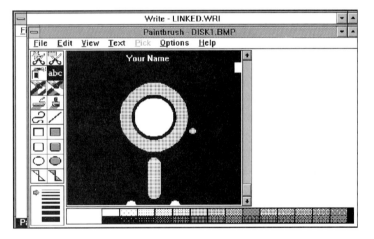

12. Pull down the **File** menu and click the **Save** command to save your changes.

Updating the Linked Graphic

13. Press Alt + Tab↹ to return to the Write application, and your name should now appear on the graphic.

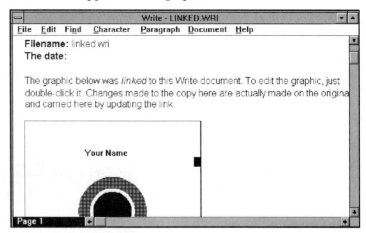

14. Pull down the **File** menu and click the **Save** command to save your changes to the document.

15. Make a printout of the document if time permits.

Checking the Original Graphic

16. Close Write, and you return to the Paintbrush application.

17. Pull down Paintbrush's **File** menu and click the **New** command to clear the screen.

18. Open the original *disk1.bmp* file, and you'll see that the changes you made in the linked graphic were made in the original file.

Finishing Up

19. Close all open applications.

IMPORTING DATA STORED IN ANOTHER FORMAT

Many Windows applications make it easy for you to open data created by another application. For example, you can use an application such as Word to open a document created with WordPerfect. Or you can use Excel or 1-2-3 to open a file created with dBASE. When you select the file to be opened, the Windows application analyzes it to see if it can identify the application that created it. If it can, it uses a built-in conversion program, called a *filter*, to convert the file from one format to another.

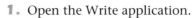

▶▶ TUTORIAL

1. Open the Write application.

2. Pull down the **File** menu and click the **Open** command to display a dialog box.

3. Change to drive A and select the *notepad* directory, then type ***.txt** in the **File Name** text box in place of **.wri,* and press ⟨Enter←⟩ to display files ending with the extension *.txt.*

Enter ***.txt** to list files ending with that extension.

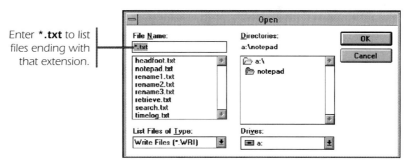

5. Double-click *notepad.txt* to open the document, and a dialog box asks if you want to convert the file to Write format.

6. Click the **Convert** command button, and the file is automatically converted into Write's file format and loaded into Write.

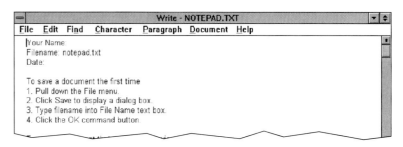

7. Double-click Write's Control-menu box to close the application, and a dialog box tells you that the document has been changed. (It's been converted to Write's format.) The box asks if you want to save the changes.

8. Click the **No** command button to abandon the converted document and close the Write application.

▶▶ SKILL-BUILDING EXERCISES

1. Drawing a House

1. Open the Paintbrush application or clear its screen of other work and maximize its window.

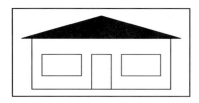

ROOF

Action	Cursor Position
Draw from	33, 93
Drag to	529, 93
Click at	280, 30
"	33, 93

2. Pull down Paintbrush's **View** menu and click the **Cursor Position** command to turn it on if it isn't already. This displays an indicator to the right of the menu bar that gives you the position of the cursor by column and row.

3. Select the Box tool and draw the rectangular parts of the house. To do so, move the pointer to the Start point, hold down the left mouse button, drag to the End point indicated in the table, and release the button.

Element	Tool	Start	End
House	Box	63, 93	499, 250
Left window	Box	94, 139	219, 203
Right window	Box	343, 139	467, 203
Door	Box	250, 139	311, 250

LOOKING AHEAD: ADJUSTING THE SPEED OF THE MOUSE POINTER

If you cannot get the cursor to stop at the positions shown in these exercises, you probably need to reduce the speed at which your mouse pointer moves across the screen. To find out how to do this, read the section "Customizing Your Mouse" in the next PicTorial.

4. To enter the roof, select the Filled Polygon tool. Then move the pointer to the *Draw from* point given in the table at the left, hold down the left mouse button, drag to the *Drag to* point indicated in the table, and release the button. Then click at each of the other points indicated.

5. Save the graphic as *house* in the *paint* directory and make a printout.

2. Drawing a Stop Sign

1. Open the Paintbrush application or clear its screen of other work and maximize its window.

2. Pull down Paintbrush's **View** menu and click the **Cursor Position** command to turn it on if it isn't already. This displays an indicator to the right of the menu bar that gives you the position of the cursor by column and row.

3. With the left mouse button, click the white color on the Palette to select it as the foreground.

4. With the right mouse button, click the black color on the Palette to select it as the background.

5. To draw the outer polygon in the sign, select the Filled Polygon tool. Then move the pointer to the *Draw from* point given in the table at the left, hold down the left mouse button, drag to the *Drag to* point indicated in the table, and release the button. Then click at each of the other points indicated.

6. With the left mouse button, click the black color on the Palette to select it as the foreground.

7. To draw the inner polygon in the sign, move the pointer to the *Draw from* point given in the table at the left, hold down the

OUTER POLYGON

Action	Cursor Position
Draw from	87, 0
Drag to	211, 0
Click at	298, 87
"	298, 211
"	211, 298
"	87, 298
"	0, 211
"	0, 87
"	87, 0

INNER POLYGON

Action	Cursor Position
Draw from	90, 6
Drag to	206, 6
Click at	290, 90
"	290, 208
"	208, 290
"	90, 290
"	6, 206
"	6, 90
"	90, 6

left mouse button, drag to the *Drag to* point indicated in the table, and release the button. Then click at each of the other points indicated.

8. Click the white color on the Palette with the left button to select it as the foreground color.

9. Pull down the **Text** menu and click the **Fonts** command to display a list of the fonts on your system. Select Arial, Bold, 48 points, and then click the **OK** command button.

10. Click the text tool, move the cursor to 65, 180 and click, then type **STOP**.

11. Save the graphic as *stopsign* in the *paint* directory and make a printout.

PICTORIAL 7 ▶VISUALQUIZ

1. List the names of the screen elements labeled in this illustration.

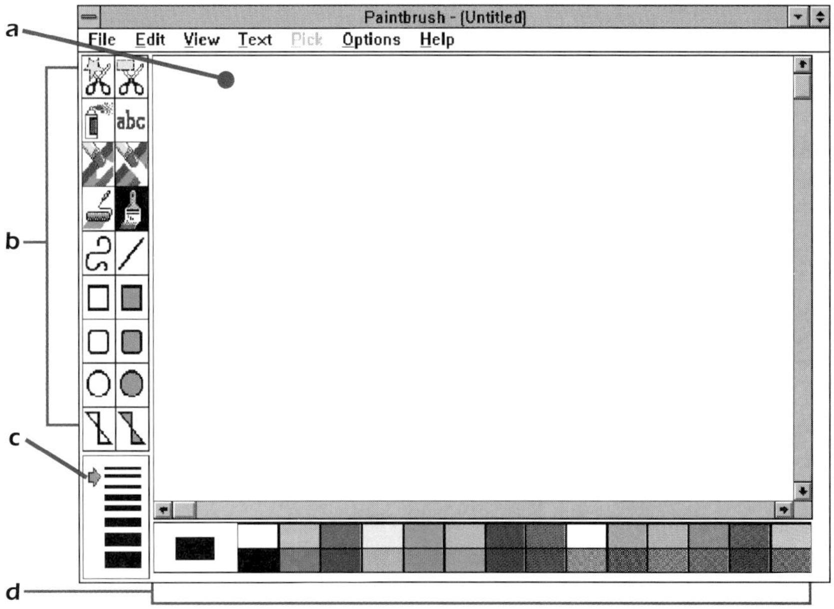

a. _____

b. _____

c. _____

d. _____

2. Match the labeled tools in the illustration with their names.

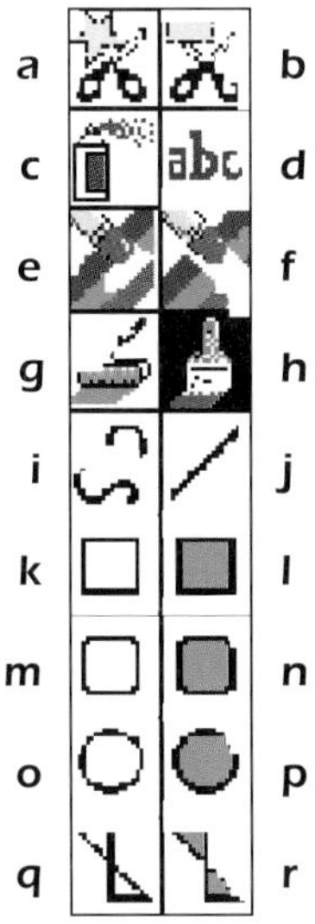

___ Airbrush	___ Eraser	___ Paint Roller
___ Box	___ Filled Box	___ Pick
___ Brush	___ Filled Circle/Ellipse	___ Polygon
___ Circle/Ellipse	___ Filled Polygon	___ Rounded Box
___ Color Eraser	___ Filled Rounded Box	___ Scissors
___ Curve	___ Line	___ Text tool

3. The box at the left end of the Palette displays the selected colors. What is the name of this box? _____

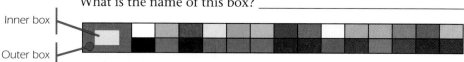

Inner box

Outer box

How do you change the inner color, and is it the foreground or background color?_____

_____

How do you change the outer color, and is it the foreground or background color?_____

_____

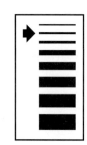

4. This figure shows the Linesize box. List three tools that can be affected by changing the selected drawing width with this box.

1. _____

2. _____

3. _____

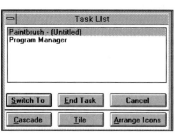

5. This illustration shows the Task List. Describe two ways that you can display this list.

1. _____

2. _____

6. This illustration shows two application windows tiled on the screen. List the steps you would follow to duplicate this screen.

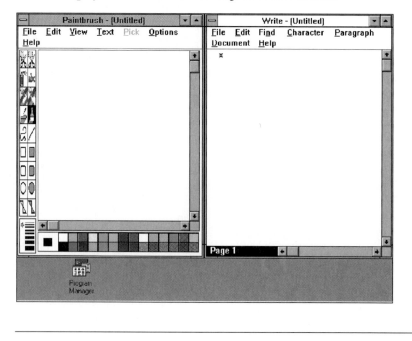

_____

_____

_____

7. This illustration shows a window in the middle of the screen that lists an open application. Describe how you display a window such as this.

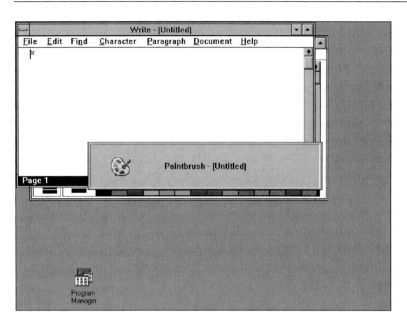

8. This illustration shows a painting created with Paintbrush embedded or linked in a Write document.

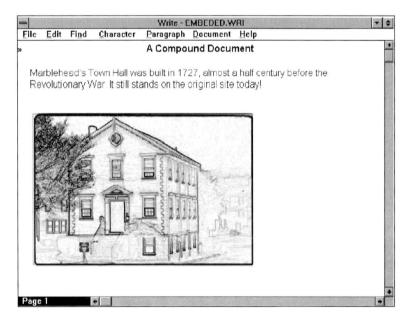

a. Write is the _____ application.

b. Paintbrush is the _____ application.

c. The Write document is known as a _____ document.

True-False (Circle T if the statement is true or F if it is false.)

T F **1.** When you use a Windows application to create a file containing data, the file is referred to as a *document*.

T F **2.** To start an application, you click its icon.

T F **3.** When you have finished working with Windows for the day, just turn it off and everything will automatically take care of itself.

T F **4.** When working on a Notepad document, double-clicking in the text selects the entire paragraph.

T F **5.** When you save a document the first time, its name can be only 8 characters long but you can use any of the characters that you can type on the keyboard.

T F **6.** Windows applications assign their own file extensions to files so you can tell which application created which file.

T F **7.** Many printers can print in either portrait or landscape orientation. Portrait orientation is the one we are most familiar with since it is used for letters, reports, and most other documents.

T F **8.** When you use a Windows application to print a document, it is normally printed to the disk before it is sent to the printer.

T F **9.** When you print documents, you must wait until each is finished printing before you start the next.

T F **10.** The lineup of jobs waiting to be printed is called a *cue*.

T F **11.** When you cut or copy data in a document, it is automatically moved or copied to the Clipboard.

T F **12.** Once data is on the Clipboard, it remains there until you exit Windows.

T F **13.** Once data is on the Clipboard, you can paste it into either the current application or another application.

T F **14.** To see what data is on the Clipboard, double-click the Clipboard icon to open the Clipboard Viewer.

T F **15.** When using the Write application, you repaginate a document by changing the page numbers that print at the bottom of each page.

T F **16.** To select an entire paragraph in Write, double-click next to it in the selection area.

T F **17.** When using **Find** or **Replace**, searching for *test* when **Match Case** is on will find *tester*, *testing*, and *tester* but not *Testy* or *Testify*.

T F **18.** When using **Find** or **Replace**, searching for *test* when **Match Whole Word Only** is on will find *tester*, *testing*, and *tester* but not *Testy* or *Testify*.

T F **19.** To completely specify a font, you must give its name, style, and size.

T F **20.** A hanging indent has the first line of a paragraph indented more than the lines that follow it.

T F **21.** To use the Ruler to change indents, you drag the two indent markers or the first line indent marker.

T F **22.** When using Paintbrush to create a drawing, you use the Palette to select colors.

T F **23.** The foreground color that you select is the color that will be used for lines, boxes, circles, and text.

T F **24.** The background color that you select will be used for fills.

T F **25.** Selecting a thicker or thinner drawing width in the Linesize box affects only the width of lines created with the Line tool.

T F **26.** To draw a perfect square or circle with the Box or Circle/Ellipse tool, you should measure it with a ruler before releasing the mouse button.

T F **27.** When you run more than one application, only one of them can be active.

T F **28.** To display the Task List, double-click any exposed area of the desktop not covered by an icon or a window.

T F **29.** You can switch between open applications by pressing [Alt]+[Tab↹].

T F **30.** When you embed data into a document, you can no longer edit it but when you link it you can.

T F **31.** Files in which you embed graphics are bigger than those in which you link them.

T F **32.** You can only use linking and embedding with applications that support object linking and embedding (OLE).

T F **33.** You can open a document that was created with another application provided the application you are using has a filter to convert the other application's documents.

 Multiple Choice (Circle the correct answer.)

1. To open an application program, you ___.

   a. Click its icon

   b. Click its icon and then pull down the **File** menu and click the **Run** command

   c. Double-click its icon

   d. Click its icon and then pull down the **File** menu and click the **Open** command

2. To close or exit an application properly, you ___.

   a. Click its Minimize button

   b. Double-click its Control-menu box

   c. Turn off the computer

   d. Pull down Program Manager's **File** menu and click the **Exit** command

3. To open an existing file, you must know ___.

   a. Its name and the drive it's on

   b. How large it is

   c. The date and time it was created

   d. What characters are legal in filenames

4. To save a file the first time, you must assign it a filename that ___.

   a. Contains 10 or fewer characters in the name and 3 in the extension

   b. Contains only the characters *a* through *z* in lowercase

   c. Contains 8 or fewer legal characters in the name

   d. Can be easily remembered

5. Print Manager appears on the desktop whenever you print a document so you can ___.

   a. Change the quality of the printout

   b. Specify which pages to print

   c. Pause the printer or delete a print job

   d. Add pages numbers to the document

6. Once you have copied data to the Clipboard, you can ___.

   a. Copy it into another document

   b. Move it elsewhere in the same document

   c. Save it into a file on the disk

   d. All of the above

7. When using Write's **Find** command to find all words that exactly match the word *hello*, you would turn on the ___.

   a. **Match Whole Word Only** check box

   b. **Match Case** check box

   c. Both the **Match Whole Word Only** and **Match Case** check boxes

   d. None of the above

8. When you use the phrase *font style*, you are referring to ___.

   a. Whether a font has serifs or not

   b. The overall appearance or design of the font

   c. How stylish the font looks

   d. Whether the font is normal, bold, or italic

9. If you were formatting a list of numbered items (such as this list of questions), you would use ___ indents.

   a. Double

   b. Left

   c. Right

   d. Hanging

10. To create a hanging indent by dragging markers on the Ruler, you would ___.

   a. Drag the left indent marker to the left of the first line indent marker

   b. Drag the first line indent marker to the left of the left indent marker

   c. Drag both the left indent marker and the first line indent marker to the same position

   d. None of the above

11. To clear a drawing from the Paintbrush screen, you just double-click the ___.

    a. Control-menu box

    b. Eraser tool

    c. Color Eraser tool

    d. Scissors tool

12. To change the inner and outer colors displayed in the Selected Colors box, you ___.

    a. Click a color with the left button to change the inner color and with the right button to change the outer color

    b. Click a color with the right button to change the inner color and with the left button to change the outer color

    c. Click a color with the right button to change the inner color and double-click to change the outer color

    d. None of the above

13. When you select a new drawing width in the Linesize box, you affect ___.

    a. The width of lines and the border around boxes

    b. The size of the Brush tool

    c. The area covered by the Airbrush tool

    d. All of the above

14. To switch among open applications, you use ___.

    a. The Task List

    b. The [Alt]+[Esc] keys

    c. The [Alt]+[Tab⇆] keys

    d. Any of the above

15. If you want to include a graphic in a Write document so you can edit it and have the changes you make not affect the original graphic, you ___.

    a. Link it

    b. Embed it

    c. Copy it

    d. Embed or copy it

16. If you are creating a compound document and want to keep the file as small as possible, you ___ the objects to or in it.

    a. Link

    b. Embed

    c. Copy

    d. Embed or copy

Fill in the Blank (Enter your answer in the space provided.)

1. To start an application, you _____ its icon.

2. To quickly close an application, you double-click its _____.

3. To open a document, you pull down the **File** menu and click the **Open** command to display a dialog box. You then select a

_____ so the names of the files are displayed, select one of the _____, and then click the _____ command button.

4. To save a document the first time, you pull down the **File** menu and click the **Save** command to display a dialog box. You then select a _____, type a _____, and then click the _____ command button.

5. Filenames can have a name of up to _____ characters followed by a _____ and up to _____ more characters.

6. Normally letters are printed in _____ orientation with text printed across the narrow width of the paper.

7. When more than one job is waiting to be printed, it is called a print _____.

8. When you copy or cut data in any Windows application, it is copied or moved to the _____.

9. Data on the Clipboard can be _____ elsewhere in the document.

10. To see the data on the Clipboard, you double-click the _____ icon to display the _____.

11. In a printed document, a line of a paragraph that prints by itself at the bottom of a page is called a(n) _____ and one that prints by itself at the top of the page is called a(n) _____.

12. When using Write, to join two paragraphs into one you delete the _____ that separate them.

13. To protect your work, you should save the last version of it as well as the current version. The saved last version of the document is called a _____.

14. When pointing to Write's selection area, _____ to select a line, _____ to select a paragraph, and hold down _____ while you click to select the entire document.

15. When you change the format of a word from bold to italic, you have changed its _____.

16. When you specify the size of a font, you normally do so in _____. One of these units is about _____ of an inch.

17. When you want a line of text to print at the top of every page, you enter it as a(n) _____. When you want a line to print at the bottom of every page, you enter it as a(n) _____.

18. To change the size of Paintbrush's Brush tool, you select a new _____.

19. To look at enlarged details of a Paintbrush drawing, you use the _____ command.

20. To draw a perfect square or circle, you hold down _____ while you drag the tool.

21. To arrange windows side by side so they don't overlap, you _____ them. To arrange them so they overlap one another, you _____ them.

22. To place a graphic in a Write document you can either _____ it, _____ it, or _____ it.

23. You can import a document created with another application if the application you are using has a(n) _____ designed to convert the file.

Projects

Project 1. Formatting a Document

1. Open the *overview.wri* document stored in the *write* directory on the *Windows Student Resource Disk* and make a printout of the document.

2. Open the *educom.wri* document supplied on the *Windows Student Resource Disk*. You'll see that it is an unformatted version of the *overview.wri* document that you retrieved and printed in Step 1.

3. Format the *educom.wri* document so it matches your printout of the *overview.wri* document.

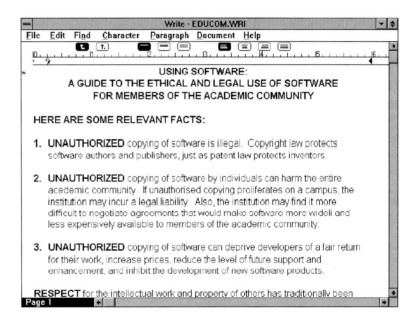

4. Save the formatted document and make a printout.

PICTORIAL **8**

MANAGING YOUR DESKTOP

After completing this PicTorial, you will be able to:

▶ Use the Control Panel to change screen colors, customize the mouse, and customize the desktop

▶ Install new Windows applications

▶ Add and delete group windows

▶ Add new application icons to groups and copy or move them between existing groups

▶ Change the properties of group windows and application icons

▶ Associate file extensions with applications so you can open or print them by dragging their icons or clicking

After Windows has been set up on the system you are using, you can customize it to suit your personal taste or needs. Some of the settings change subjective aspects such as the colors, patterns, or images displayed on the desktop. Other settings, such as printer or font setup, are essential to the proper operation of the system. To customize the system, you use the Control Panel.

EXPLORING THE CONTROL PANEL

To change Windows settings, double-click the Control Panel icon in the main group window to display the Control Panel group window. Then double-click any of the icons in this window or pull down the **Settings** menu and select a setting to change it.

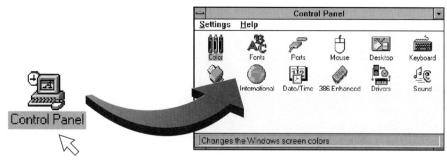

The icons and **Settings** menu choices on your system may vary depending on what devices have been installed on your system. For example, if you are connected to a network, a network icon is displayed. Here are brief descriptions of some of the icons you might see.

▶ *Colors* changes the colors on your Windows screen.

▶ *Fonts* adds and removes TrueType fonts to your system from floppy disks on which they are distributed.

▶ *Ports* sets communication options for your system's serial port. For example, you can set the port to the baud rate, data bits, parity, stop bits, and flow control suggested in your printer manual.

▶ *Mouse* adjusts the speed of the mouse and the double-click speed, and switches the functions of the buttons for left-handed users.

▶ *Desktop* changes the image and pattern on the desktop and turns the screen saver on or off.

▶ *Printers* installs and configures printers.

▶ *Drivers* installs and configures drivers for optional devices that may be added to your system. Such devices include sound cards and pen tablets.

▶ *Midi Mapper* creates, selects, or changes MIDI setups when a synthesizer is connected to your system.

▶ *Sound* assign sounds to specific Windows events such as loading or exiting Windows; or typing an asterisk, question mark, or exclamation point. This works only if your system has a sound card installed.

▶ *Network* is displayed only if your system is connected to a network. You use this icon to specify your system's network connections. The choices vary depending on the type of network your system is connected to. However, typical settings allow you to log on and off the network or change your user ID and password.

▶ *Keyboard* adjusts how quickly your keyboard begins to repeat when you hold down a key and the rate at which it repeats.

▶ *International* specifies international settings such as the country, language, keyboard layout, measurement system, list separator, and formats for dates, times, currencies, and numbers.

▶ *Date/Time* sets the system's date and time. You can change the format in which the date and times are displayed with the **Date Format** and **Time Format** commands in the International Settings dialog box.

 ▶▶ **TUTORIAL**

1. Load Windows so Program Manager is displayed.

2. Double-click the Control Panel icon in the Main group window to open the Control Panel group window. The icons in this window are the ones you use to customize various aspects of your system.

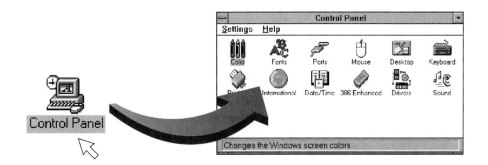

3. Pull down the **Settings** menu, and you'll see commands that duplicate the icons. You can change the settings either by using these commands or by double-clicking the matching icons.

You can change setting with icons or menu commands.

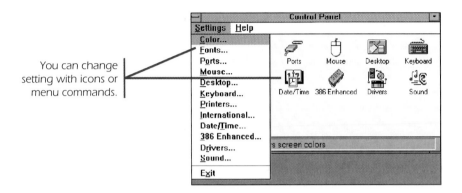

4. Click anywhere but on the menu to close it.

1 Click to display a list of available color schemes, then click one to select it.

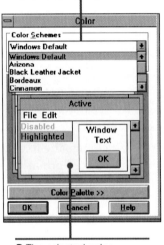

2 The selected color scheme is previewed here.

CHANGING SCREEN COLORS

To change screen colors, double-click the Control Panel's Color icon to display the Color dialog box. Drop down the list of **Color Schemes** and click any name to select it. A sample of how the colors will look is shown in the box.

To create your own color scheme, click the **Color Palette** command button to display a grid of the available colors. Then click the element you want to change in the sample area or select it from the **Screen Element** drop-down list. Finally, click the color you want to apply to it.

1 Select an element to change.

2 Click the new color you want.

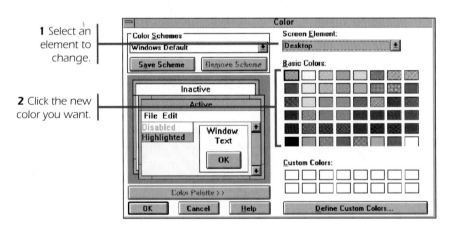

When you have the colors the way you want them, click the **OK** command button to return to Windows.

▶▶ TUTORIAL

1. Double-click the Control Panel's Color icon to display a dialog box.

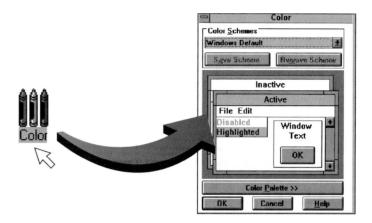

2. Click the **Color S̲chemes** drop-down arrow to display a list of Windows color schemes. Then press ⬇ and ⬆ to move the selection cursor through the choices, and each is previewed for you in the sample window below. Select *Fluorescent* and press [Enter◄┘] or click the **OK** command button.

3. Repeat Steps 1 and 2 until you have explored a number of color schemes and found the one that you like the best.

THE MOUSE DAILOG BOX

Controls how closely the mouse pointer follows mouse movements

Adjusts the speed at which Windows recognizes a double-click

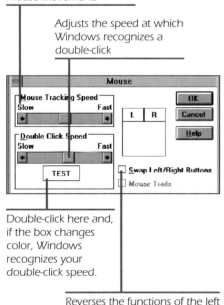

Double-click here and, if the box changes color, Windows recognizes your double-click speed.

Reverses the functions of the left and right mouse buttons

CUSTOMIZING THE MOUSE

When using a mouse, you can customize it for your personal preferences. For example, you can switch the functions of the left and right buttons, change the speed at which the mouse pointer moves across the screen, and change the speed at which you must click a second time to have Windows recognize it as a double-click. For example, if you are both left handed and a slow clicker, you can move most functions to the mouse's right button and increase the time allowed between clicks when double-clicking.

To customize the mouse, double-click the Control Panel's Mouse icon to display a Mouse Manager or Mouse dialog box, depending on which software you have (Mouse Manager replaced Mouse in version 9). Make your adjustments and then click the **OK** command button to close the dialog box.

THE MOUSE MANAGER DAILOG BOX

Opens a dialog box that lets you reverse the functions of the left and right mouse buttons

Opens a dialog box that lets you adjust the double-click speed and the sensitivity of the mouse pointer to mouse movements

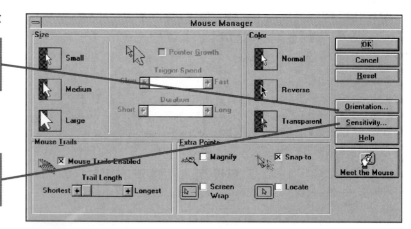

▸▸ **TUTORIAL**

1. Double-click the Control Panel's Mouse icon to display a dialog box. If the box title is Mouse Manager, continue here. If the title is Mouse, go to Step 5.

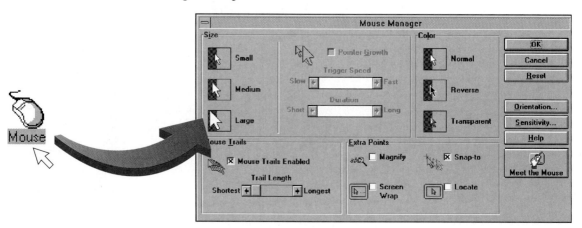

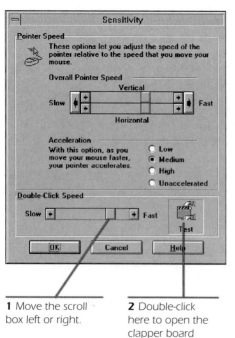

1 Move the scroll box left or right.

2 Double-click here to open the clapper board

2. Click the **Sensitivity** command button to display the Sensitivity dialog box. Move the scroll box under the **Overall Pointer Speed** heading below the **Pointer Speed** command to adjust the speed at which you can move the mouse pointer. Then move the mouse as fast as you can to see if the mouse pointer keeps up with you. When you set the speed to Slow, there will be a noticeable lag.

3. Move the scroll box under the **Double-Click Speed** command to adjust the speed. Then, double-click the Test box to see if you can open and close the clapper board. When you can't click fast enough, the clapper board doesn't open. Try it with the scroll box dragged all the way over to the Fast end of the scroll bar. At this setting, most people can't double-click fast enough to open the clapper board.

4. Click the **Cancel** command button to close the dialog box without saving your changes and return to the Mouse Manager dialog box. Then click the **OK** command button to close that dialog box. You have now completed this tutorial. Skip to the next section, "Customizing the Desktop."

5. With some versions of the mouse software, the dialog box displayed by double-clicking the Control Panel's Mouse icon is named Mouse.

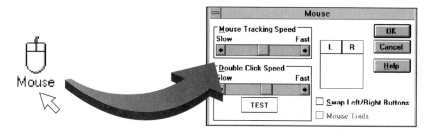

6. Move the scroll box under the **Mouse Tracking Speed** command to adjust the speed at which you can move the mouse pointer. Then move the mouse as fast as you can to see if the mouse pointer keeps up with you. When you set the speed to Slow, there will be a noticeable lag.

Move the scroll box left or right.

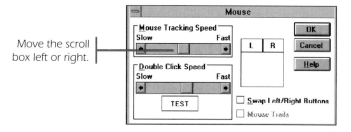

7. Move the scroll box under the **Double Click Speed** command to adjust the speed. Then double-click the TEST box to see if you can change it from white to black or black to white. When you can't click fast enough, the color of the box doesn't change. Try it with the scroll box dragged all the way over to the Fast end of the scroll bar. At this setting, most people can't double-click fast enough to change the color of the box.

1 Move the scroll box left or right.

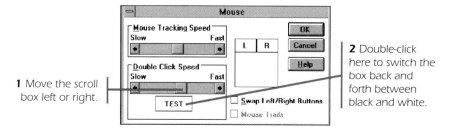

2 Double-click here to switch the box back and forth between black and white.

8. Click the **Cancel** command button to close the dialog box without saving your changes.

CUSTOMIZING THE DESKTOP

You can change the colors and patterns of your desktop and, more importantly, turn on a screen saver that hides your screen display when you stop using the computer for a specified period of time. On some systems, the screen saver also prevents an image from being burned into the screen. To make these settings, and others, double-click the Control Panel's Desktop icon to display the Desktop dialog box.

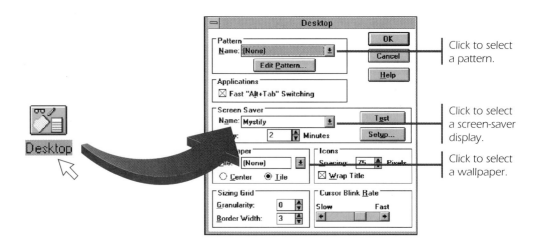

Click to select a pattern.

Click to select a screen-saver display.

Click to select a wallpaper.

There are many settings on the Desktop dialog box, but the ones you are most likely to use are those that select a pattern or wallpaper for the desktop background or that specify a screen saver. All three commands are executed by clicking drop-down list box arrows, scrolling though the list of available choices, and clicking to select the one you want to use.

▶▶ TUTORIAL

1. Double-click the Control Panel's Desktop icon to display a dialog box.

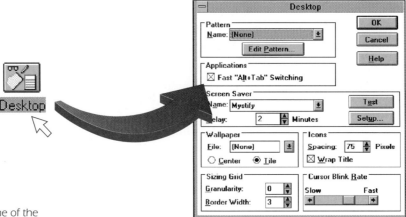

1 Click to display a drop-down list.

2 Click one of the patterns to select it.

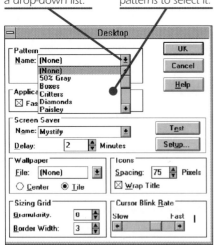

Changing the Desktop Pattern

2. Click the **Name** drop-down list in the Pattern section of the dialog box, and a list of patterns is displayed. The current choice is highlighted. Jot down its name in the space provided so you can select it again later.

Original pattern name: _____

3. Scroll up and down through the list of patterns and click one to select it.

4. Click the **OK** command button to return to the Control Panel.

5. Minimize all windows except the Control Panel's, and you'll see the new pattern used on the desktop.

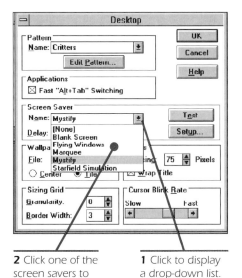

2 Click one of the screen savers to select it.

1 Click to display a drop-down list.

Turning on a Screen Saver

6. Double-click the Desktop icon to display the Desktop dialog box again.

7. Click the **Name** drop-down list in the Screen Saver section of the dialog box, and a list of screen savers is displayed. The current choice is highlighted. Jot down its name in the space provided so you can select it again later.

Original screen saver name: _____

8. Click one of the screen savers to select it.

9. Click the **Test** command button to see how it looks on your screen.

10. Click anywhere to end the display, then repeat Steps 7 through 9 until you get a screen saver you like.

11. Click the up or down scroll arrow in the **Delay** list box to set the delay time to 5 minutes.

12. Click the **OK** command button to return to the Control Panel. Now if you don't press a key or move the mouse for 5 minutes, the screen saver will activate and the image you chose will be displayed on the screen. No part of it remains in one place very long, so no image will be burned into the screen. When a screen saver is displayed on the screen, press a key or move the mouse to turn it off and return to where you were.

COMMON WRONG TURNS: BLANK SCREEN

Many new users are confused when the screen saver kicks in and their screen goes blank or displays a moving pattern. If this happens to you, just press any key, and the Windows screen reappears.

Changing the Desktop Wallpaper

13. Double-click the Desktop icon to display the Desktop dialog box one more time.

14. Click the **File** drop-down list in the Wallpaper section of the dialog box, and a list of images is displayed. The current choice is highlighted. Jot down its filename in the space provided so you can select it again later.

Original wallpaper file: _____

15. Scroll up and down through the list of files and click one to select it. (Note that *leaves.bmp* and *tarten.bmp* are dramatic-looking choices.)

16. Click the **Tile** option button in the Wallpaper section of the dialog box to turn it on if it isn't already.

17. Click the **OK** command button to return to the Control Panel. Note that the file you selected is now used as the image on the desktop, replacing the pattern you chose earlier in this tutorial.

18. Repeat Steps 13 through 17 until you have changed the wallpaper a few times.

Finishing Up

19. Double-click the Control Panel's Control-menu box to close the application.

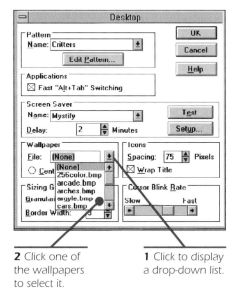

2 Click one of the wallpapers to select it.

1 Click to display a drop-down list.

INSTALLING A NEW WINDOWS APPLICATION

Before you can use a new Windows application or an updated older application, you must first install it. This installation process, called *setup*, copies the application's files from the floppy disks on which they are distributed to your system's hard disk drive. It also normally creates a new group window for the application and installs application icons in it.

There is some variation in the way you install Windows applications, but by far the most common procedure is to use the **Run** command on Program Manager's **File** menu. To begin, you insert the first disk into drive A, then click the Run command to display the **Run** dialog box. You then either type **a:\setup** into the **Command Line** text box or use the **Browse** command button to select the *setup.exe* file on drive A. (A common variation of *setup.exe* is *install.exe*.)

After selecting *setup.exe*, you follow the instructions that appear on the screen. These vary widely from application to application, but frequently you are asked to confirm the drive and directory on which the application is to be installed and have to enter your name, company, and the application's serial number.

Enter the name of the file to run.

Click to browse through directories for the name of the file to run.

NOTE: PAINT SHOP PRO

The Paint Shop Pro application that you install on your system in the following tutorial is known as *shareware* and has been provided by its developer, JASC, Inc. If you like this application and find yourself using it, you must order the complete version from JASC. Doing so is not just the morally correct thing to do, it also qualifies you for a copy of the most recent version of the application, a complete user's manual, technical support by phone, and information on future updates on the application. Complete information on how to order can be found in the *psp* directory of the *Windows Student Resource Disk* in a file named *readme.txt* which you can open with Notepad.

NOTE: IF YOU CAN'T USE DRIVE C

This tutorial explains how to install Paint Shop Pro on drive C of your system. If you do not have access to this drive, ask your instructor for the letter of another drive that you can use, or skip this tutorial.

Getting Started

1. Insert your *Windows Student Resource Disk* into drive A.

Installing an Application

2. Pull down Program Manager's **File** menu and click the **Run** command to display a dialog box.

3. Type **a:\psp\setup** (the application's files are stored on your disk in the *psp* directory) and then click the **OK** command button to begin.

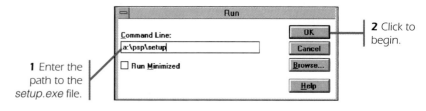

1 Enter the path to the *setup.exe* file.

2 Click to begin.

A dialog box is displayed asking you to confirm the source and destination drives and directories.

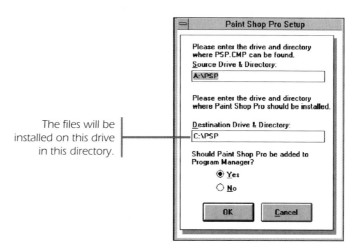

4. Click the **OK** command button to confirm, and a dialog box keeps you informed of the installation process. When finished, a dialog box tells you installation is complete.

5. Click the **OK** command button, and you'll see the new Paint Shop Pro group window and the Paint Shop Pro application icon.

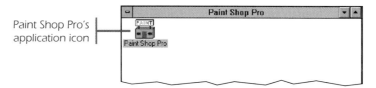

Paint Shop Pro's application icon

Exploring Paint Shop Pro

6. Double-click Paint Shop Pro's icon to open the application. Then click its Maximize button to display it full screen. If a screen entitled *Paint Shop Pro Shareware Notice* appears, read it carefully, then click the **OK** command button to clear it from the screen.

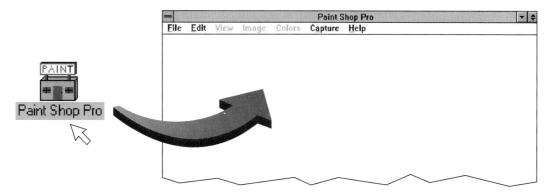

7. Pull down the **File** menu and click the **Open** command to display a dialog box. Set the drive to *a* and the directory to *psp*, and then select the file named *doorway.bmp*. This dialog box differs from the one you have become familiar with.

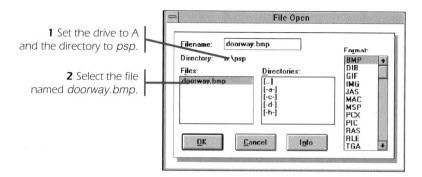

1 Set the drive to A and the directory to *psp.*

2 Select the file named *doorway.bmp.*

▶ To change drives, click the drive letter.

▶ To move up the directory tree one level, double-click [..].

▶ To move down, click any directory name.

8. Click the **OK** command button, and in a moment the photograph appears on your screen.

9. Pull down the **Colors** menu and click the **Grey Scale** command to convert the image from color to a gray scale (a series of grays ranging in darkness from pure white to pure black).

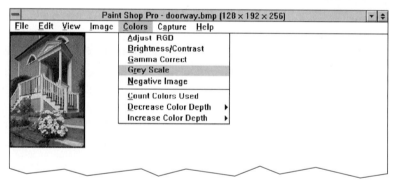

10. Pull down the **Image** menu and click the **Resample** command to display a dialog box.

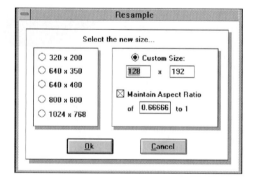

11. In the **Custom Size** text boxes, type the numbers **256** and **384** to specify a picture twice the size of the original.

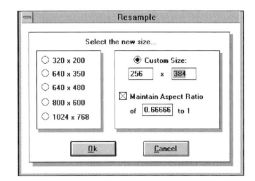

12. Click the **OK** command button, and the photograph is enlarged on the screen.

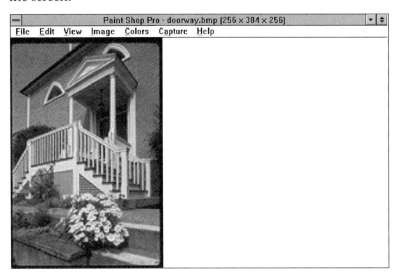

13. Pull down the **Image** menu and click the **Mirror** command to reverse the image left to right.

14. Pull down the **Colors** menu and click the **Negative Image** command to reverse the colors in the image.

15. Pull down the **Image** menu and click the **Apply Standard Filter** command to display a dialog box. Scroll the **Emboss** command into view in the **Filter Type** window and click it to select it.

Select the Emboss command.

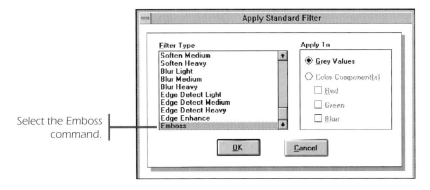

16. Click the **OK** command button, and the image is embossed on your screen.

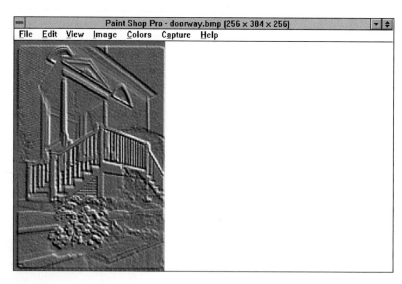

Finishing Up

17. Pull down the **File** menu and click the **Print** command to print your revised photograph.

18. Pull down the **File** menu and click the **Close** command to abandon the changes you have made. A dialog box warns you that your changes have not been saved.

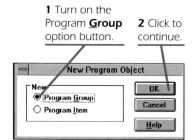

19. Click the **No** command button to close the document without saving the changes. Now you'll be able to open the photograph again and experiment further.

20. Double-click the application's Control-menu box to close it.

CREATING NEW GROUP WINDOWS

When you first install Windows, it creates the group windows Main, Accessories, Applications, StartUp, and (on DOS 6 systems) Microsoft Tools. However, you can easily add new groups—for example, to display just the icons for the applications you use most frequently.

To create a new group window, display Program Manager, pull down the **File** menu, and click the **New** command to display a dialog box.

1 Turn on the Program **Group** option button.   **2** Click to continue.

Click the **Program Group** option button, and then click the **OK** command button to display another dialog box.

1 Enter a label for the title bar and icon.

2 Name of the file the group's settings are stored in—leave blank.

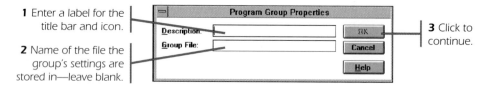

3 Click to continue.

In the **Description** text box, enter a description of the group. The text you enter here will appear in the window's title bar and as the label for its icon. Leave the **Group File** text box blank, and Windows will name the file in which the settings for the group are stored.

▶▶ TUTORIAL

1. Display Program Manager.

2. Pull down the **File** menu, and click the **New** command to display a dialog box.

3. Click the **Program Group** option button to turn it on.

Click to turn on.

4. Click the **OK** command button to display another dialog box.

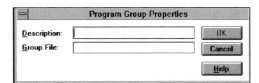

5. In the **Description** text box, type **My Group**.

Type the name of the new group.

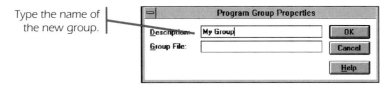

6. Click the **OK** command button to close the dialog box. The new (empty) group window is displayed on the screen. The text you entered in the **Description** text box is displayed on the window's title bar.

The title you added

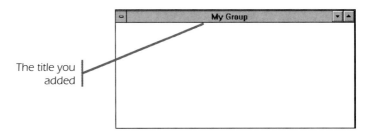

7. Click the window's Minimize button to reduce it to an icon. (If you can't see the icon, minimize other windows that may be hiding it.) The text you entered in the **Description** text box is used as the label for the group's icon.

The title you added

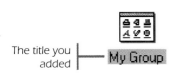

ADDING ICONS TO A GROUP WINDOW

At any point, you can add icons for new or existing applications to any group window, or you can copy or move them from one group to another. For example, you can copy or move icons into the Startup group window so the applications load automatically when you load Windows. Or you can create a new group window and copy to it only those icons that you use most frequently.

ADDING NEW ICONS

To add a new icon to a group window, first click the group window to make it active. Then pull down the **File** menu and click the **New** command to display a dialog box.

1 Turn on the Program **Item** option button.

2 Click to continue.

Click the **Program Item** option button and then click the **OK** command button to display another dialog box.

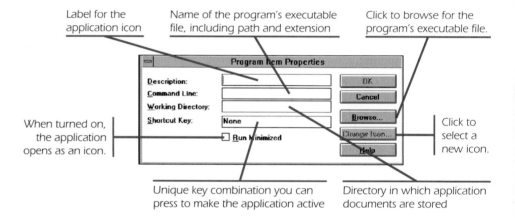

Label for the application icon

Name of the program's executable file, including path and extension

Click to browse for the program's executable file.

When turned on, the application opens as an icon.

Click to select a new icon.

Unique key combination you can press to make the application active

Directory in which application documents are stored

Enter the required information and then click the **OK** command button to add the application's icon to the active group window.

COPYING OR MOVING ICONS FROM ONE GROUP WINDOW TO ANOTHER

To copy or move an application icon from one group window (the source) to another (the destination), begin by arranging the desktop so you can see both groups. The source window must be open, but the destination can either be open or displayed as an icon.

▶ To move an application icon, drag it from the source window and release it in the destination window.

▶ To copy an application icon, hold down Ctrl while dragging it to a new group window and then drop it.

▶▶ TUTORIAL

Getting Ready

1. To add an icon for an application, you must first know the name of its executable program file and where this file is located on your system. In this section, we'll show you how to add an icon for the application called QBASIC (or BASIC or BASICA on DOS 4 and earlier versions) that is stored in the DOS directory on drive C. If your instructor wants you add an icon for another application, he or she will supply you with the following information:

Question	Example	Your Information
Name of application:	Microsoft QBASIC	
Name of its executable file:	*qbasic.exe*	
Path to the executable file:	*c:\dos*	
Command you use to exit the application:	Alt + F , X	

Adding a New Icon

2. Double-click the *My Group* icon to open it into a window.

3. Pull down the **File** menu and click the **New** command to display a dialog box. The **Program Item** option button should be on.

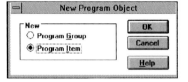

4. Click the **OK** command to display another dialog box.

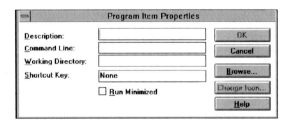

5. Enter the following information:

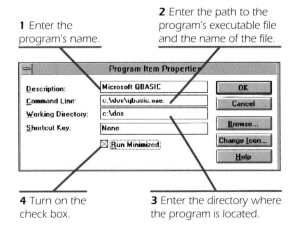

1 Enter the program's name.

2 Enter the path to the program's executable file and the name of the file.

3 Enter the directory where the program is located.

4 Turn on the check box.

▶ Enter **Microsoft QBASIC** in the **Description** text box.

▶ Enter the path **c:\dos\qbasic.exe** in the **Command Line** text box.

▶ Enter the path **c:\dos** in the **Working Directory** text box.

▶ Click the **Run Minimized** check box to turn it on.

6. Click the **OK** command button, and an icon for the application is added to the *My Group* window.

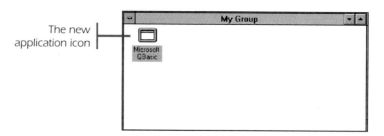

The new application icon

Copying Icons from Other Groups

7. Maximize Program Manager's window.

8. Open the *My Group*, *Accessories*, and *Main* group windows and run all other groups as icons.

9. Pull down the **Window** menu and click the **Tile** command. (The group windows may not be in the order shown here, but it doesn't matter.)

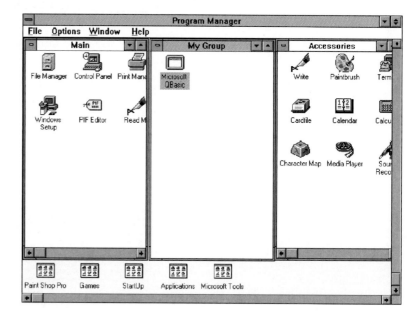

10. Click the *Accessories* group window to select it, pull down the **Window** menu, and click the **Arrange Icons** command so all of the icons in the window can be seen. Do the same for the *Main* window.

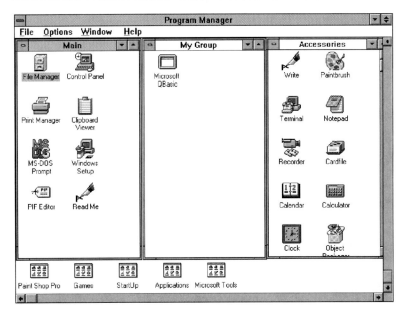

11. Click the Write icon in the *Accessories* group window, hold down [Ctrl], and drag the icon into *My Group*.

Copy of icon being dragged to a new window

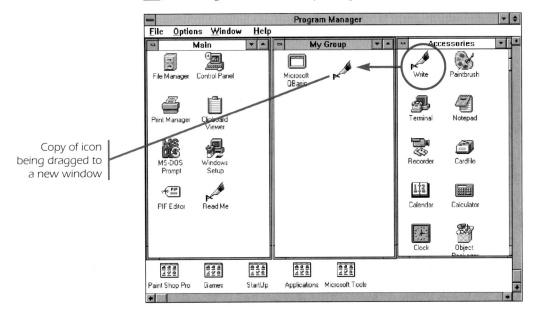

12. Release [Ctrl] and the mouse button, and a copy of the icon is now in *My Group*.

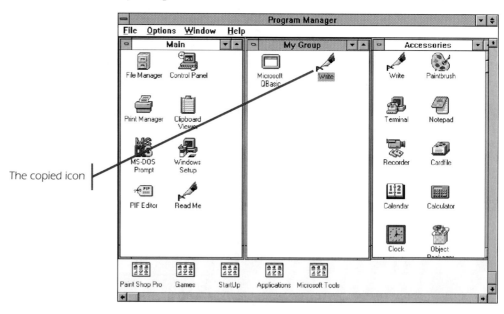

The copied icon

CHANGING THE PROPERTIES OF A GROUP WINDOW OR ICON

You can change the description of a group window if you want different text displayed on the title bar or icon label. You can also change the icon that represents an application. To change the properties of an application, do any of the following:

▶ Make the group the active window, pull down the **File** menu, and click the **Properties** command.

▶ Make the group the active window and press [Alt]+[Enter ↵].

▶ Hold down [Alt] and double-click the group's icon.

To change the properties of a group window, you use the same commands; however, the window must be displayed as an icon.

Any of these commands displays a dialog box in which you enter your changes.

Current settings

Current icon

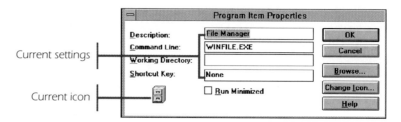

Clicking the **Change Icon** command button displays another dialog box where you can select a new icon to represent the application.

Icons available for selection

Clicking the **Browse** command button displays a list of files that may or may not contain additional icons. For example, if you select the *moricons.dll* file and click the **OK** command button, additional icons are displayed in the Change Icon dialog box.

Icons in the *moricons.dll* file that you can select

You can click one of the new icons to select it (use the scroll bar to see them all), and then click the **OK** command button. Your application will then display the new icon when you click its Minimize button.

▶▶ **TUTORIAL**

Changing the Properties for a Group Window

1. Close the *My Group* window to an icon.

2. Click the *My Group* icon to select it and open its Control menu.

3. Click anywhere on the desktop to close the menu but leave the icon selected.

4. Pull down Program Manager's **File** menu and click the **Properties** command to display a dialog box.

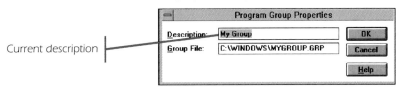

Current description

5. Type your first and last name into the **Description** text box in place of the previous text.

Enter your name.

6. Click the **OK** command button, and now the icon has your name under it.

Your name —— First Last

7. Double-click the icon to open it, and your name is now in the window's title bar.

Changing the Properties for an Application

8. Click the *Microsoft QBASIC* application icon to select it.

9. Pull down Program Manager's **File** menu and click the **Properties** command to display a dialog box.

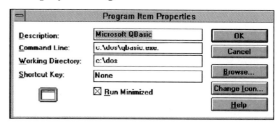

10. Click the **Change Icon** command button to display a dialog box telling you there are no icons available.

11. Click the **OK** command button to display the Change Icon dialog box.

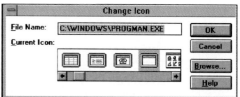

12. Click the **Browse** command button to display a dialog box just like the ones you use to open files. Scroll the file *moricons.dll* into view and then click it to select it.

Select the
moricons.dll file.

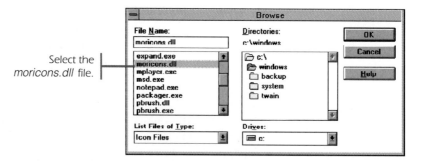

13. Click the **OK** command button, and new icons are loaded into the Change Icon dialog box.

When you select the
moricons.dll file,
many new icons are
made available.

14. Scroll through the entire collection until you find an icon you like. Then click it to select it and click the **OK** command button. The new icon will replace the previous one in the Program Item Properties dialog box.

15. Click the **OK** command button to close the dialog box, and the new icon is displayed in your group window.

DELETING APPLICATION ICONS AND GROUP WINDOWS

At any point, you can delete icons and group windows from your desktop by selecting them and pressing Del. When you do so, a dialog box asks you to confirm the deletion. Clicking the **Yes** command button does not delete the files for the application from your disk, so you can always add the icons and group windows back to your desktop. Normally, you would delete the application icons from a group window and then, when the group window is empty, delete it. However, you can delete a group window and all the application icons within it by displaying it as an icon and pressing Del.

COMMON WRONG TURNS: DISAPPEARING ICONS AND GROUP WINDOWS

Since it is so easy to delete an application's icon or even a group window, it's sometimes done inadvertently. Should this happen to you, just recreate the group window or add the missing icon for the application to an existing group window. Lots of people think deleting the icon deletes the program files. But now you know it doesn't.

▶▶ TUTORIAL

1. Click each of the icons in the group window that you named with your first and last name, and press Del to display a dialog box that asks for confirmation. Click the **Yes** command button in each case until all of the icons are deleted.
2. With the empty group window the active window, press Del to display a dialog box that asks for confirmation. Click the **Yes** command button to delete the group window.

WORKING WITH ASSOCIATED FILES

Each Windows application assigns a unique extension to the filenames you assign. For example, Write assigns the extension *.wri*, and Notepad assigns the extension *.txt*. These extensions allow Windows to match each document file with the application that created it. These matches are called *associations*, and many of them are built into Windows. For example, if you double-click a file with the extension *.wri* when it's listed on File Manager's contents list, first the Write application is loaded and then the document you double-clicked. You can also open associated files by dragging and dropping them onto an application icon or title bar, or print them by dragging and dropping them onto Print Manager's icon or title bar.

To specify or change an association between a application and a file-name extension, open File Manager and click a file with the desired extension on the contents list to select it. Then pull down the **File** menu and click the **Associate** command to display a dialog box.

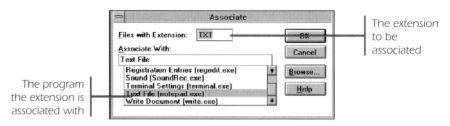

The extension to be associated

The program the extension is associated with

The extension of the selected file is shown in the **Files with Extension** text box, and the application the extension is associated with is highlighted on the **Associate With** list. Click another application on the list to change the association, or click the **Browse** command button and browse through the directories for the program file that you want the extension associated with.

PRINTING ASSOCIATED FILES BY DRAGGING AND DROPPING

Associations allow you to print files by dragging their icons from File Manager's contents list and dropping them onto Print Manager's icon or title bar. This causes the associated application to be loaded, then the document. Then the usual Print dialog box is displayed so you can specify print quality and the pages to be printed. After the document is printed, the application and document are both automatically closed.

You can also print associated documents by selecting them on File Manager's contents list, then pulling down the **File** menu and clicking the **Print** command to display a dialog box listing the filename. If you then click the **OK** command button, the printing sequence proceeds just as if you had dropped the document's icon onto Print Manager's icon.

OPENING ASSOCIATED FILES BY DRAGGING AND DROPPING

When an application is running, you can open an associated document by dragging the document's icon from File Manager's contents list and dropping it onto the application's title bar or icon.

OPENING ASSOCIATED FILES BY PLACING THEIR ICONS IN THE APPLICATION'S GROUP WINDOW

You can drag a document's file icon from the contents list and drop it into the same Program Manager group as its associated application's icon. The document icon looks just like its parent application's icon, but you can identify it by its name. When you double-click the document's icon, both the application and the document are loaded. To remove the document's icon, just click it to select it, and then press [Del] just as you would to remove any other icon. The document file is not deleted when you remove the icon.

▶▶ TUTORIAL

Getting Ready

1. Open File Manager.

2. Insert your *Windows Student Resource Disk* into drive A and display the contents list for the root directory on that drive.

Trying to Open a Non-Associated File

3. Double-click the file named *read.me* on the contents list, and a dialog box is displayed telling you that no application is associated with the file. (If Notepad opens, someone has previously made an association. Double-click Notepad's Control-menu box to close the application and continue at Step 5.)

4. Click the **OK** command button to remove the dialog box.

Associating a File

5. Click the file named *read.me* on the contents list to select it.

6. Pull down the **File** menu and click the **Associate** command to display a dialog box.

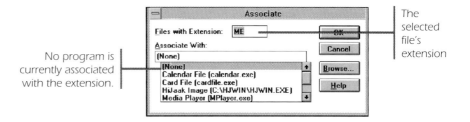

7. Scroll the list of files in the **Associate With** list and click *Text File (notepad.exe)* to select it.

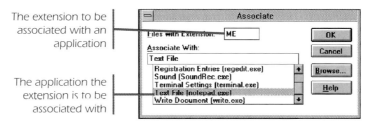

8. Click the **OK** command button to complete the association.

Opening an Associated File

9. Double-click the filename *read.me* on the contents list to start the Notepad application and then open the document. Enter your name and the date and then save the document.

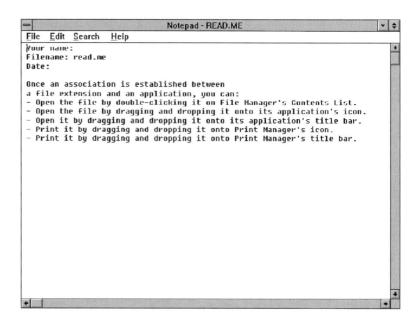

10. Pull down the **File** menu and click the **New** command to clear the Notepad screen.

11. Drag and size the File Manager and Notepad windows so you can see the file named *read.me* on the contents list and you can also see Notepad's title bar. You'll probably have to drag File Manager's split bar to see the files in the smaller window.

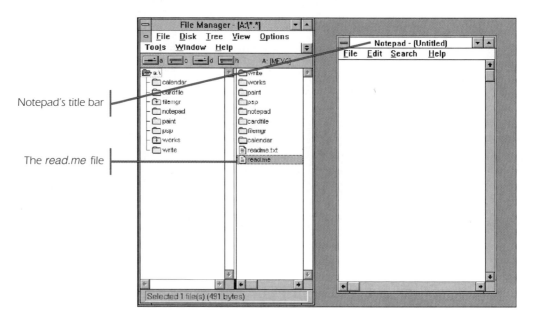

Notepad's title bar

The *read.me* file

12. Drag the *read.me* filename from the contents list to Notepad's title bar.

File dragged to Notepad's title bar

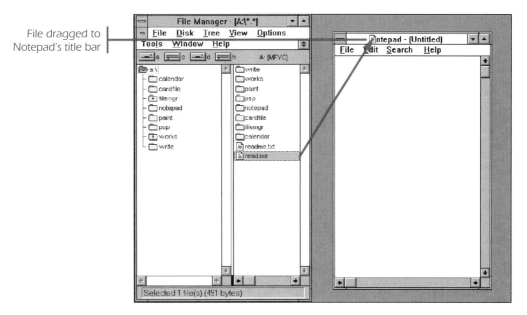

13. Drop the file onto the title bar to open the document.

When you drop the file onto Notepad's title bar, it is opened.

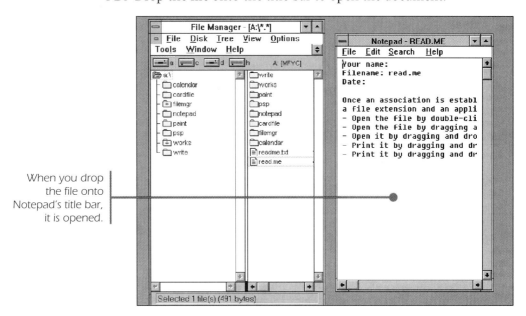

14. Double-click Notepad's Control-menu box to close the application.

Printing an Associated File By Dragging and Dropping

15. Open the Main group and double-click the Print Manager icon to open it. Then click its Minimize button to run it as an icon. Arrange the screen so you can see it and the file named *read.me* on File Manager's contents list.

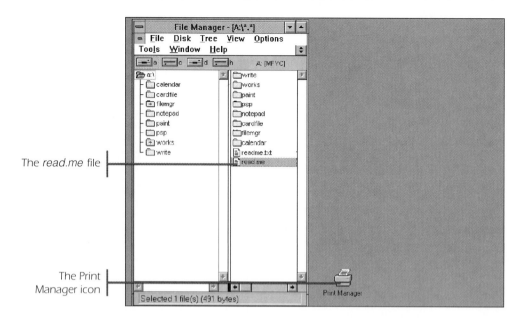

The *read.me* file

The Print
Manager icon

16. Reduce Program Manager to an icon, then drag the *read.me* filename from the contents list to Print Manager's icon and drop it to
print the document.

17. When the document has finished printing, the Notepad application is automatically closed.

▶▶ SKILL-BUILDING EXERCISES

1. Resetting Windows

In one of this topic's tutorial sections you reset the Windows desktop
pattern, wallpaper, and screen saver. Reset each of them to their original settings, which you wrote down in the spaces provided in the
tutorial.

2. Using Paint Shop Pro

If you installed Paint Shop Pro in this PicTorial, you can use it to
open and revise the files with the extensions *.bmp* in the *paint* directory of the *Windows Student Resource Disk*. After revising them, make
printouts. You should also use Notepad to open the file named
readme.txt in the *psp* directory and read it on the screen or make a
printout.

PICTORIAL 8 ▶VISUALQUIZ

1. This illustration shows the window that appears when you double-
click the Color icon on the Control Panel. Describe what each of the
labeled parts is used for.

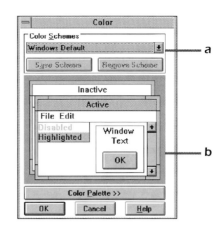

a. _____

b. _____

2. Describe how each of these controls affects the mouse attached to your system.

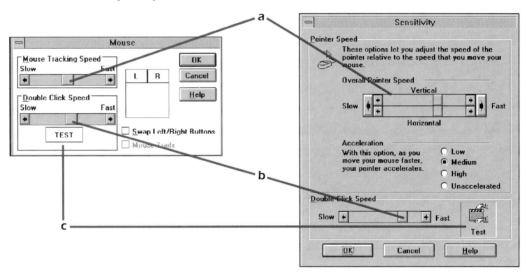

a. _____

b. _____

c. _____

3. This illustration shows the window that appears when you double-click the Desktop icon on the Control Panel. Describe what each of the labeled parts is used for.

a. _____

b. _____

c. _____

d. _____

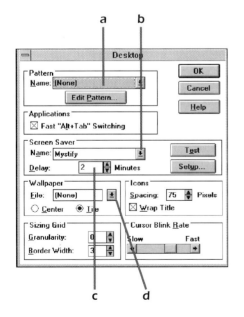

4. What command would you enter in the **Command Line** text box (a) to install a program such as Microsoft Word from a disk in drive A? What would be the result of turning on the **Run Minimized** check box (b)?

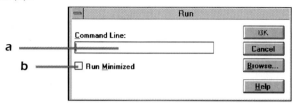

a. _____

b. _____

5. When you add a new application icon or change one's properties, you can enter text in the **Description** text box. What two places does this text then appear after you close the dialog box?

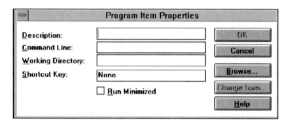

6. When you add a new application icon, this dialog box appears. Briefly describe what you do with each of the labeled elements.

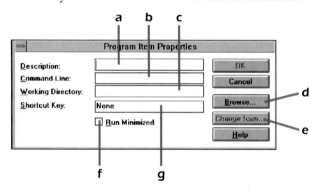

a. _____

b. _____

c. _____

d. _____

e. _____

f. _____

g. _____

7. Were you to make these dialog box choices, what would happen if you:

```
Associate
Files with Extension:   ME                      OK
Associate With:
Text File                                       Cancel
  Registration Entries (regedit.exe)    ↑
  Sound (SoundRec.exe)                          Browse...
  Terminal Settings (terminal.exe)
  Text File (notepad.exe)                       Help
  Write Document (write.exe)            ↓
```

a. Double-clicked a filename *you.me* on the contents list?

_____

_____

b. Dragged a filename *who.me* onto Print Manager's icon?

_____

_____

c. Dragged a filename *give.me* into the same group window as Notepad's icon?

_____

_____

d. Dragged a filename *give.me* into the same group window as Write's icon?

_____

_____

PicTorial 9

Using DOS and DOS Applications

After completing this topic, you will be able to:

▶ Display the DOS command prompt without leaving Windows

▶ Run non-Windows applications

▶ Undelete files

▶ Defragment your disk

Windows runs on top of the DOS operating system, which must be loaded before Windows is loaded. You can access the DOS command prompt without leaving Windows, and you can run non-Windows applications (those designed to run under DOS and not Windows) within Windows. On systems running DOS 6 you can also perform several useful functions from the Windows desktop. For example, you can easily check for and remove viruses that may be on your system, undelete any files that you have mistakenly deleted, and defragment the files on your hard disk so it works faster and better.

UNDERSTANDING STANDARD AND ENHANCED MODES

Windows has been designed to take advantage of features available only on high-end PCs. At the same time, however, it can run on less powerful computers. The way it does this is by switching *modes*, or methods of operation. On more powerful computers (those with 386, 486, or Pentium processors) Windows runs in *enhanced mode*. On less powerful computers, Windows runs in *standard mode*. The difference between these two modes is significant. For example, in enhanced mode, you can run non-Windows applications in windows. In standard mode you can't—they can only be run full screen. In enhanced mode, Windows stores parts of large active programs and files on the hard disk until it needs them. In a way this makes the space on the disk act as if it were part of the computer's internal random access memory, or RAM. In standard mode, Windows can't do this, so you can't work on applications or data files that are as large.

To see what mode your system is using, pull down Program Manager's **Help** menu and click the **About Program Manager** command. A dialog box tells you what mode your system is running in. Click the **OK** command button to close the dialog box.

▶▶ **TUTORIAL**

1. Display Program Manager.

2. Pull down the **Help** menu and click the **About Program Manager** command to display a dialog box that tells you what mode your system is in. Note the mode.

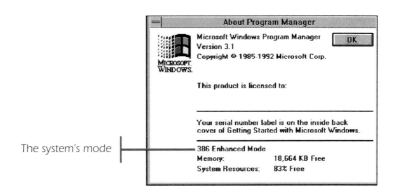

The system's mode

3. Click the **OK** command button to close the dialog box.

ACCESSING AND EXITING THE DOS COMMAND PROMPT

Any time you are using Windows, you can access the DOS command prompt to run DOS applications or use DOS commands that are not available on File Manager's menus.

To display the DOS command prompt, double-click the DOS icon in the Main or Accessories group window. When you double-click the DOS icon, the DOS command prompt is displayed.

If your system is running in enhanced mode, you can press [Alt]+[Enter←] to run DOS in a window, or if it is running in a window, press [Alt]+[Enter←] to run it full screen. When DOS is displayed in a window, you can use the window's Minimize and Maximize buttons just as you do on any other window.

To exit DOS, type **exit** and press [Enter←]. You can't exit Windows without first exiting DOS. If you try to, you'll get an error message.

Click to close the dialog box, then exit the application.

TIP: FORGETTING THAT WINDOWS IS STILL RUNNING

It's not unusual to access the DOS prompt from Windows and then forget that Windows is still loaded. If you do forget and turn off the computer without first returning to Windows and exiting it correctly, you can lose work. To have the DOS command prompt remind you that Windows is still loaded, add a line such as *SET WINPMT=Type Exit and press Enter to return to Windows $_$_PG* to your *autoexec.bat* file.

▶▶ TUTORIAL

1. Open the Main group window and double-click the DOS icon to display the DOS command prompt. (Your DOS icon may be different from the one shown here and if the Windows on your system was upgraded from an earlier version, the DOS icon may be in the Accessories group window.)

2. Insert your *Windows Student Resource Disk* into drive A.

3. If your system is running in enhanced mode, press [Alt]+[Enter ↵] to display DOS in a window. Otherwise, skip to Step 5.

4. Press [Alt]+[Enter ↵] again to display DOS full screen.

PAUSING FOR PRACTICE

Switching DOS applications back and forth between full-screen and windowed operation is a basic skill. Continue pressing [Alt]+[Enter ↵] a few times to switch back and forth between running DOS full screen and running it in a window.

5. Type **a:** and press [Enter ↵] to change the default drive to drive A.

6. Type **dir** and press [Enter ↵] to display a directory of the files on your disk.

7. Type **exit** and press (Enter←) to end your DOS session and return to Windows. If DOS was running in a window, its window closes automatically.

USING NON-WINDOWS APPLICATIONS

There are times when you want to stay in Windows to use an application designed to run with DOS but not with Windows. The DOS versions of Lotus 1-2-3 and WordPerfect are widely used examples of these *non-Windows applications*. To open a non-Windows application, you can add its icon to one of Program Manager's group windows and double-click it just as you do with Windows applications. However, if the application has not been added to a group window, you can open it in a number of other ways. You can:

▶ Double-click the application's executable program filename in File Manager's contents list. For example, to load WordPerfect, double-click the file named *wp.exe*.

▶ Use the **Run** command located on Program Manager's **File** menu. This command displays a dialog box into which you can type the path and filename of the executable program file that starts the application. Alternatively, you can click the dialog box's **Browse** command button and then browse through directories on your disks to locate the desired file.

▶ Access the DOS command prompt and type the application's path and executable program filename.

Enter the path and executable filename of the program you want to run.

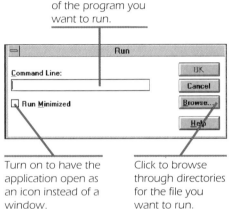

Turn on to have the application open as an icon instead of a window.

Click to browse through directories for the file you want to run.

TIP: EXECUTABLE FILES

If you use File Manager to look in a directory containing one of your applications, you will see many filenames. However, only one of the files is the one you load to open the application. This file is an *executable program file* and almost always ends with the extension *.exe* or *.com*. For example, the executable program file for Windows is *win.com* and for Write it is *write.exe*. To start such a program, you double-click the executable program file's name or you pull down the **File** menu, click the **Run** command, type the filename (not including the extension), and press (Enter←).

Once the application is running, you can press (Alt)+(Enter←) to switch back and forth between running it in a window or running it full screen if your system is running in enhanced mode. When a non-Windows application is running in a window, it takes up more memory and may operate more slowly, but you can click its Minimize button to run it as an icon, drag and resize its window (within limits), and otherwise treat it much like a Windows application.

To close a non-Windows application, you must first exit it using its own exit command. This removes the application from the computer's memory and removes its display or icon from the desktop. If you try to exit Windows without first exiting an open non-Windows application, a warning is displayed.

If you are running a non-Windows application and it misbehaves, you may find that you can't exit it in the normal way. If this happens, click the window's Control-menu box to display the Control menu. Click the **Se_t_tings** command, and then click the **Terminate** command button. Be careful with this command and use it only as a last resort, since it is similar to a local reboot and you could lose data. If you can't display the Control menu, you can still press [Ctrl]+[Alt]+[Del] and follow the instructions displayed on the screen to exit the application.

▶▶ TUTORIAL

Getting Ready

1. To load a DOS application, you must first know its name and where it is located on your system. In this section, we'll load an application called QBASIC (or BASIC or BASICA on DOS 4 and earlier versions) that is stored in the DOS directory on drive C. If your instructor wants you to load another application, he or she will supply you with the following information:

Question	Example	Your Information
Name of application:	Microsoft QBASIC	_____
Name of its executable file:	qbasic.exe	_____
Path to the executable file:	c:\dos	_____
Command you use to exit the application:	[Alt]+[F], [X]	_____

Loading a DOS Application Using the Browse Command

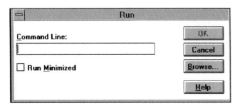

2. Pull down Program Manager's **File** menu and click the **Run** command to display a dialog box.

3. Click the **Browse** command button to display the Browse dialog box. This box is identical to the Open dialog box that you use to open documents.

4. Make these settings:

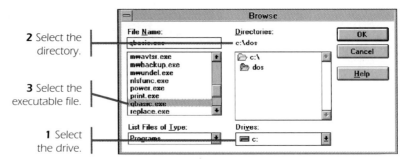

2 Select the directory.

3 Select the executable file.

1 Select the drive.

▶ Select the drive and directory where your DOS files are located. For example, select drive C in the **Drives** drop-down box, then the *dos* directory in the **Directories** box. This will display a list of the files in that directory in the **File Name** box.

▶ Select the name of the executable file that runs your application. For QBASIC, scroll the *qbasic.exe* filename into view and click it to select it.

COMMON WRONG TURNS: CAN'T FIND A DIRECTORY

When you use the **Browse** command, it may display a dialog box for a directory other than the one you want. Often you have to move up to the root directory to find the directory you are looking for. For example, clicking the **Browse** command button may display the files in the *c:\windows* directory. To see the files in the *c:\dos* directory you have to first double-click *c:* in the **Directories** box to move up to the root directory and then double-click the *dos* directory. Be sure to check the path listed under the heading **Directories** to be sure of your current location.

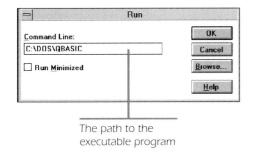

The path to the executable program

5. Click the **OK** command button to return to the Run dialog box.
6. Click the **OK** command button to run the selected application.

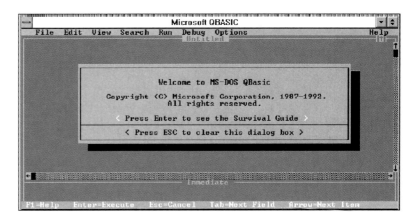

7. If you loaded QBASIC, press Esc to clear the opening screen.

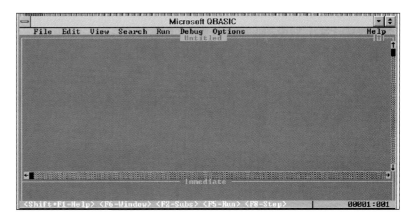

8. If the application is displayed in a window, press Alt + Enter↵ to display it at full screen.

Closing a DOS Application

9. If you loaded QBASIC, press Alt + F to pull down the **File** menu, then press X to exit the application and return to Windows. If you loaded another application, use its exit command instead. When you exit the application, it is no longer displayed on the desktop.

Loading a DOS Application by Typing Its Name

10. Pull down Program Manager's **File** menu and click the **Run** command to display a dialog box.

The path to the executable program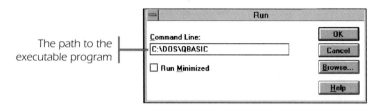

11. Type **c:\dos\qbasic** (or the path and application name you are using) and click the **OK** command button to load the application. This method of loading a application is faster if you know the executable file's exact name and path.

Finishing Up

12. If you loaded QBASIC again, press [Esc] to clear the opening screen. Then exit the program as you did in Step 9. If you loaded another application, use its exit command instead.

EDITING AND CREATING PIF FILES

When you load a non-Windows application, Windows looks for a PIF file (Program Information File) that contains information needed to run the application efficiently. If Windows cannot find a PIF file for the application that you are loading, it uses a default PIF file named *_default.pif*. However, applications can often be made to operate better with a PIF file designed specially for them. PIF files for many, but not all, applications are supplied with Windows. If one doesn't exist for your application, you can create or edit PIF files with the PIF Editor application found in the Main group window.

TIP: PIF NAMES AND FILE LOCATIONS

When you click an application icon or filename, Windows tries to locate a PIF file with the same name. For example, if the application is loaded by typing **wp**, it looks for a file named *wp.pif*. Windows first looks for this file in the application's directory, then the current directory, then the *windows* directory, then the *systems* subdirectory under the *windows* directory, and finally all of the directories specified in the *path* command. If Windows cannot locate a file with the same name, it uses the PIF file named *_default.pif*.

PIF Editor

To create a new PIF file, double-click the PIF Editor icon in the Main group window.

The mode that your system is running in determines which dialog box you see when you run PIF Editor. In standard mode there are fewer options available when running applications.

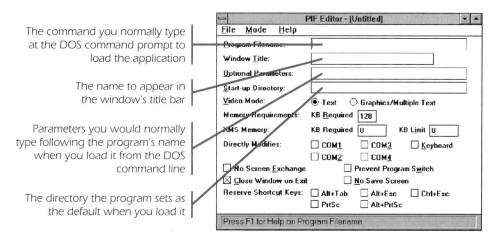

The command you normally type at the DOS command prompt to load the application

The name to appear in the window's title bar

Parameters you would normally type following the program's name when you load it from the DOS command line

The directory the program sets as the default when you load it

In *enhanced mode* so there are more options from which to choose.

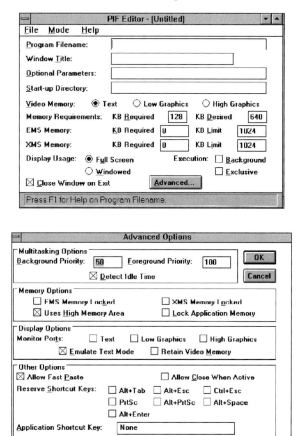

When you create a new PIF file, save it under the same name as the main program file but with the extension *.pif*. For example, if the application is normally loaded from the DOS command prompt by typing **word** and then pressing Enter⏎, name the file *word.pif*.

▶▶ TUTORIAL

Getting Ready

1. Begin by collecting the information that you need to edit a PIF file for a non-Windows application. In this section, instructions are given for the QBASIC application on a system running in enhanced mode. If your instructor wants you to edit a PIF file for another application or a system running in standard mode, he or she will supply you with the necessary information.

Opening a PIF File

2. Open the Main (or Accessories) group window and double-click the PIF Editor icon to display a dialog box. Which one is displayed depends on whether your system is running in standard or enhanced mode.

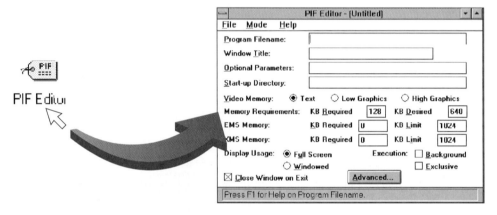

PIF Editor

3. Pull down the **File** menu and click the **Open** command to display a dialog box. The application automatically displays the files ending with the extension .*pif* in the *c:\windows* directory.

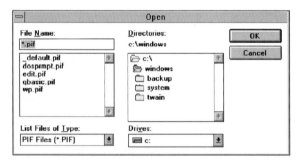

4. Click the *qbasic.pif* file in the **File Name** window to select it, and then click the **OK** command button. The settings for QBASIC are loaded into the PIF Editor screen.

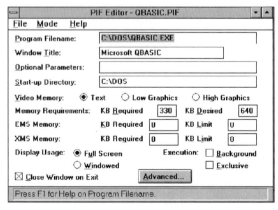

COMMON WRONG TURNS: CLICKING THE WRONG MENU

It's rare that two menus are displayed at the same time. However, if Program Manager isn't closed when you open the PIF Editor, both windows display menus. If, by mistake, you try to pull down Program Manager's **File** menu instead of PIF Editor's **File** menu, Program Manager becomes the active window and may hide the PIF Editor. If this happens, minimize Program Manager, and the PIF Editor can be seen again.

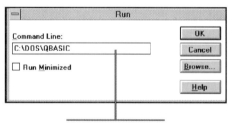

The path to the executable program

Editing and Saving a PIF File

5. Click the **Windowed** option button to turn it on and click the **Close Window on Exit** check box to turn it off.

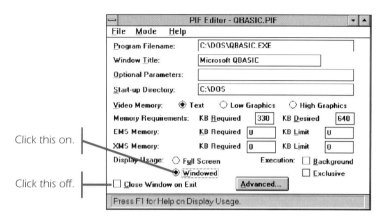

Click this on.

Click this off.

6. Pull down the PIF Editor's **File** menu and click the **Save** command to save the revised file.

7. Double-click the PIF Editor's Control-menu box to close the application.

Running the Application

8. Pull down Program Manager's **File** menu and click the **Run** command to display a dialog box.

9. Type **c:\dos\qbasic** (or the path and application name you are using) and click the **OK** command button to load the application. Notice how it now runs in a window instead of full screen, because you turned on the **Windowed** option button.

Exiting the Application

10. If you loaded QBASIC again, press `Esc` to clear the opening screen. Press `Alt`+`F` to pull down the **File** menu, then press `X` to exit the application and return to Windows. If you loaded another application, use its exit command instead. Notice how the application window doesn't close when you exit it because you turned off the **Close Window on Exit** check box.

11. Open the Main (or Accessories) group window and double-click the PIF Editor icon to display a dialog box.

12. Pull down the **File** menu and click the **Open** command to display a dialog box. Click the *qbasic.pic* file in the **File Name** window to select it, and then click the **OK** command button.

13. Click the **Windowed** option button to turn it off, and click the **Close Window on Exit** check box to turn it on.

14. Pull down the PIF Editor's **File** menu and click the **Save** command to save the revised file.

15. Double-click QBASIC's Control-menu box to close the application window.

PROTECTING AGAINST VIRUSES (DOS 6 ONLY)

A growing problem in the microcomputer field is the introduction of viruses by antisocial users. A virus is a small program, either stored on a disk by itself or appended to an existing file. When an application containing a virus is run, the virus loads itself into the computer's memory. Once there, it can secretly attach itself to other files or programs or store itself on any other disks run on the computer, including the hard disk. What happens next depends on the intent of the vandal who created the virus.

▶ The virus may cause problems immediately.

▶ It may count specific occurrences, for example, how many times it is copied, and then cause damage.

▶ It may look at the computer's clock and cause damage on a specific date.

▶ It may reproduce itself and then cause damage. Like a biological virus, a computer virus can infect other files and then spread from them.

The number of instances in which viruses cause damage is increasing. Once introduced, viruses are hard to detect and remove. For individual users, the best defense is to use only commercial applications and not to exchange files with other users. Using a virus scan application will help you detect the presence of viruses on your system and then delete them. DOS 6 has one of these applications, called Anti-Virus, built in.

Keep in mind that this antivirus application recognizes only a certain set of viruses. It does so by looking for a sequence of code that uniquely identifies each one. This code is called a *virus signature*. Since new viruses are being introduced daily, you should look at an antivirus application as only a first line of defense. You can, however, add new virus signatures by downloading them from a Microsoft *bulletin board system* (BBS). *Downloading* is the term used to describe transferring programs or data from another computer to yours using a modem and the telephone lines. Adding these signatures will help you identify new viruses, but to delete them, you must also update the Anti-Virus application periodically. A subscription plan is available for this service.

In Windows, the icon for this Anti-Virus application is located in the Microsoft Tools group window.

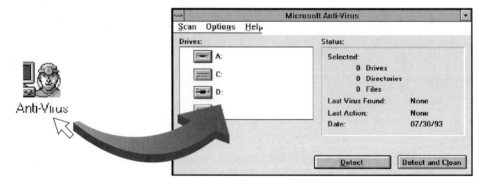

COMMON WRONG TURNS: NO TOOLS GROUP!

If your system does not have a **Tools** name on the File Manager Menu bar or a Tools group in Program Manager, DOS 6 may not be installed on your system. However, even if DOS 6 has been installed, you may not find the name *Tools*, because some companies that distribute DOS for Microsoft have changed the name of these items. If your system has such a renamed command, substitute that name in any of the following instructions that refer to the name *Tools*.

You can also access the Anti-Virus application by pulling down File Manager's **Tools** menu and clicking the **Anti-Virus** command.

Once the Anti-Virus application is open, you can pull down the **Scan** menu and click the **Virus List** command to display a list of the viruses it can detect and remove. The most common name for each virus is listed first. If it is also known by aliases, these are indented following the main entry. In addition to names, the list also gives the type of virus, its size, and the number of known variations.

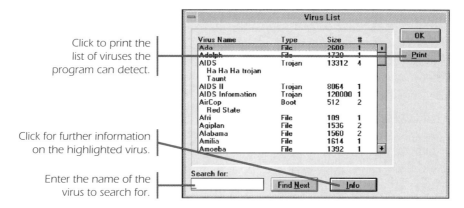

Click to print the list of viruses the program can detect.

Click for further information on the highlighted virus.

Enter the name of the virus to search for.

The list identifies three types of viruses: file, boot, and Trojan horse. A *file virus* infects program files and is executed when you run the application. A *boot virus* infects the boot sector on the disk that contains the information your system needs to start. The virus loads itself into memory when you boot the system. A *Trojan horse* virus looks just like a real program, but when you run it, it damages your system. Trojan horse viruses are typically the most damaging.

TIP: CONTINUOUSLY SCANNING FOR VIRUSES

DOS 6 comes with a application named *vsafe.com* that when loaded into memory will automatically scan the system for signs of unusual activity that may indicate the presence of a virus. If you add the line *c:\dos\vsafe* (your path may be different from *c:\dos*) to your *autoexec.bat* file, this application will be loaded into memory whenever you turn on the system.

THE VIRUSES ARE COMING

▸ A virus introduced into the computers at several universities counted the number of times it copied itself to other disks. When it had reproduced itself four times, it erased all files on the current disks in the computer.

▸ ARC, a major shareware program used to compress files so that they take up less space on the disk and can be telecommunicated faster, was altered and then uploaded to bulletin board systems. When it was then downloaded to a user's computer and run, it erased the part of the hard disk that is needed to boot the computer.

▸ A Christmas message sent over IBM's worldwide network looked up the mailing list of each person it was sent to and then sent itself to all those people. The avalanche of messages that were sent to more and more people slowed down the system and eventually brought it to a halt.

▸ A virus attached to Aldus's Freehand application displayed a peace message on users' screens on March 2, the anniversary of Apple's introduction of the Macintosh II. This was the first virus to be inadvertently distributed in a commercial application.

▸▸ TUTORIAL

Getting Ready

1. Insert your *Windows Student Resource Disk* into drive A.

Scanning a Disk for Viruses

2. Open the Microsoft Tools group window and double-click the Anti-Virus icon to display a dialog box. (Your system may be set to automatically scan a drive when you load this application. If it is, a message appears telling you that the drive's directories are being read, a dialog box with a progress bar appears, and then the application closes if no viruses are found. If your system does this, ask your instructor how to proceed.)

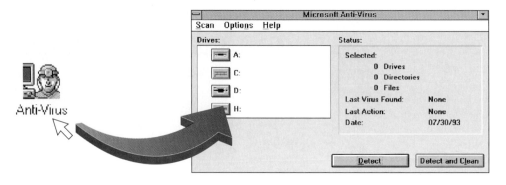

3. Click the icon for drive A, and a dialog box asks you to wait while it reads the directories for that drive. After the directories have been read, their number and the number of files on the disk are listed in the **Status** box.

Click the drive A icon to scan that drive.

Drives, directories, and files read (your numbers may be different)

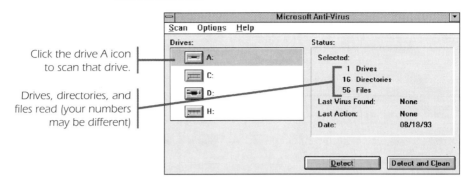

4. Click the **Detect** command button to begin scanning drive A.

Click to detect viruses.

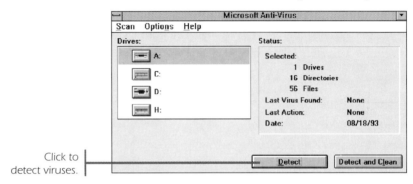

A progress bar keeps you informed of the scanning processes, and if a virus is found, a dialog box appears listing its name. To remove the virus, click the **Clean** command button in the dialog box.

Progress report

Viruses found, if any

Click to pause.

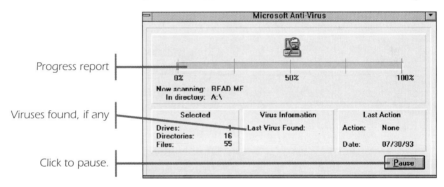

5. When the selected drives have been scanned, the Statistics dialog box is displayed. It tells you the number of disks and files scanned and how many were infected and cleaned. It also tells you how long the scanning and cleaning operation took.

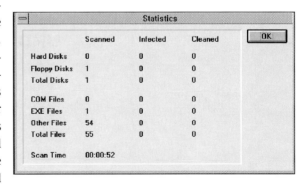

6. Click the **OK** command button to remove the Statistics dialog box.

Examining the List of Virus Signatures

7. Pull down the **Scan** menu and click the **Virus List** command to display a list of the viruses the Anti-Virus application can detect.

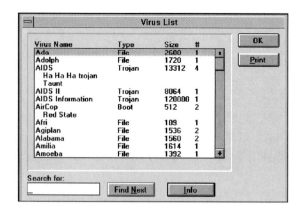

8. Click any virus described as *File* in the Type column and click the **Info** command button to learn more about the virus.

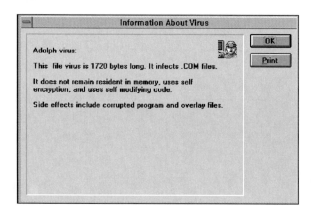

9. Click the **OK** command button when you are through reading the description.

10. Repeat Steps 8 and 9 but select any virus described as *Boot* or *Trojan* in the Type column before you click the **Info** command button.

Finishing Up

11. Double-click the Control-menu boxes for the virus list and Anti-Virus windows to close them.

UNDELETING FILES (DOS 6 ONLY)

It's easy to delete files by mistake. For example, you may select a file by mistake or delete a directory that contains a subdirectory you didn't mean to delete. When this happens, if you notice the mistake soon enough you can recover the deleted file or directory. The reason you can do so is that a deleted file or directory is not actually deleted from the disk. Instead, the first letter of its name is changed in the disk's directory, indicating to DOS that the space on the disk occupied by the file or directory is available for overwriting by another file. If you then save files on the disk, the new files may overwrite part or all of the deleted file or directory and it will be lost forever. For this reason, if you delete a file or directory by mistake, you should not save any files on the disk until you have used the Windows Undelete application to attempt to recover it.

UNDELETING FILES AND DIRECTORIES

To undelete deleted files or directories, you can use the Windows Undelete application introduced with DOS 6. (A similar *undelete* command, included with DOS 5, can be used from the DOS command prompt.) In Windows, the icon for this Undelete application is located in the Microsoft Tools group window. You can also access the Undelete application by pulling down File Manager's **File** menu and clicking the **Undelete** command. When you do either, a dialog box displays a list of the deleted files on the current drive and directory.

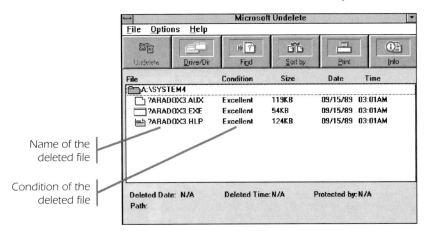

Name of the deleted file

Condition of the deleted file

The files listed on the screen are all assigned a condition depending on how likely it is that you can recover them. Files listed as *Perfect* have been protected by DOS's Data Sentry level of protection and can be easily recovered. Those listed as *Excellent* have been protected by DOS's Data Tracker level of protection and can be recovered if not overwritten by part of another file. Those listed as *Good* may be partially recovered, and those listed as *Poor* may be recovered using the DOS version of the Undelete application. Those listed as *Destroyed* cannot be recovered. When the files are listed, all but those listed as Perfect have a question mark in place of the first character in their filename. When you click the **Undelete** command button for one of these files, a dialog box appears so you can reenter the first character. Files that are listed as Poor or Destroyed are dimmed to indicate that you cannot select them for undeletion.

SPECIFYING THE LEVEL OF PROTECTION

The Windows Undelete application offers three levels of security. To choose one, you pull down File Manager's **File** menu and click the **Undelete** command to display the Undelete screen. You next pull down the **Options** menu and click the **Configure Delete Protection** command to display a dialog box. You then select **Delete Sentry**, **Delete Tracker**, or **Standard**.

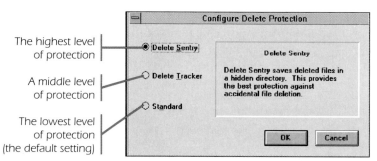

The highest level of protection

A middle level of protection

The lowest level of protection (the default setting)

Standard is the default setting. It provides the lowest level of security but requires no memory and no computer disk space.

Delete Sentry provides the highest level of protection and requires a small amount of memory. Delete Sentry saves your deleted files in a hidden directory named *Sentry*. You can choose how long you want to save the deleted files and what portion of your disk space to allocate to the hidden directory.

Delete Tracker provides the middle level of protection. It keeps a record of where the deleted files were stored on your disk, making them easier to recover. It requires the same amount of memory as Delete Sentry but minimal disk space.

 ►► **TUTORIAL**

Specifying Delete Sentry Protection for the Disk in drive A

1. Pull down File Manager's **File** menu and click the **Undelete** command to display the Undelete window.

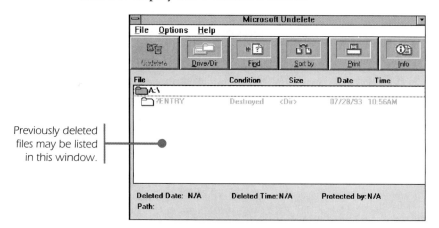

Previously deleted files may be listed in this window.

2. Pull down the Undelete window's **Options** menu and then click the **Configure Delete Protection** command to display a dialog box. One of the three levels of protection will be selected. The default choice is **Standard.**

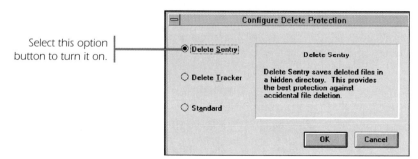

Select this option button to turn it on.

3. Click the **Delete _Sentry_** option button to turn it on (if it isn't already) and then click the **OK** command button to display another dialog box.

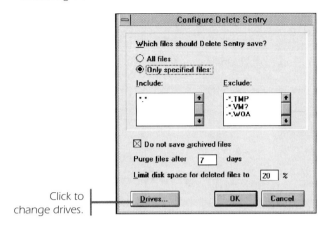

Click to change drives.

4. Click the **_Drives_** command button to display a list of the drives on your system. If drive A isn't highlighted, click it to select it.

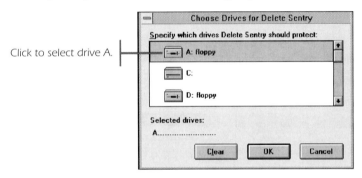

Click to select drive A.

5. Click the **OK** command buttons on the next two screens to display an Undelete Alert notice that you must reboot your computer. Click the **OK** command button.

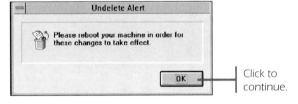

Click to continue.

LOOKING BACK: SELECTING NONADJACENT FILES

To select nonadjacent files on the contents list, hold down Ctrl and click each file-name individually.

6. Exit Windows and then either turn your computer off and back on or press Ctrl + Alt + Del to reboot the system.

Deleting Files

7. Load Windows, open the Main group window, and double-click the File Manager icon to open it.

8. Insert your *Windows Student Resource Disk* into drive A and choose that drive.

9. Display the files in the *filemgr* directory of the disk in drive A, and select the files named *chpt1.wri*, *file1.txt*, and *rename1.txt*.

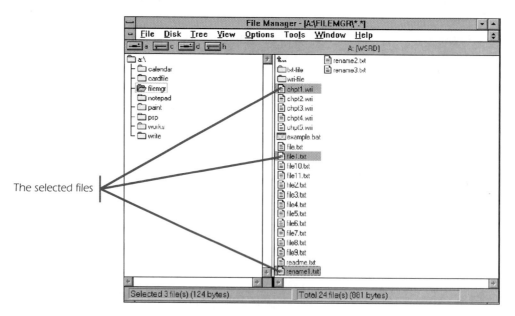

The selected files

10. Pull down the **File** menu and click the **Delete** command to display a dialog box.

11. Click the **OK** command button to confirm that you want to delete the files.

12. Click the **Yes to All** command button to delete all of the selected files.

Undeleting Files

13. Minimize File Manager so it is displayed as an icon.

14. Open the Microsoft Tools group window and double-click the Undelete icon to display the Undelete window. Any files previously deleted from the current directory are listed.

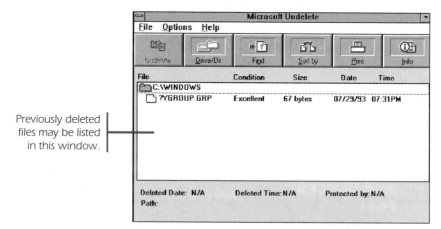

Previously deleted files may be listed in this window.

15. Click the **Drive/Dir** command button to display a dialog box. The path in the **Change to Directory** text box is highlighted.

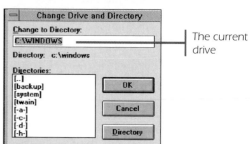

The current drive

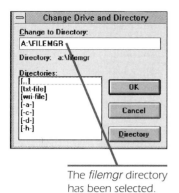

The *filemgr* directory
has been selected.

16. Double-click *[-a-]* in the **Directories** window to change to drive A;
then double-click the *[filemgr]* directory name to open it.

17. Click the **OK** command button, and any deleted files found in the
filemgr directory on the disk in drive A are listed on the screen. The
Condition column indicates your chances of recovering each file.

Any files that
were previously
deleted from the
directory are listed.

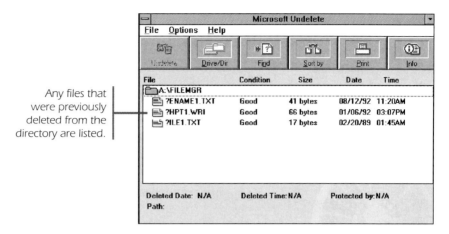

18. Click the *?hpt1.wri* file.

2 Click to recover
the selected file.

1 Click to select
the *?hpt1.wri* file.

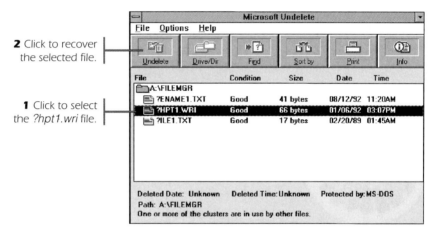

19. Click the **Undelete** command button, and the file's condition
changes to *Recovered*. (If a dialog box asks you to type a new first
letter, type C and then click the **OK** command button.)

The file is now listed
as recovered.

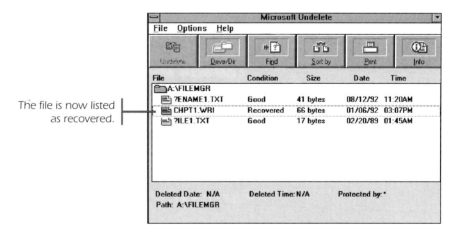

20. In turn, click each of the other two files and then the **Undelete** command button. When you do so, each file's condition should change to *Recovered*. (If a dialog box asks you to type a new first letter, type **R** for the *?ename1.txt* file and type **F** for the *?ile1.txt* file and click the **OK** command button.)

Finishing Up

21. Double-click the Undelete window's Control-menu box to close the window.

Contiguous and Noncontiguous Sectors
Disks with files located in contiguous sectors put less wear and tear on the drive and allow faster file saving and retrieving.

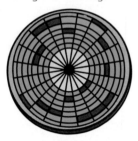

When a file is stored in noncontiguous sectors, parts of it are scattered about the disk. For the disk drive to retrieve such a file, it must move back and forth all over the disk.

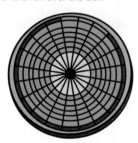

When a file is stored in contiguous sectors, it is stored on the disk in adjacent sectors. The disk drive can retrieve such a file in one smooth, continuous operation.

DEFRAGMENTING FILES FOR FASTER PERFORMANCE (DOS 6 ONLY)

When you save a file on a new disk, it is stored neatly on adjacent sectors around adjacent tracks on the disk. But after the disk begins to fill up and you delete some files and add others, the disk drive has to work harder to store a file. It stores different parts of the file wherever it can find free sectors. After a while, a file may end up scattered all over the disk on *noncontiguous sectors* (parts of the file that do not adjoin each other on the disk). Files stored this way are called *fragmented files*.

When files are stored in widely separated sectors, the drive's read/write head will have to move back and forth more frequently. This puts increased wear and tear on the drive because the drive's read/write head must keep moving over the disk's surface to reach parts of the files. It also makes opening and saving the files go slower.

When files become fragmented, some sections may become lost and not be retrievable. To determine if there are any such sections, called *lost allocation units*, use the *chkdsk* command. For example, to check the status of all files on drive C, type **chkdsk c:*.*** and press Enter⏎. This command tells you if all files occupy contiguous, or adjacent, blocks (as they should) or lists the files that contain noncontiguous, or scattered, blocks.

If your system does have fragmented sectors, use the *defrag* command to move the fragmented sectors back together. This application has on-line help, so if you need help at any point, just press F1.

To lessen the wear and tear on your drive, speed operations, and avoid lost files, you must perform this routine maintenance on your hard disk on a regular basis. Heavy users may do this as often as once a week. People who only use the computer occasionally should do so monthly or every other month. It only takes a few seconds if you do it periodically.

COMMON WRONG TURNS: CORRUPTED FILES

You must exit Windows before using the *chkdsk* or *defrag* commands. Do not use these commands after double-clicking the DOS icon to access DOS. Using them from within Windows can corrupt your files.

▶▶ **TUTORIAL**

1. Exit Windows and display the DOS command prompt.

2. Insert your *Windows Student Resource Disk* into drive A.

3. Type **chkdsk a:*.*** and press ⌷Enter⏎⌷ to see if there are any lost allocation units on the disk. If there are, type **chkdsk a:*.* /f** and press ⌷Enter⏎⌷, then press ⌷Y⌷ when asked whether to convert them to files. These files will be stored in the root directory as *file0000.chk*, *file0001.chk*, and so on.

4. Type **defrag a:** and press ⌷Enter⏎⌷ to display the Optimize screen. In a moment, a recommendation screen indicates the type of optimization that is suggested.

5. The dialog box that appears depends on whether or not your disk needs to be optimized:

   ▶ If the disk doesn't need to be optimized, click the **OK** command button or press ⌷Enter⏎⌷ to continue, and the **Optimize** menu is pulled down. Press ⌷B⌷ for **Begin Optimization** anyway to see how optimization works.

   ▶ If the disk needs to be optimized, click the **Optimize** command button, and optimizing begins automatically.

   As the disk is optimized, a grid shows you the progress being made. When optimization is completed, a dialog box indicates that it is finished condensing.

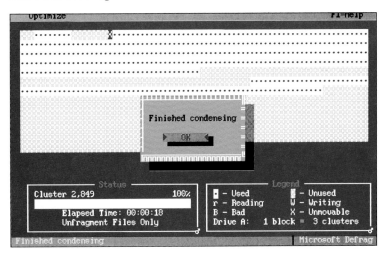

6. Click the **OK** command button or press [Enter↵] to continue. Another dialog box tells you optimization is complete and offers you three options; defragment another drive, configure Defrag, or exit.

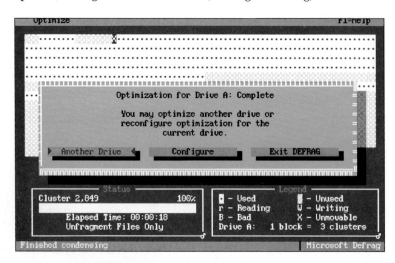

7. Click the **Exit DEFRAG** command button or press [Tab↹] to move the selection cursor to that command and press [Enter↵] to return to the command prompt.

►► SKILL-BUILDING EXERCISES

1. Running DOS Programs

1. Ask your instructor for the names of other executable program files that are on your system and enter information about them in the spaces provided.

Question	Program 1	Program 2
Name of application	_____	_____
Name of its executable program file	_____	_____
Path to the executable program file	_____	_____
Command you use to exit the program	_____	_____

2. Run each of these applications and then exit them.

2. Exploring PIF Files

Use the PIF Editor application to open two of the PIF files in the *c:\windows* directory and list the following information about each of them.

Information	PIF 1	PIF 2
Program filename	_____	_____
Window title	_____	_____
Optional parameters	_____	_____
Start-up directory	_____	_____

1. Explain how you display the DOS command prompt shown here without leaving Windows.

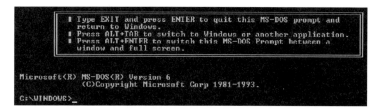

How do you then return to Windows?

_____

2. What keys do you press to run DOS in a window like this?

_____

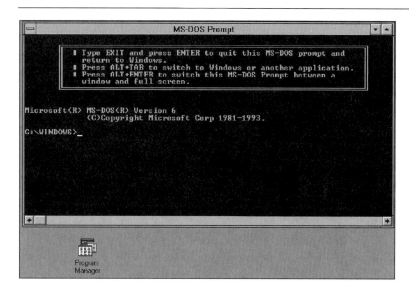

What mode does your system have to be in when you do so?

_____

3. What information would you list in each of these PIF Editor text boxes to create a PIF file for a program in the directory named *word-perf* on drive C that you normally loaded by typing **wp /x** from the DOS command prompt?

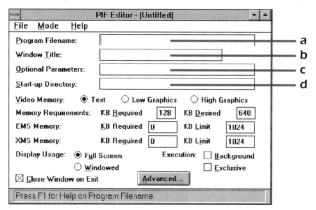

a. _____

b. _____

c. _____

d. _____

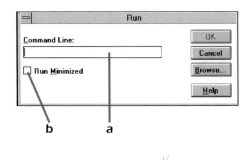

4. What command would you enter in the **Command Line** text box (a) to run a program in the directory named *lotus* on drive C that you normally loaded by typing **123** from the DOS command prompt? What would be the result of turning on the **Run Minimized** check box (b)?

a. _____

b. _____

5. When undeleting files, the screen may list any of five conditions. List the five conditions and briefly describe what each means.

Condition   **Description**

a. _____

b. _____

c. _____

d. _____

e. _____

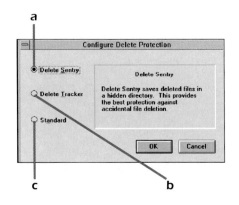

6. When specifying a level of protection, you have the three choices shown in this dialog box. Briefly describe the protection offered by each, what each level's memory requirements are, and which is the default setting.

a. _____

b. _____

c. _____

7. When your screen looks like this, describe what is happening and how you do it.

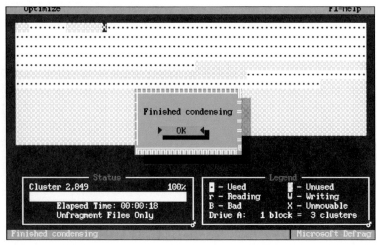

_____

_____

_____

True-False (Circle T if the statement is true or F if it is false.)

T F **1.** When you change the wallpaper on your system, you only see the change when you can see part or all of the desktop.

T F **2.** Changing the pattern on the desktop has only a subtle effect.

T F **3.** If you are left-handed, you can only use Windows easily by buying a left-handed mouse that has the buttons reversed.

T F **4.** You can easily copy an application icon into another group window.

T F **5.** To delete a group window, you must first delete all of the application icons in it one by one.

T F **6.** You can tell what mode your system is running in by pulling down Program Manager's Help menu and clicking the **About Program Manager** command.

T F **7.** In standard mode, you can run DOS applications in windows and full screen.

T F **8.** To display the DOS command prompt, you must always first exit Windows.

T F **9.** If you display the DOS command prompt without exiting Windows, you return to Windows by typing **quit** and pressing ⏎ Enter ◄┘ .

T F **10.** When you try to run a non-Windows application, there must be a PIF file for it in the Windows directory.

T F **11.** The Anti-Virus program that comes with DOS 6 can identify all harmful viruses that may damage your system.

T F **12.** Viruses are funny, and you should look upon the people who create and distribute them with great respect.

T F **13.** Once you have deleted a file or directory, it is gone forever.

T F **14.** DOS 6 provides three levels of Undelete security.

T F **15.** If you change the level of Undelete protection, you must reboot your system for the change to take effect.

T F **16.** Hard disks are so well designed, you never have to worry about how your files are being stored on them of perform any maintenance functions.

T F **17.** A file that is split up in noncontiguous blocks is called a fragmented file.

Multiple Choice (Circle the correct answer.)

1. To change the bit-mapped image on your desktop, you change the ___ .

a. Screen saver

b. Pattern

c. Wallpaper

d. Pattern or wallpaper

2. Using the Control Panel, you can ___.

   a. Change the appearance of the Windows desktop

   b. Change the colors of the screen

   c. Install new fonts or printers

   d. All of the above

3. To copy an application icon from one group window to another, you hold down ___ while dragging it.

   a. [Alt]

   b. [Ctrl]

   c. [⇧ Shift]

   d. None of the above

4. When you associate a file's extension with an application, you can then ___.

   a. Open the file by double-clicking a file with the extension on the contents list

   b. Print the file by dragging a file with the extension from the contents list and dropping it onto Print Manager's icon

   c. Add an icon for a document with the extension by dragging the file from the contents list and dropping it into the same group window as the application's icon

   d. All of the above

5. To switch back and forth between running a non-Windows application in a window and running it full screen, you ___.

   a. Press [Alt]-[Enter ←]

   b. Pull down the **W**indow menu and click the **R**efresh command

   c. Press [Ctrl]-[Enter ←]

   d. None of the above

6. To run a non-Windows application, you ___.

   a. Double-click the application's executable program filename in File Manager's contents list

   b. Use the **R**un command located on Program Manager's **F**ile menu

   c. Access the DOS command prompt and type the application's executable program filename

   d. Any of the above

7. When you try to run a non-Windows application, Windows looks for a PIF file for it in ___.

   a. The program's directory and the current directory

   b. The *windows* directory and the *systems* subdirectory under the *windows* directory

   c. All of the directories specified in the *path* command

   d. All of the above

8. Viruses fall into categories such as ___ based on how they operate and what they infect.

    a. File virus

    b. Boot virus

    c. Trojan horse virus

    d. All of the above

9. DOS 6 provides a ___ level of Undelete protection.

    a. Standard

    b. Delete Tracker

    c. Delete Sentry

    d. All of the above

Fill in the Blank (Enter your answer in the space provided.)

1. Many of the commands that you use to control how Windows looks and runs on your system are stored together in a window called the _____ Panel.

2. The image displayed on the desktop is called the _____ or _____.

3. To protect your screen, you can have a _____ turn on automatically after a specified period of time.

4. To slow down how fast the mouse pointer moves when you move the mouse, you can adjust the _____.

5. Normally, to install a new Windows application, you pull down Program Manager's _____ menu, click the _____ command, and enter _____ in the **Command Line** text box.

6. If you want to store a group of related icons together, you can create a new _____ window.

7. To copy an icon from one group window to another, you hold down _____ when you drag it.

8. When you create a new group window or add a new icon, you enter text into the **Description** text box. This text later appears on both the _____ and the _____.

9. To delete both a group window and the icons that it contains in a single step, the window must first be _____.

10. To change the text that appears on a group window's title bar, you would first select it, then pull down the _____ menu and click the _____ command.

11. If you can print a document by dragging its filename from the contents list and dropping it onto Print Manager's icon, the file has an _____.

12. Windows can only run DOS in a window when it is running in _____ mode. To switch back and forth between running it in a window and running it full screen, press _____.

13. If you double-click the DOS icon to access the DOS command prompt, you return to Windows by typing _____ and then pressing _____.

14. When you try to exit Windows while a DOS application is still running, a _____ is displayed. You must then _____ the application before exiting.

15. When you run a non-Windows application, Windows looks for a _____ file. If it can't find one specifically designed for the application, it uses one named _____.

16. DOS's Anti-Virus program can identify a virus by its _____.

17. To have your system continually monitored for signs of virus activity, you run the _____ program.

18. DOS provides three levels of Undelete protection: _____, _____, and _____. The default level of protection is _____.

19. When parts of a file are stored all over a disk, it is said to be _____ or stored in _____ sectors.

20. To optimize a disk so files are stored in adjacent sectors, you must _____ the disk.

 ## Projects

Project 1. Using SYSEDIT

There is an application named *sysedit.exe* in the *system* subdirectory under the *windows* directory. This application automatically opens the *config.sys*, *autoexec.bat*, *win.ini*, and *sys.ini* files so you can look at them or revise them. Create a new group window named *Key Files* and add an icon for this application to it. Then double-click the icon to display the four files. When finished looking at the files, double-click the window's Control-menu box to close it, then delete both the icon and the group that you created.

Project 2. Adding a Dos Application to the Applications Group

In Exercise 1 of PicTorial 9 you gathered information about DOS programs on your system. Use this information to add one of these programs to Program Manager's Applications group. Run the program and exit it, then remove it from the Applications group.

QUICK REFERENCE
TOPIC LOOKUP CHART

BASIC OPERATIONS

LOADING WINDOWS

▶ Boot the system, then type **win** and press Enter←⏎.

▶ To load Windows and open an application, type **win**, press Spacebar, and type the name used to load the application. For example, to load Windows and open the Paintbrush application, type **win pbrush** and press Enter←⏎.

EXITING WINDOWS

Do any of the following:

▶ Pull down the **File** menu and click the **Exit Windows** command.

▶ Make Program Manager the active window and press Alt + F4.

▶ Double-click Program Manager's Control-menu box.

▶ Click Program Manager's Control-menu box or icon to display the Control menu, then click the **Close** command.

USING A MOUSE

▶ *Pointing* refers to moving the mouse on the desktop so it moves the mouse pointer on the screen to a place where you want it.

▶ *Clicking* refers to quickly pressing and then releasing the left mouse button.

▶ *Double-clicking* refers to pointing to an object on the screen and then quickly pressing the left button twice in rapid succession.

▶ *Dragging* means pointing to an object on the screen and then holding down the left mouse button while you move the mouse to drag the object. When the object is where you want it, you release the mouse button.

USING SCROLL BARS

▶ To scroll up or down one line, click the up or down scroll arrow.

▶ To scroll the screen continuously, point to the up or down arrow and hold down the mouse button.

▶ To scroll up or down one screen, point to the scroll bar above or below the scroll box and click. Use the same procedure to scroll one screen left or right.

▶ To move quickly to any point in the document, drag the scroll box to where you want it and then release it. The scroll bar represents the total length of the document and the scroll box represents your current position. For example, if you drag the scroll box halfway down the scroll bar and release it, you move halfway down the document.

USING MENUS

▶ To pull down a menu, point to the menu name on the menu bar and click.

▶ To choose a command from a pulled-down menu, click it. Commands listed on menus follow the con-

ventions described in the table "Menu Conventions."

▶ To close a menu without selecting a command, point anywhere outside of the menu or menu bar and click.

Menu Conventions	
Convention	**Description**
Dimmed or hidden	The command is not available from the point at which you are in a procedure. For example, you may not yet have selected an item to be affected by the command.
Followed by an ellipsis (...)	Choosing the command displays a dialog box listing options you can choose.
Followed by a check mark (✔)	The command has already been selected. Choosing it again removes the check mark and unselects the command.
Followed by a key combination	The listed keys can be used instead of the menu as a shortcut to executing the command.
Followed by a right-pointing triangle	Choosing the item displays a cascading menu listing additional commands.

USING DIALOG BOXES

▶ *Text boxes* are spaces where you type in data. To enter data in a text box, click it to move the insertion point into it. If you press Tab⇆ to move to a text box that already has an entry, or double-click it, the entire entry will be selected. The first character that you type deletes this previous entry.

To edit an entry in a text box, press one of the arrow keys or Home or End to remove the highlight; position the insertion point where you want to insert characters; and type them in. To delete characters, press Del or ←Bksp. You can also double-click a word to select it and press Del to delete it. Or you can move the insertion point to a character, hold down the left mouse button, and drag the highlight over adjacent text and then press Del. Holding down ⇧Shift while you press an arrow key also extends the selection.

▶ *List boxes* display a list of choices. Lists too long to be displayed in the window can be scrolled with the box's scroll bar. To select an item on the list, click it.

▶ *Drop-down list boxes* are displayed as a rectangular box with the current selection listed. To see other options, click the down arrow to the right of the box, then use the scroll bar to scroll through the list.

▶ *Command buttons* such as **OK, Cancel,** and **Options** execute a command when you click them. If the command button is followed by an ellipsis (...), another dialog box is displayed. If it is marked with greater-than signs (>>), the active dialog box is expanded.

▶ *Option buttons* offer mutually exclusive options (only one can be on at a time). The one that is on contains a black dot. If you click a button that is off, you turn it on and turn off any other related button.

▸ *Check boxes* offer nonexclusive options (one or more of them can be on at the same time). To turn on an option, click it to display an X in the box. To turn it off, click the X to remove it. If the name of one of the check boxes is dimmed, it can't be chosen from where you are in a procedure. If the check box itself is shaded, it may mean that additional choices relate to the option.

▸ To cancel a command that you have not yet executed, click the **Cancel** command button or double-click the dialog box's Control-menu box.

USING ON-LINE HELP

1. Pull down the **Help** menu, click a **Help** command button, or press F1.
2. Choose one of the Help commands described in the table "Help Menu Commands" or click one of the command buttons described in the table "Help Buttons."
3. Once Help has been displayed, you can use any of the menu commands described in the table "Help Window Menu Commands."

Help Menu Commands	
Command	**Description**
Contents	Lists Help topics from which you can choose by clicking one.
Search for Help On	Displays a dialog box so you can choose a topic from a list or type a topic to search for into a text box.
How to Use Help	Displays information on how to use Help.
About (application name)	Displays the current application's name and version number and lists the memory available on your system.

Help Buttons	
Command	**Description**
Contents	Displays a list of Help topics from which you can choose by clicking one.
Search	Displays a dialog box so you can choose a topic from a list or type a topic to search for into a text box.
Back	Backs you up through previously displayed Help screens.
His**t**ory	Displays a list of all Help screens you have viewed since loading Windows in the current session.
Glossary	Displays a list of terms you can click to display definitions. To remove a definition, click anywhere.
<<	Displays the previous topic in a series of related topics (dimmed when you are on the first topic in the series).
>>	Displays the next topic in a series of related topics (dimmed when you are on the last topic in the series).

Help Window Menu Commands	
Command	**Description**
File	Displays a menu with the following choices: ▸ **O**pen displays a list of Help files from other Windows applications. ▸ **Print Topic** prints the displayed Help topic. ▸ **P**rint Setup connects you to the printer setup commands that all Windows applications share. ▸ **Exit** quits the Help program and removes the Help window from the screen.
Edit	Displays a menu with the following choices: ▸ **C**opy copies the displayed Help topic to the Clipboard so it can be transferred to other programs. ▸ **A**nnotate adds your own comments to a Help screen and displays a paper clip next to the screen's title. When you click the paper clip, your annotation is displayed.
Bookmark	Defines a bookmark that is then listed on the menu so you can quickly return to a specific screen by clicking the bookmark's name.
Help	Displays a menu with the following choices: ▸ **How to Use Help** displays help on how to use the on-line Help system. ▸ **Always on T**op keeps the Help screen on top of any other windows on the desktop. ▸ **About Help** displays the current application's name and version number and lists the memory available on your system.

ACCESSING THE DOS COMMAND PROMPT

To display the DOS command prompt, double-click the DOS icon. If your system is running in enhanced mode, press Alt + Enter↵ to switch it from running full screen to running in a window and back again.

MANAGING WINDOWS AND ICONS

MINIMIZING, MAXIMIZING, AND RESTORING WINDOWS

The ways you switch a window from one size to another are summarized in the following table:

Minimizing, Maximizing, and Restoring Windows		
Window Display	**To Change To**	**Do This**
Icon	Original size	Double-click icon
		Click to display Control menu, then click **Restore** command
	Full screen	Click to display Control menu, then click **Maximize** command
Original size	Icon	Click **Minimize** button
		Click window's Control-menu box, then click **Minimize** command
	Full screen	Click **Maximize** button
		Click window's Control-menu box, then click **Maximize** command
Full screen	Icon	Click **Minimize** button
		Click window's Control-menu box, then click **Minimize** command
	Original size	Click Restore button
		Click window's Control-menu box, then click **Restore** command

PROGRAM MANAGER'S INITIAL GROUPS

When Windows is first installed, it contains the groups described in the table "Initial Windows Groups."

Initial Windows Groups	
Group	**Description**
Main	Contains application icons for File Manager, Control Panel, Print Manager, Clipboard Viewer, MS-DOS Prompt (may be in the Accessories group), Windows Setup, and PIF Editor.
StartUp	Contains icons for applications that you want to start automatically when you start Windows.
Applications	Contains icons for other applications on the disk.
Accessories	Contains icons for the Windows applications such as Write and Paintbrush.
Microsoft Tools	If you are using DOS 6, this window contains icons for Anti-Virus, Backup, and Undelete applications.
Games	Contains the Solitaire and Minesweeper games.

USING CONTROL MENUS

1. To display a window's Control menu, click its Control-menu box in the upper-left corner of the window.

2. Choose any of the commands described in the table "Control-Menu Box Commands." (The commands listed on the menu vary depending on what program you are using.)

Control-Menu Box Commands	
Command	**Description**
Restore	Restores a window to its previous size after reducing it to an icon or maximizing it to fill the screen or window.
Move	Uses the arrow keys on the keyboard to move the window on the desktop.
Size	Uses the arrow keys to change the size of the window.
Minimize	Reduces the window to an icon.
Maximize	Enlarges the window to its maximum size.
Close	Closes a document window or closes an application window and quits the application.
Switch To	Displays the Task List so you can switch between running applications or use the menu to arrange windows and icons on the desktop.
Edit	When running non-Windows applications in a window, displays a menu with the following commands:
	▸ **Mark** lets you select text with the keyboard so you can copy it to the Clipboard.
	▸ **Copy** copies selected text to the Clipboard.
	▸ **Paste** copies text from the Clipboard.
	▸ **Scroll** displays information not visible in the window.
Settings	Displays a dialog box where you can enter or change multitasking options (non-Windows applications only).
Fonts	Displays a dialog box where you can enter or change font options (non-Windows applications only).
Next	Switches between open windows and icons in document windows.

SIZING AND ARRANGING WINDOWS

▸ To change the size of a window, point to its frame so the mouse pointer turns into a double-headed arrow. Hold down the left mouse button and drag the window's border to where you want it, then release the button.

▸ To drag a window to a new location, point to its title bar, hold down the left mouse button, and drag the window to where you want it, then release the button.

▸ To rearrange windows so they overlap with their title bar displayed, pull down Program Manager's **Window** menu and click the **Cascade** command.

▸ To rearrange windows so they are side by side, pull down Program Manager's **Window** menu and click the **Tile** command.

▸ To rearrange windows, double-click anywhere on the desktop (other than in an open window) or click the active window's Control-menu box and click the **Switch To** command to display the Task List. Then click the **Cascade** or the **Tile** command button.

REARRANGING ICONS

▸ To rearrange icons on the desktop, double-click anywhere on the desktop (other than in an open window) or click the active window's Control-menu box and click the **Switch To** command to display the Task List.

Click the **Arrange Icons** command button to line up the icons along the lower portion of the window.

▶ To rearrange application icons in a group window, select the group window, pull down Program Manager's **Window** menu, and click the **Arrange Icons** command. This command evenly spaces application icons within the window. If all application icons cannot be displayed in a group window, the window displays a scroll bar so you can scroll through the icons in the window.

▶ To rearrange open group icons, first click one of the icons to select it and then click the desktop to close its Control menu. Pull down Program Manager's **Window** menu and click the **Arrange Icons** command to evenly space application icons along the lower portion of the Program Manager window.

▶ To have application icons in group windows automatically rearrange themselves when you change their window's size, pull down the **Options** menu and put a check mark (✔) in front of the **Auto Arrange** command.

AUTOMATICALLY REDUCING PROGRAM MANAGER TO AN ICON

To have Program Manager automatically reduced to an icon when you start an application, pull down its **Options** menu and put a check mark (✔) in front of the **Minimize on Use** command.

SAVING CHANGES TO THE DESKTOP LAYOUT

▶ Pull down the **Options** menu and click the **Save Settings on Exit** command to remove the check mark (✔) from in front of the command. Then press [Alt]+[⇧ Shift]+[F4] to save the settings.

▶ Pull down the **Options** menu and click the **Save Settings on Exit** command to place a check mark (✔) from in front of the command. When you then exit Windows, your settings will be saved. Be sure to remove the check mark the next time you load Windows unless you want subsequent changes to be saved.

CHANGING PROPERTIES

▶ To specify properties of a group or program, click it to select it (a group must be displayed as an icon to select it). Then either pull down the **File** menu and click the **Properties** command, or press [Alt]+[Enter ←] to display its Properties dialog box.

▶ Hold down [Alt] and double-click an icon to display its Properties dialog box.

USING FILE MANAGER

CHANGING DEFAULT DRIVES

Do either of the following:

▶ Click the drive icon on the directory window.

▶ Pull down the **Disk** menu and click the **Select Drive** command to display a dialog box listing all of the drives on your system. Choose one of the drives on the list.

CHANGING THE CURRENT DIRECTORY

▶ To move to any directory or subdirectory on the current drive, click its name or icon on the menu tree.

▶ To move up a level, double-click the Up icon that is displayed before the first entry on the contents list.

UNDERSTANDING FILE ICONS ON THE CONTENTS LIST

File icons on the contents list indicate the type of file that each name represents. See page 68 for an illustration and explanation of the five icon types.

DISPLAYING THE DIRECTORY TREE AND/OR THE CONTENTS LIST

1. Pull down the **View** menu.
2. Click the **Tree and Directory, Tree Only,** or **Directory Only** command.

DISPLAYING PARTIAL DETAILS

1. Pull down the **View** menu.
2. Click the **Partial Details** command to display a dialog box. Turn on or off any of the options described in the table "Partial Details Options."

Partial Details Options	
Option	**Description**
Size	The size of each file in bytes.
Last Modification Date	The date the file was last modified, based on the computer's system clock.
Last Modification Time	The time the file was last modified, based on the computer's system clock.
File Attributes	Whether the file is a read-only file (R), a hidden file (H), or a system file (S) and whether the file has been changed since a backup copy was last made with the Windows/DOS Backup command (A , for *archive*).

DISPLAYING SPECIFIC FILE TYPES

1. Pull down the **View** menu.
2. Click the **By File Type** command to display a dialog box. Turn on or off any of the options described in the table "By File Type Options."

By File Type Options

Option	Description
Name	Displays files based on the filename specifications you enter in this text box. For example, *.bak displays all files with the extension .bak.
Directories	Displays all subdirectories in the current directory.
Programs	Displays all files that have the extension .exe, .com, .pif, or .bat.
Documents	Displays all files that are associated with an application.
Other Files	Displays all other files (those that are not displayed by the **Programs** or **Documents** choices).
Show Hidden/ System Files	Displays all hidden and system files in the active directory. If you display these, don't rename or delete them or your system may have troubles.

WORKING WITH MULTIPLE DIRECTORY WINDOWS

▶ To open a new directory window without closing the current one, double-click the drive icon.

▶ To arrange multiple directory windows one above another, pull down the **Window** menu and click the **Tile** command.

▶ To arrange directory windows side by side, pull down the **Window** menu, then hold down ⇧Shift when you click the **Tile** command.

▶ To arrange multiple windows so they overlap, pull down the **Window** menu and click the **Cascade** command.

EXPANDING AND COLLAPSING DIRECTORY LEVELS WITH MENU COMMANDS

1. Pull down the **Tree** menu.

2. Choose one of the options described in the table "The Tree Menu's Options."

The Tree Menu's Options

Option	Description
Expand One Level	Expands just the selected directory to display one level of subdirectories.
Expand Branch	Expands just the selected directory to display all levels of subdirectories.
Expand All	Displays all subdirectories in the menu tree.
Collapse Branch	Hides all subdirectories in the selected directory.
Indicate Expandable Branches	Marks all expandable directories with a plus sign (+).

▶ To expand or collapse a directory's subdirectories, double-click their directory's name on the directory tree.

▶ To expand all levels of directories, hold down ⇧Shift when you click a drive icon.

FORMATTING FLOPPY DISKS

1. Insert the disk you want to format into one of the drives (usually drive A).

2. Pull down the **Disk** menu and click the **Format Disk** command to display a dialog box.

3. Point to the **Label** text box and click to move the cursor into the box, type a volume label (up to 11 characters), and then click the **OK** command button to display the Confirm Format Disk box.

4. Click the **Yes** command button, and the drive spins and its light comes on as the disk is formatted. When the disk has been formatted and the Format Complete box appears, either click the **No** command button to return to File Manager or insert a new disk in the same drive and click the **Yes** command button to format it.

SELECTING DISKS FOR YOUR SYSTEM

The disks you use must be appropriate for your system. Some of the possible combinations are shown in the tables "Formatting and Reading 5¼-Inch Disks" and "Formatting and Reading 3½-Inch Disks."

Formatting and Reading 5¼-Inch Disks

Procedure	360KB Drive	1.2MB Drive
Format a 360KB disk	Yes	Yes
Format a 1.2MB disk	No	Yes
Read a 360KB disk	Yes	Yes
Read a 1.2MB disk	No	Yes

Formatting and Reading 3½-Inch Disks

Procedure	720KB Drive	1.44MB Drive
Format a 720KB disk	Yes	Yes
Format a 1.44MB disk	No	Yes
Read a 720KB disk	Yes	Yes
Read a 1.44MB disk	No	Yes

MAKING SYSTEM DISKS

This command does not erase files from a disk.

1. Insert a formatted disk into one of the drives (usually drive A).

2. Pull down the **Disk** menu, click the **Make System Disk** command, and then click the **Yes** command button to transfer the system files needed to make the floppy disk a self-booting system disk. For this command to work successfully, the disk must have room for the files, and its root directory must have space for two more entries.

SPLITTING THE SCREEN DIFFERENTLY

1. Point to the split bar between the directory tree and contents list until the pointer turns into a double-headed arrow.

2. Hold down the left mouse button while you drag the bar to where you want it and then release it.

SPECIFYING FILE INFORMATION DISPLAYED ON THE CONTENTS LIST

1. Pull down the **View** menu.

2. Click one of the commands described in the table "Contents List Display Options"

Contents List Display Options	
Command	**Description**
Name	Displays just filenames.
All File Details	Displays the size of each file in bytes, the date and time the file was last saved, and the file's attributes. These attributes tell you if the file is a read-only file (R), a hidden file (H), or a system file (S) and whether the file has been changed since a backup copy was last made with the Windows/DOS Backup command (A, for *archive*).
Partial Details	Similar to **A**ll File Details command, but it lets you choose what information is displayed about the files. To display size, date, time, or file attribute information, click the appropriate check boxes to turn them on (Xs) or off (no Xs). Windows displaying only a directory tree are not affected by these options.
Sort by Name	Arranges the filenames in ascending alphabetical order by their filename. Files that begin with A are listed before those that begin with B.
Sort **b**y Type	Arranges the filenames in ascending alphabetical order first by their extension and then by their filename.
Sort by **S**ize	Arranges the filenames in descending order by their size. Larger files are listed before smaller files.
Sort by **D**ate	Arranges the filenames in descending order by date. More recent files are listed before older files.

USING WILDCARDS TO DISPLAY SPECIFIC FILES

1. Pull down the **View** menu and click the **By File Type** command to display a dialog box.

2. Enter a filename specification in the **Name** text box. The default filename specification is *.*, which displays all files. The filename specification you enter into the **Name** text box can contain text and wildcards. For example, if you want to display only the file named *myfile.txt*, you enter that filename. However, you can also use the ? and * wildcards to specify groups of files.

▸ The question mark substitutes for any single character in a given position.

▸ The asterisk represents any character in a given position and all following characters in the part of the filename (either the name or extension) where it is used.

3. You can turn the check boxes on or off for any of the options described in the table "By File Type Options" on page 284.

4. When you have finished, click the **OK** command button to display filenames based on the choices you have made.

COPYING DISKS

1. Pull down the **Disk** menu and click the **Copy Disk** command to display a dialog box if your system has more than one floppy disk drive.

2. Specify the source and destination drives. When using this command, keep the following points in mind:

▸ The destination disk will be formatted if necessary before files are copied to it.

▸ You cannot use this command to copy files to a disk that already contains files unless you want to erase the existing files.

▸ You can only use the **Copy Disk** command to copy files between disks with identical storage capacities. For example, do not use **Copy Disk** between a high-density 5¼-inch disk in a high-density drive and a disk in a 360KB drive. If you do so, the target disk may not be usable. Also, do not use **Copy Disk** between 5¼-inch and 3½-inch drives.

▸ The command copies not only files but also directories and subdirectories.

3. Click the **OK** command button and follow the instructions displayed on the screen.

LABELING DISKS

1. Pull down the **Disk** menu and click the **Label Disk** command to display a dialog box.

2. Type the name of the disk into the **Label** text box (up to 11 characters) and then click the **OK** command button.

RENAMING FILES OR DIRECTORIES

1. Click the file or directory you want to rename.

2. Pull down the **File** menu and click the **Rename** command to display a dialog box. The current name is displayed in the **From** text box.

3. Type the new name into the **To** text box and click the **OK** command button to rename the file.

TURNING CONFIRMATION ON AND OFF

1. Pull down the **Options** menu and click the **Confirmation** command to display a dialog box.

2. Turn check boxes on for those actions where you want Windows to prompt you for confirmation. The options are described in the table "Confirmation Options." It is recommended that you leave all of these options on until you become an experienced Windows user.

Confirmation Options	
Option	**Description**
File **D**elete	Prompts you for confirmation when you delete a file.
Directory Delete	Prompts you for confirmation when you delete a directory. If you turn this off and delete a directory, it, its files, and all subdirectories can be deleted without your being asked to confirm your deletion command.
File **R**eplace	Prompts you for confirmation when you copy or move a file into a directory that already has a file with the same name.
Mouse Action	Prompts you for confirmation when you copy or move files by dragging them with the mouse.
Dis**k** Commands	Prompts you for confirmation when you format or copy disks.

SELECTING FILES IN THE CONTENTS LIST WITH THE SELECT FILES COMMAND

1. Pull down the **File** menu and click the **Select Files** command to display a dialog box.

2. Enter a filename specification and click the **Select** command button to select the files or the **Deselect** command button to unselect them. Rectangular boxes surround filenames that match the specification you entered.

3. Click the **Close** command button to return to the directory, and any selected files are now highlighted. The number selected and their total size is indicated on the status bar. (You can turn the display of this bar on and off with the **Status Bar** command on the **Options** menu.)

SELECTING FILES BY POINTING AND CLICKING

▶ To select a single file on the contents lists, click it.

▶ To extend the selection over sequential files, click the first filename to select it, and then hold down ⇧Shift while you either click the last filename or use the arrow keys to extend the highlight over sequential items in the list.

▶ To select nonsequential items, hold down Ctrl while you click each item. To cancel a selection, hold down Ctrl and click the item again.

▶ To select more than one sequential group, click the first filename to select it, and then hold down ⇧Shift while you either click the last filename or use the arrow keys to extend the highlight over sequential items in the list. To select the next group, hold down Ctrl while you click the first item. Then hold down Ctrl+⇧Shift while you click the last item.

COPYING AND MOVING FILES USING MENU COMMANDS

1. Select the files on the contents list.

2. Pull down the **File** menu and click the **Copy** command to display a dialog box.

3. Specify the path to where you want the file copied in the **To** text box. For example, to copy a file from drive B to drive A, you would enter the path **a:** or **a:**. If you copy a file to a disk or directory that already has a file by the same name, a dialog box appears if you have turned confirmation on for Replace.

COPYING AND MOVING FILES BY DRAGGING AND DROPPING

1. Make sure both the source and destination are visible in the directory window or windows. (You can use the **Window** menu's **Cascade** or **Tile** command to do this.)

2. Select the files to be copied or moved.

3. Drag the files or directories to the destination's drive icon, directory window, or directory icon as follows:

▶ To move them to another location on the same disk, drag them there and release the mouse button to drop them.

▶ To move them to another disk, hold down ⇧Shift while dragging them. To drop them, release the mouse button and then release ⇧Shift.

▶ To copy them to another disk, drag them there and release the mouse button to drop them.

▶ To copy them to another location on the same disk, hold down Ctrl while dragging them. To drop them, release the mouse button and then release Ctrl.

4. If a confirmation box appears, read it and choose the appropriate option.

Keys to Hold Down When Dragging & Dropping Files & Directories		
Destination	**Copy**	**Move**
Same Disk	Ctrl	None
Another Disk	None	⇧Shift

MAKING DIRECTORIES

1. Display the directory tree.

2. Select the directory under which you want the new directory to appear.

3. Pull down the **File** menu and click the **Create Directory** command to display a dialog box.

4. Type the name of the new directory into the **Name** text box and then click the **OK** command button. Directory names follow the same conventions that you use for filenames. However, you should not use a period and extension, or you might confuse directories with filenames at some later date.

DELETING FILES AND DIRECTORIES

1. Select the unneeded files or directories on the contents list or directory tree.

2. Pull down the **File** menu and click the **Delete** command to display the Delete dialog box listing the selected files. Click the **OK** command button to delete them. If confirmation is on, and if you are deleting a directory containing files, additional confirmation boxes may appear. (Tip: When the confirmation box appears, if you are deleting a number of files and directories, you can turn the prompt off for each deletion by choosing the **Yes to All** command button.)

Using Applications—The Basics

OPENING APPLICATIONS

Do any of the following:

▶ Double-click the application's icon.

▶ To open it as an icon, hold down ⇧Shift while you double-click the icon.

▶ Drag the application icon into Program Manager's StartUp group. Any application whose icon is in this group starts automatically when you load Windows. Applications are loaded in the order in which their icons appear in the window, from left to right beginning with the first line. (To have the StartUp group ignored when you load Windows, hold down ⇧Shift when you first see the Windows logo and don't release it until Windows is completely loaded.)

▶ Double-click an application's executable program filename in a File Manager window.

▶ Use the **Run** command on the **File** menu.

▶ Display the DOS command prompt and type its executable program filename (for non-Windows applications).

▶ Enter the application's executable program filename following **win** when you load Windows from DOS. For example, to load Windows and open Write, type **win write** and press Enter⏎ from the DOS command prompt.

EXITING APPLICATIONS

Do any of the following:

▶ Pull down the **File** menu and click the **Exit** command.

▶ Click the Control-menu box to display the Control menu and click the **Close** command.

▶ Double-click the Control-menu box.

▶ Press Alt + F4.

TERMINATING A MISBEHAVING APPLICATION (LOCAL REBOOT)

To terminate a misbehaving application, press Ctrl + Alt + Del (called a local reboot) to display an instruction screen telling you how to proceed. Your choices include returning to the application, quitting the application, and rebooting the system. All but the first may cause you to lose data. You normally perform a local reboot only when your system has stopped responding.

SWITCHING AMONG APPLICATIONS

Do any of the following:

▶ If you can see any part of the application's or document's window, click it.

▶ If the application is running as an icon, double-click the icon.

▶ To return to the application you last used, press Alt + Tab↹.

▶ To cycle through all open applications, press Alt + Esc.

▶ Hold down Alt and press Tab↹ repeatedly to display the names of open applications in the middle of the screen. When the name of the application you want to switch to is displayed, release Alt.

▶ To switch to another open application, double-click anywhere on the desktop (other than in an open window) or click the active window's Control-menu box and click the **Switch To** command to display the Task List. Double-click the application's name to choose it or click its name to select it and then click the **Switch To** command button.

OPENING DOCUMENTS

Do any of the following:

▶ With the application open, pull down the **File** menu and click the **Open** command to display a dialog box. Specify the drive and directory where the file is stored, then double-click the name of the document you want to open.

▶ Drag the document's icon from File Manager's contents list and drop it onto the open application's icon or title bar (if an association exists).

▶ Drag the document's file icon from File Manager's contents list to the same Program Manager group window as the application's icon. When you then double-click the file's icon, the application and document are both loaded (if an association exists).

SWITCHING AMONG DOCUMENT WINDOWS WITHIN APPLICATIONS

▶ To cycle through document windows within an application such as File Manager's document windows, press Ctrl + F6.

▶ Most applications have a **Window** menu that lists the open document windows so you can select the one you want to make active.

SAVING DOCUMENTS

▶ To save a file the first time, pull down the **File** menu and click the **Save** command to display a dialog box. Type the file's name into the **File Name** text box, select the drive and directory to save it to, then click the **OK** command button.

▶ To save a file under a new name, pull down the **File** menu and click the **Save As** command to display a dialog box. Type the file's new name into the **File Name** text box, select the drive and directory to save it to, then click the **OK** command button.

PRINTING DOCUMENTS

Do either of the following:

▶ Pull down the **File** menu and click the **Print** command to display a dialog box. Make any changes in the box, then click the **OK** command button.

▶ Open Print Manager and File Manager. Drag the document's icon from File Manager's contents list onto the Print Manager icon.

USING PRINT MANAGER

PAUSING AND RESUMING THE PRINTER

1. Double-click the Print Manager icon to open it to full screen.
2. Click the name of the printer you want to pause or resume.
3. Click the **Pause** command button to pause the printer or the **Resume** command button to resume printing.

DELETING A PRINT JOB FROM THE QUEUE

1. Double-click the Print Manager icon to open it to full screen.
2. Click the name of the print job that you want to delete.
3. Click the **Delete** command button to delete the print job.

SPEEDING PRINTING OR EDITING

1. Double-click the Print Manager icon to open it to full screen.
2. Pull down the **Options** menu and click any of the commands described in the table "Priorities."

Priorities	
Command	**Description**
Low Priority	Allocates most of the computer's processor to tasks other than printing. This allows you to work on other documents without being held up by delays due to printing.
Medium Priority	Allocates the processor's time equally between printing and other tasks.
High Priority	Allocates most of the computer's processor to printing so it is completed faster.

CHANGING PRINTERS

1. Double-click the Print Manager icon to open it to full screen.
2. Pull down the **Options** menu and click any of the commands described in the table "Changing Printers."

Changing Printers	
Command	**Description**
N̲etwork Settings	Specifies how Print Manger interacts with a network printer.
Network C̲onnections	Connects and disconnects you to network printers.
P̲rinter Setup	Installs printers and changes printer settings.

USING THE CLIPBOARD

The Windows Clipboard is used to copy or move data within or between applications. To use it, you first copy or cut data to the Clipboard and then paste it in where desired. The data remains on the Clipboard until you copy or cut other data to it or exit Windows.

COPYING OR CUTTING DATA TO THE CLIPBOARD

1. Select the data to be copied or cut.
2. Pull down the application's **Edit** menu and click the **Copy** or **Cu̲t** command.
   - ▶ **Copy** leaves the original data intact and makes a copy of it on the Clipboard.
   - ▶ **Cut** removes the original data from the application's file and transfers it to the Clipboard.

COPYING DATA FROM THE CLIPBOARD

1. Move the insertion point to where you want it pasted.
2. Pull down the **Edit** menu and click the **Paste** command. The data is pasted into the application in a format that the application recognizes.

COPYING A SNAPSHOT OF THE SCREEN TO THE CLIPBOARD

In 386 enhanced mode:

- ▶ To copy a snapshot (bitmap) of the entire screen to the Clipboard, press `PrtScr`. If this doesn't work, try pressing `Alt`+`PrtScr` or `Shift`+`PrtScr`.
- ▶ To copy a snapshot (bitmap) of just the active window to the Clipboard, press `Alt`+`PrtScr`. If this doesn't work on your system, try pressing `Shift`+`PrtScr`.

DISPLAYING THE CLIPBOARD'S CONTENTS

1. Double-click the Clipboard icon to open the Viewer.
2. Select any of the menu commands described in the table "Clipboard Viewer Menu Commands."

Clipboard Viewer Menu Commands

Command	Description
File	Displays a menu with the following choices:
	▶ **Open** displays a dialog box you use to retrieve a previously saved Clipboard file. If the Clipboard contains data when you open a new file, you are prompted to clear it. You can only open files with the *.clp* extension.
	▶ **Save As** displays a dialog box into which you enter the name of the file to be saved. Windows adds the extension *.clp* to Clipboard files. You can precede the filename with a path if you want to store the file in a directory other than the default.
	▶ **Exit** close the Clipboard Viewer.
Edit	Displays a menu with the command **Delete** that clears data from the Clipboard.
Display	Displays a menu of formats in which you can view the data.
Help	Displays a Help menu.

KEYBOARD SHORTCUTS

Although Windows is designed to be best used with a mouse, you can operate it from the keyboard. This is occasionally necessary should you be working on a mouseless computer such as a notebook or laptop. In this section, you can find the keys you need to execute the most essential commands.

Clipboard Viewer Keyboard Shortcuts

Action	Press
Delete contents of Clipboard	Del
Copy a selection from a document to the Clipboard	Ctrl + Ins
Move a selection from a document to the Clipboard	Shift + Del
Paste the Clipboard's contents into a document	Shift + Ins
Copy an image of the screen to the Clipboard	PrtScr
Copy an image of the active window to the Clipboard	Alt + PrtScr

Cursor Movement Keyboard Shortcuts

Action	Press
Up or down one line	↑ or ↓
Left or right one character	← or →
Left or right one word	Ctrl + ← or Ctrl + →
Beginning or end of line	Home or End
Up or down one screen	PgUp or PgDn
Beginning or end of document	Ctrl + PgUp or Ctrl + PgDn

Dialog Box Keyboard Shortcuts

Action	Press
Move between options	Tab or Shift + Tab
Move directly to an option	Alt + underlined letter in option's name
Move among options within a group	arrow keys
Move to first or last option	Home or End
Open the highlighted list	Alt + ↓
Select or unselect an item in a list	Spacebar
Extend the selection in a text box	Shift + arrow key
Execute a command	Enter ↵
Close a dialog box without executing the command	Esc or Alt + F4

Editing Keyboard Shortcuts

Action	Press
Delete character to left of insertion point	← Bksp
Delete character to right of insertion point	Del
Copy a selection from a document to the Clipboard	Ctrl + Ins
Move a selection from a document to the Clipboard	Shift + Del
Paste Clipboard's contents into a document	Shift + Ins
Undo last editing action	Alt + ← Bksp
Select text one character at a time	Shift + ← or Shift + →
Select text one line at a time	Shift + ↑ or Shift + ↓
Select to beginning of line	Shift + Home
Select to end of line	Shift + End
Select previous word	Ctrl + Shift + ←
Select next word	Ctrl + Shift + →
Select to beginning of document	Ctrl + Shift + Home
Select to end of document	Ctrl + Shift + End

File Manager Keyboard Shortcuts

Action	Press
Move selection cursor among directory tree, contents list, and drive icons	`Tab`
Move selection cursor between items within the directory tree, contents list, and drive icon areas	`←` or `→`
Expand or collapse a directory's subdirectories	`Enter ←`
Open a new window showing just the contents of the selected directory	`Shift`+`Enter ←`
Move the selection cursor up or down directory levels	`←` or `→`
Move the selection cursor between directories at the same level	`Ctrl`+`↑` or `Ctrl`+`↓`
Move the selection cursor to the drive icons	`Tab`
Select any drive	`Ctrl`+drive letter
Select the drive highlighted by the selection cursor	`Spacebar`
Select a file on the contents list	arrow keys
Select adjacent files on the contents list keys	`Shift`+arrow keys
Select all items on contents list	`Ctrl`+`/`
Cancel all selections on the contents list except the current selection	`Ctrl`+`\`
Open a new directory window for the drive highlighted by the selection cursor	`Enter ←`

Help Keyboard Shortcuts

Action	Press
Display Help	`F1`
Move between jumps	`Tab` or `Shift`+`Tab`
Highlight all jumps	`Ctrl`+`Tab`
Copy Help screen to the Clipboard	`Ctrl`+`Ins`
Quit Help	`Alt`+`F4`

Menu Keyboard Shortcuts

Action	Press
Select or unselect first item on the menu bar	`Alt` or `F10`
Choose a menu or command	underlined letter in name
Move selection cursor between menu names	`←` or `→`
Move selection cursor between menu commands	`↑` or `↓`
Choose the highlighted menu name or command	`Enter ←`
Cancel a command or close the menu	`Esc`

Program Manager Keyboard Shortcuts

Action	Press
Move selection cursor between icons in a group window	arrow keys
Move between group windows or group icons	`Ctrl`+`Tab`
Start the selected application	`Enter ←`
Tile open group windows	`Shift`+`F4`
Cascade open group windows	`Shift`+`F5`
Close the active group window	`Ctrl`+`F4`
Exit Windows	`Alt`+`F4`

System Keyboard Shortcuts

Action	Press
Display Help	`F1`
Display Task List	`Ctrl`+`Esc`
Switch to last application used	`Alt`+`Tab`
Switch to next application	`Alt`+`Esc`
Copy image of screen to the Clipboard	`PrtScr`
Copy image of active window to the Clipboard	`Alt`+`PrtScr`
Display application's Control menu	`Alt`+`Spacebar`
Display document window's Control menu	`Alt`+`-`
Close a window or quit an application	`Alt`+`F4`
Close the active group or document window	`Ctrl`+`F4`
Switch a non-Windows application between running in a window and running full screen	`Alt`+`Enter ←`

GLOSSARY

Accessories group. The Program Manager group that contains icons for the Write, Paintbrush, Notepad, and Terminal applications plus a calculator, clock, calendar, cardfile, character map, media player, object packager, recorder, and sound recorder.

active window. The window in which you are currently working. Its title bar will be highlighted. To make a window the active window, click it or use the **Switch To** command on the Task List.

application. Any task on which you work with a computer.

application icon. An icon that starts an application when you double-click it.

application program. Any computer program such as a spreadsheet or database manager that you use to perform useful work.

application window. The window in which an application runs.

Applications group. The Program Manager group that contains the applications the Windows Setup program found on your hard drive when Windows was first installed.

ASCII text file. A document that contains just printable ASCII (pronounced "ask-ee") characters with little or no formatting information, so that it can be easily moved between applications.

associated file. A file whose filename extension has been connected ("associated") with an application so you can open or print the file by double-clicking its filename or by dragging and dropping.

boot. Turn on a computer so it can load the operating system.

cascade. Arrange windows to overlap so that parts of each can be seen.

character format. The style, size, and font of a character; in Windows applications such as Write, these elements can be individually formatted.

check box. A small box found on dialog boxes that you click to turn on and off.

choose. Execute a command by clicking an icon, a menu command, or a command button.

click. Quickly press and then release the mouse button (usually the left one).

client application. The application into which you embed or link data from another application. Compare *server application*.

cold boot. Same as *boot;* compare *warm boot*.

command button. A button in a dialog box that you click to execute commands.

compound document. A document in which data has been embedded or linked from another document.

computer literacy. Knowing how to use application programs to perform useful work.

contents list. The area of File Manager's directory window that displays the contents of the selected directory; either the right side or the whole window.

context-sensitive help. A Help screen that provides information relevant to the procedure you are currently in.

Control menu. A menu, displayed when you click the Control-menu box or an application icon, that lists commands for manipulating a window.

Control-menu box. The box in the upper-left corner of a window. Clicking it displays the Control menu. Double-clicking it closes the window.

copy. Copy data from an application to the Clipboard.

cursor. See *insertion point*. In Paintbrush, a mark of varying shapes indicating the point where an action will begin in the drawing area.

cut. Move data from an application to the Clipboard.

desktop. The full area of the screen on which Windows can display applications when you open them.

destination. The location you copy or move files to. Compare *source*.

destination document. The document into which an object is linked or embedded. Compare *source document*.

directory. A division of a disk in which you can store files and which you can further divide into subdirectories.

directory path. A listing on the title bar of File Manager's directory window that shows the path to the directory currently displayed on the contents list.

directory tree. A listing in File Manager's directory window of the directories and subdirectories on a disk; occupies the left side or the whole window.

directory window. The File Manager window that displays the directory tree and the contents list.

document. Any file of data created with a Windows application. Also called *file*.

document icon. An icon in File Manager's contents list that classifies files by type.

document window. A window within an application window.

double-click. Press and then release the mouse button (usually the left one) twice in quick succession.

down scroll arrow. The arrow on a scroll bar that you click to scroll the screen down a document or list.

download. Transfer programs or data from another computer to your computer using a modem and the telephone lines.

drag. Hold down the left mouse button while you move the mouse to move the item under the mouse pointer.

drag and drop. Drag a file icon with the mouse from File Manager's contents list to an icon or title bar and then release it.

drawing area. The area of the Paintbrush window where you create or edit a drawing using the tools in the Toolbox.

drive icon. An icon in the File Manager directory window that you click to select a drive.

drop-down list box. A type of list box that is displayed when you click a drop-down arrow.

embed. Insert an object into one document (the destination) from another (the source), in a way that allows editing in the destination without changing the source. Double-clicking the embedded object in the destination document opens the source application to allow for the editing. Embedding is possible only in applications that support OLE.

end mark. The mark at the end of a Write document past which there is no text.

enhanced mode. A mode in which Windows can run non-Windows applications in windows and can utilize free disk space as if it were RAM (random access memory). Windows can use this mode only on computers that have a 386 or better processor.

extend a selection. Expand the highlight when selecting text so other characters are included in a selection.

file. See *document*.

file extension. An optional identifier that follows a file name; it consists of a period and 3 legal characters. Many applications automatically add a particular extension. For example, files saved from the Clipboard have the extension *.clp*.

File Manager. A Windows application that manages files. It has commands to format disks; copy, move, and delete files; and create directories.

file name. The name used to identify a file on the disk; it consists of 8 or fewer legal characters.

filename. The name and extension assigned to a file on the disk.

filename specification. Any combination of text and wildcards that you enter in a Name text box to control which filenames are affected by a command.

filter. A program built into an application allowing it to convert files created in another application into its own format.

font. A typeface with its own unique design; for example, Arial, Courier, and Times New Roman.

font size. The height of a font specified in points. One point is about $\frac{1}{72}$ of an inch.

font style. A variation of a font: regular, bold, italic, and bold italic.

footer. A line of text that prints at the bottom of pages.

fragmented file. A file stored on noncontiguous sectors of a disk.

Games group. The Program Manager group that contains icons for Solitaire and Minesweeper, two games included with Windows.

Glossary. A part of the on-line Help system that defines terms for you.

graphical user interface. A screen display where commands are chosen from icons and menus and where text and graphics are shown almost exactly as they will appear in print. Abbreviated GUI (pronounced "goo-ee"). See *WYSIWYG*.

group icon. The icon for a group window that has been minimized. Double-click it to see the application icons that it contains.

group window. A Program Manager window that contains application icons.

GUI. See *graphical user interface*.

hanging indent. A paragraph indent in which the first line is indented less than the other lines in the paragraph or not indented at all.

header. A line of text that prints at the top of pages.

Help. On-screen guidance for Windows; accessible from most points in most programs by pressing F1 or clicking a **Help** command or command button.

horizontal scroll bar. The scroll bar at the bottom of a window that you use to move the window's contents left and right.

icon. A graphic representation of an application, a command, or a file.

indent. Offset all or part of a paragraph from the left or right margin.

insertion point. A flashing vertical bar, sometimes called a *cursor*, that indicates where the next character you type will appear. It moves to the right as you type.

jump. A highlighted hot spot on a Help screen that jumps you to another screen when you click it.

justified text. Text that is evenly aligned with both left and right margins.

landscape mode. The orientation in which text prints across the length of the page. Compare *portrait mode*.

launch. Start (a program); as in "I launched File Manager."

left indent. A paragraph indent in which all lines are moved in from the left margin by a specified amount.

legal character. A character that DOS allows you to use in a filename.

Linesize box. In Paintbrush, the box where you can choose drawing widths to control the thickness of the lines or the cursor used with certain of the tools.

link. Insert a reference in one or more destination documents to an object in a source document, in a way that allows changes in the source to be carried forward to the destinations. Double-clicking the linked object in a destination document opens the source document and its application to allow for editing; and any editing of the source is carried through to all linked destinations. Linking is possible only in applications that support OLE.

list box. A box, usually inside a dialog box, that lists available choices, such as commands or files. If the list is longer than the box, a scroll bar is included.

local reboot. Canceling a Windows application by pressing Ctrl + Alt + Del. Compare *warm boot*.

lost allocation unit. A section of a fragmented file that has become detached from the rest and is not retrievable into the file.

Main group. The Program Manager group that contains icons for File Manager, Control Panel, Print Manager, Clipboard Viewer, MS-DOS Prompt, and PIF Editor. In the regular Windows installation, the Main group window is open within Program Manager when Windows is started.

manual page break. A page break that you insert in a Write document by pressing `Ctrl`+`Enter ←`.

Maximize button. The upward pointing triangle in the upper-right corner of a window that enlarges the window to full screen when you click it.

menu. A list of available commands; shown in a window's menu bar.

menu bar. The list of menu names at the top of an application window.

Microsoft Tools group. The Program Manager group added by DOS 6 containing icons for Anti-Virus, Backup, and Undelete.

Minimize button. The downward pointing triangle in the upper-right corner of a window that reduces the window to an icon when you click it.

mode. See *enhanced mode; standard mode*.

mouse. A hand-held device used to move the mouse pointer on the screen; it contains buttons you click to execute commands.

mouse pointer. The arrow or other shape on the screen that moves when you move the mouse.

noncontiguous sectors. Sectors of a disk that are discontinuous; when a file is stored in them, it is said to be fragmented.

non-Windows application. An application designed to run with DOS but not with Windows. Windows can usually run a non-Windows application, but it does not look or act like a Windows application.

object. Any piece of data created by a Windows application that you can link or embed into another document.

object linking and embedding (OLE). A method of copying and transferring information between applications used by Windows. See *object; link; embed*.

OLE (pronounced "oh-lay"). See *object linking and embedding*.

on-line help. Help that is built into an application so you can access it from within the application, usually by pressing `F1` or clicking a **Help** command or command button.

open. Retrieve data from a file on a disk into an application.

option button. A round button in a dialog box that offers one of a set of mutually exclusive options. The one that is turned on contains a black dot. If you click a button that is off, any other related button that is on automatically turns off.

optional hyphen. A hyphen that breaks a line and is printed only when it falls at the right margin. To insert an optional hyphen in a Write document, press `Ctrl`+`⇧ Shift`+`-`.

orientation. The direction in which text prints on a page. See *portrait mode; landscape mode*.

orphan. The first line of a paragraph printed by itself at the bottom of the page.

page break. A line across a document on the screen that indicates where one page will end when printed and the next will begin.

Palette. An area of the Paintbrush screen containing colors that can be selected for use when drawing with some of the tools.

paragraph mark. An invisible code in a Write document that indicates the end of a paragraph.

paste. Copy data from the Clipboard into a document.

path. A listing of directories and subdirectories that specifies exactly where a file is stored on a disk. To specify a path, you indicate the drive, then the name of all subdirectories leading to the destination. All elements must be separated from one another by backslashes (\); for example, *c:\letters\new*.

PIF. See *Program Information File*.

point. Move the mouse pointer to a specific location on the screen.

portrait mode. The orientation in which text prints across the narrow width of the page. Compare *landscape mode*.

print queue. In Print Manager, a list of jobs waiting to be printed.

Program Information File (PIF). A file containing information Windows uses to run a non-Windows application. Windows contains custom PIFs for many applications and uses a default PIF for all others.

Program Manager. The Windows application that is always in memory when Windows is loaded. You use it to start all other Windows applications.

pull-down menu. A list of commands that descends from the menu bar when you click a menu name.

ragged margin. The uneven right margin when text is left-aligned or the uneven left margin when it is right-aligned.

repaginate. Break a document into pages.

resolution. The number of dots printed per inch.

Restore button. The double triangle in the upper-right corner of a window that appears when you click the Maximize button. When you click the Restore button, the window returns to its original size.

retrieve. See *open*.

right indent. A paragraph indent in which all lines are pulled in from the right margin by a specified amount.

root directory. The highest level of directory on a disk. Normally specified as *a:\, b:\,* or *c:*.

sans serif font. A font, such as Arial, that does not have small cross bars (serifs) at the base of the letters.

save. Store data in the computer's memory in a file on the disk so it can be opened again later.

screen saver. A moving graphic that appears on the screen if you don't type a key or move the mouse for a specified period of time.

scroll arrow. An arrow on a scroll bar that you click to scroll the screen.

scroll bar. A bar at the right side or bottom of a window that you use to scroll the screen; contains scroll arrows and a scroll box.

scroll box. A box-shaped element of a scroll bar that you drag to scroll the screen.

select. Click an item to indicate you want to perform some action on it.

selection area. A narrow, invisible strip just inside the left edge of the Write document window. When you point to this area, the mouse pointer turns into an inward-pointing arrow.

selection cursor. The outlined or reverse video box that you use to highlight menus, commands, icons, filenames, and other objects on the screen.

serif font. A font, such as Times New Roman, that has small cross bars (serifs) at the base of the letters.

server application. The application from which you embed or link data into another application. Paintbrush is a server application.

setup. The procedure you perform to install an application in Windows. The process copies the application's files from the floppy disks on which they are distributed to your system's hard disk drive. It also normally creates a new group window for the application and installs application icons in it.

shareware. Software distributed free of charge by its owners, who request that you register it and pay a fee if you use it and like it. Registering your copy usually entitles you to free technical support and notification of program updates.

shortcut key. A key you can press to execute a command instead of using the mouse.

source. The location you copy or move files from. Compare *destination*.

source document. The document containing an original object. Compare *destination document*.

split bar. The vertical bar that separates a directory window's directory tree from the contents list in File Manager.

standard mode. A Windows mode that doesn't permit non-Windows applications to run in windows and in which memory available to programs is limited to free RAM (random access memory). The only mode Windows can run in on a computer using a 286 processor.

startup drive. The drive the computer looks to for the operating system files when you turn it on. It first looks to drive A, then to drive C.

StartUp group. The Program Manager group that contains the icons for applications you want to open when you load Windows.

status bar. The bar at the bottom of a window that displays information about the window's contents.

string. Any sequence of characters. For example, both *howdy* and *?*0* are strings.

subdirectory. A directory within a directory.

subscript. A character that print in a type size smaller than the text, sunk below the line.

superscript. A character that print in a type size smaller than the text, raised above the line.

system disk. A disk that contains the DOS files the computer needs to start up.

Task List. A menu that you use to switch between applications and perform other tasks such as cascading and tiling windows, or arranging icons. Accessed by choosing the **S**witch To command from the Control menu.

text box. A box in a dialog box into which you enter text. It contains an insertion point.

text file. See *ASCII text file*.

tile. Arrange windows side by side or one above another without any overlap.

title bar. The bar at the top of a window that gives the name of the application, the name of the open document, or both.

Toolbox. An area of the Paintbrush screen containing icons for the tools you use to create or edit drawings. To select a tool, you click its icon.

tree. See *directory tree*.

up scroll arrow. The arrow on a scroll bar that you click to scroll the screen up the document.

vertical scroll bar. The scroll bar on the right side of a window that you use to move the window's contents up and down.

virus signature. A unique code by which DOS 6's Anti-Virus program identifies a virus.

volume label. The name of a disk assigned when it was formatted or added or changed with File Manager's **L**abel Disk command.

warm boot. Pressing [Ctrl]+[Alt]+[Del] to restart the system. Compare *local reboot*.

widow. The last line of a paragraph printed by itself at the top of a page.

wildcard. A character that substitutes for one or more characters in a filename. The question mark substitutes for any single character. The asterisk represents any character in a given position and all following characters in the part of the filename (either the name or extension) where it is used.

win. The command you type to run the Windows executable program file *win.com*. Typing **win** from the DOS prompt loads Windows on most systems.

window. The frame in which applications and documents are displayed.

word wrap. A feature whereby a word that cannot fit at the end of a line without continuing past the right edge of the window automatically moves, or "wraps," to the beginning of the next line. The Write application employs word wrap.

WYSIWYG (pronounced "wizzy-wig"). A screen display that matches printed output—stands for "what you see is what you get." See *graphical user interface*.

INDEX